*"At 35 years old I realized I needed help. I started shoplifting in my late teens. I've been working since I was 16 years old and I've stolen from all of my employers. I was the "star" employee and the last person you would expect to be stealing. My double life finally caught up with me. I was confronted with stealing from my job and was fired. I knew I needed help but had nowhere to turn. I found The Shulman Center online and signed up for Terry's 10-therapy session treatment program immediately. There are no words to express my thanks to him. Therapy exposed the origins of my theft addiction and the reasons why I continued to fall back into my addiction. I've read Terry's books <u>Something for Nothing</u> and <u>Biting the Hand That Feeds</u>. I highly recommend them. I now have the tools and the support to keep me focused on my recovery. I realized I wasn't really living before. If you are reading this, you're not alone and there's a better way. I encourage you to get help now!" -- **D in PA***

---

*"I found Terry Shulman by chance on the Internet after finally coming to terms with the fact I had a shopping addiction. I was pleasantly surprised at how quickly he returned my call. Thanks to Terry and a little of my own resolve, today I'm no longer in debt and am living on my budget. He was realistic, positive, supportive, and nudged me into exploring my past and the causes of my shopping addiction. Without his help I never would've connected the dots between my shopping and its root causes. His book <u>Bought Out and $pent!</u> really opened my eyes, too. Terry is the biggest factor in the honest life I'm living today and the improvement in my relationship with my husband. I can't recommend him highly enough to anyone suffering from this disorder. Thanks, Terry!" – **SBV in NY***

---

*"I was an overshopper and gradually became a hoarder. On the outside, I looked like the most normal and organized person in the world. But my home was a disaster zone and nobody knew my secret. I felt so alone. I completed Mr. Shulman's intensive phone counseling program for compulsive shopping and hoarding and I was able to not only clear away the physical baggage but my emotional baggage, too!" -- **CW in PA***

---

*"I've always had problems following rules and doing things by the book. I lied, cheated on tests, stole and always looked for the short cut. As a result, I've been in more trouble than it was ever worth. Mr. Shulman helped me understand what got me into this and the value of honesty and playing by the rules. I feel peace and hope again!" – **TD in MI***

"Terry Shulman provides a unique glimpse into the minds and hearts of shoplifters and dishonest employees. Terry's personal work as a recovering theft addict combined with his training as a therapist and an attorney give him a rare perspective into the world of theft in the workplace. I have found his material extremely helpful in training both managers and investigators as it allows me to communicate the widespread prevalence of employee theft while putting a human perspective on the experiences of those who commit dishonest and fraudulent actions against retail companies."–Frank Borecki, CFI Senior Manager, Investigations Radio Shack (Dallas, Texas)

"Terrence Shulman's presentation "Biting The Hand That Feeds: The Employee Theft Epidemic," was a fascinating, thought-provoking, and highly informative presentation. The training provided invaluable information and tools for recipient rights investigators to understand the person, circumstances, risk factors, and theft deterrence in today's world. Terry's personal and professional background—social worker, attorney, and "in recovery" from stealing since 1990—ensures expert working knowledge of employee theft."—Denice Virgo, LMSW, President, Recipient Rights Officers Association of Michigan

---

To whom it may concern:

"Please be advised that Terrence Shulman guest spoke in June of 2004 at the annual Professionals in Pretrial Services Conference (PIPS). He was one of the most informative and professional speakers we have had in the 13 years I have served on the board of directors. His resume speaks for itself. In January of this year (2010) we purchased and implemented his theft awareness program. The feedback we get is extremely positive and we look forward to running statistics and recidivism rates. I highly recommend his theft awareness program."—Dusty J. Guidry, Dir. Pretrial Services, Baton Rouge, Louisiana District Attorney's Office

---

"Terry Shulman has been an incredible asset to our teen youth offenders program since 2001. We feel grateful to have such an expert on shoplifting and stealing speak to our group of teens several times a year. I've always had good feedback from the teens and other staff about Terry's presentation content and style. He manages to take a subject nobody really wants to talk about and bring it into the light to examine. He makes the kids feel safe, respected, and valued. I highly recommend Terry as a speaker/presenter."—Rhonda Major, Coordinator, Taylor (Michigan) Youth Assistance / Downriver Guidance Council

CLUTTERED *Lives,*

empty souls

Compulsive Stealing, Spending & Hoarding

Terrence Daryl Shulman, JD, LMSW

Author of
SOMETHING FOR NOTHING:
Shoplifting Addiction and Recovery
BITING THE HAND THAT FEEDS:
The Employee Theft Epidemic
and
BOUGHT OUT AND $PENT!
Recovery from Compulsive $hopping and $pending

PREVIEW EDITION

Copyright © 2011 by Terrence Daryl Shulman, JD, LMSW

ISBN 0-7414-6712-7

Printed in the United States of America

Published August 2011

INFINITY PUBLISHING
1094 New DeHaven Street, Suite 100
West Conshohocken, PA 19428-2713
Toll-free (877) BUY BOOK
Local Phone (610) 941-9999
Fax (610) 941-9959
Info@buybooksontheweb.com
www.buybooksontheweb.com

<u>*Dedication*</u>

I dedicate this book to the millions of people around this world who have struggled with compulsive stealing, shopping/spending, and hoarding/cluttering. May this book serve as a lifeline to recovery. You are not alone. There is hope.

I also dedicate this book to the brave souls who have contributed their stories in this book; to those who've yet to seek help; and to those who have made a difference in the lives of others by seeing with curiosity, compassion and faith the pain and the hope in each other.

Table of Contents

Table of Contents

ACKNOWLEDGMENTS

As with my first three books, there are so many people I wish to acknowledge. Please forgive me if I have forgotten any of you who have touched my life...

My beautiful & supportive wife, Tina, (Book proofreader and Creative Director of The Shulman Center)
My mother Madeline & my step-Dad Jim,
My brothers Jordy, Sam, and Marty,
My in-laws Barb, Craig, and Evan Chadick,
My nephew Devan,
My father, Robert, rest in peace,
Bunica Jennie Polak (rest in peace)
All of my relatives for their unconditional love and support,

My best buddies who have kept me strong and centered: Lee Anzicek, Tom Lietaert, Dick Halloran, Brett Koon, Scott McWhinney, Rob Koliner, Joe Sulak, Dana L. Piper, Marty Peters, Ben Goryca, Brian Kevin Lauderdale, Josh Barclay, John Stepmien, Jeff Gabrielson, Art Stone, Rich Nave, Dan McCrary, and Larry Raymond (rest in peace),

Steve Campbell, mentor and friend, rest in peace,

Dana L. Piper for back cover photograph,

Cathy Dyer, for book cover design,

My Goddess cheerleading squad: Julie Brydon, Laura Hansen-Koon, Andrea Sulak, Sharon Harris, Bryn Fortune, Mona Light, Robin Schwartz, Megan Powers, Denise Miller, Carol Klawson, Pam Landy, Karen Greenberg, Linda Fink, Gigi Colombini, Kam Flynn, & Maureen McDonald,

Nancy Rabitoy of Better Direction Design and Chick Hershberger of Dot Design,

Benji and Penelope, the love dogs,

My fellow recovering friends in C.A.S.A. (Cleptomaniacs And Shoplifters Anonymous)—metro Detroit area,

My fellow recovering friends of CASA-online,

S.O.S. (Secular Organization for Sobriety),

Landmark Education Corporation,

Stan Dale and the angels of the Human Awareness Institute,

The Detroit Area Men's Wisdom Council,

The Tuesday morning men's breakfast club,

The Mankind Project,

Dr. Eugene Ebner, PhD,

Dr. John Brownfain, PhD, rest in peace,

Elizabeth Corsale, Jack Hayes, Gary Zeune, Dr. April Benson, Dr. Gail Steketee, John Prin, and Tom Lieteart,

S.A.A. (especially Rich N. and Dan M.),

Dr. Kenneth Adams,

Challenge Day at www.challengeday.org,

Oprah Winfrey,

Those who contributed their stories in this book, and

The good folks at Infinity Publishing!

<u>DISCLAIMER</u>

The stories herein are composites of various clients I have worked with. Most of those written about have given me express permission to include their stories herein. Names and details have been changed to protect the anonymity and confidentiality of all persons.

ABOUT THE AUTHOR

Terrence Daryl Shulman is a native-Detroiter, attorney, therapist, and consultant. He's been in recovery since 1990 and founded C.A.S.A. (Cleptomaniacs And Shoplifters Anonymous), a weekly support group, in 1992 in the Detroit area. C.A.S.A. is one of only a handful of groups of its kind.

He launched the websites www.kleptomaniacsanonymous.org, www.employeetheftsolutions.com, www.shopaholicsanonymous.org, and www.hoardersanonymous.org. In 2004, Mr. Shulman founded, and has directed, The Shulman Center for Compulsive Theft, Spending & Hoarding. He specializes in counseling clients with theft addictions, compulsive shopping/spending and hoarding disorders. He works with clients both in person and by phone. Previously, he worked extensively as a chemical dependency counselor and was a clinic director.

Mr. Shulman has organized and presented on compulsive theft, spending and hoarding at numerous conferences across the U.S. He's been featured on over 100 television programs, notably Oprah, 48 Hours, 20/20, The Today Show, The Early Show, Good Morning America, CNN, MSNBC, Fox News, WETV, and CNBC. He's been heard on various local, national, and international radio shows and has been quoted or has written articles in various and newspapers and magazines, including The New York Times, The Detroit Free Press/News, The Wall Street Journal, The Washington Post, The Chicago Tribune, The L.A. Times, Lifetime, Health, Good Housekeeping, Redbook, Cosmopolitan, TV Guide, and O Magazine.

This is Mr. Shulman's fourth book.

Mr. Shulman lives in Southfield, Michigan with his wife Tina

Preface

This is a book about real people and real pain: about what causes our pain; about avoiding our pain; about misdirected cries of pain; about the ways we cry out in pain and how they, tragically, cause more pain—for ourselves and others.

This is a book about the pain which causes people to shoplift and steal, overshop and overspend, hoard and clutter, and lie, cheat, break rules, and take destructive risks.

This is a book about the pain these behaviors—these disorders—cause ourselves and others.

This is a book about pain: understanding our pain; healing our pain; learning from our pain; transforming our pain; helping others with their pain; being made more whole and finding peace within ourselves and the world.

This is a book about hope and faith: may you find them now.

....

Be honest, answer the following questions:

Have you ever shoplifted or stolen from the workplace? (Hasn't everyone?)

Does lying or bending the truth come too easily for you? (Some call it lying, others call it creativity.)

Ever envied the Joneses and then broke your budget? (Budget, what's a budget?)

Ever panicked when your doorbell rang—you weren't expecting guests—because your home was too cluttered? (Martha Stewart doesn't live here anymore.)

*Do you hate following rules, look for the short-cuts or loopholes, or take risks more than the average Joe/Jane? (*Hey, if there's a wall, there's a way around it!*)

If you answered *"yes"* to any of these questions, then this book is for you! (Of course, it's likely everyone answered *"yes"* to at least one question).

....

Thou shalt not steal.—The 8th Commandment

Thou shalt not bear false witness (lie) against thy neighbor. —The 9th Commandment

Thou shalt not covet thy neighbor's house or possessions. —The 10th Commandment

Don't worry: this book isn't about religion or sin. It's about our shifting individual and collective attitudes toward stealing, spending, and hoarding. It's about how they've shifted, why they've shifted, and the cost to each and all of us. It's about how more stuff makes us emptier and how less is often more. It's about our increasing culture of corruption, "truthiness," and envy. It's about society's mixed messages:

-"Be honest, but not too honest."

-"Your only mistake was getting caught."

-"Don't be a spendthrift but keep up with the Joneses."

-"Save your money but spend to help the economy."

-"It's only stuff but it's too good to let it go."

-"Bend the rules but don't break them."

For readers not as familiar with my personal story or background, I encourage you to read *Something for Nothing: Shoplifting Addiction and Recovery*, published in late 2003. It documents my early life, my addiction to shoplifting and stealing from age 15-25, and my recovery path since 1990. It recounts my work as an attorney and founder of the C.A.S.A. support group in 1992; my return to social work school from 1995-97; and my first six years as an addictions therapist.

Next, in early 2004, I founded The Shulman Center for Theft Addictions and Disorders. I was a guest expert on shoplifting addiction on The Oprah Show later that year. I went from being handcuffed to a jail cell wall in 1990 to appearing with Oprah 14 years later. This was nearly beyond my realm of imagination and reminds me we never know what's in store for us once we get our lives on track.

In late 2005, I published my second book, *Biting The Hand That Feeds: The Employee Theft Epidemic,* and organized and co-presented at The First International Conference on Theft Addictions and Disorders in Detroit. In early 2006, I changed my company name to The Shulman Center for Compulsive Theft & Spending as I began learning about and working more and more with compulsive shopping/spending.

In mid-2008, I published my third book *Bought Out and Spent! Recovery from Compulsive $hopping and $pending,* and later that year organized and presented at The Second International Conference on Compulsive Theft & Spending in Detroit. My counseling work continued to expand—as did the C.A.S.A. groups—and I began learning about hoarding issues in my clients (as well as some family and friends!).

In December 2008, I got a knock on my front door. I was served with a Federal lawsuit. An out-of-state organization, with whom I'd once discussed collaborating, sued me for trademark and copyright infringement. I felt the suit was frivolous; I felt I was being bullied. I knew I had to fight and stand up for myself. The lawsuit dragged on for a year. It was scary, frustrating, and very expensive; in fact, it was one of most difficult periods of my life. Along the way, I found great support from sources I had taken for granted and also found less support from sources I'd assumed were there.

They say "what doesn't kill you will make you stronger" and that a "crisis" brings both "danger" and "opportunity." The lawsuit tested my recovery, my marriage, my own sanity; and I passed. When the suit finally settled in late 2009, I felt called to re-evaluate my life—my limits, my family dynamics, and the depth of my own recovery. It was a dramatic time of growth. Often, crises beget blessings.

Now, it's 2011 and I'm finishing this fourth book. I look forward to presenting at The Third International Conference on Compulsive Theft, Spending & Hoarding later this year in Detroit. I'm changing the company name, yet again, to The Shulman Center for Compulsive Theft, Spending & Hoarding. I see too much cross-over between these disorders to think about one without considering the others.

There are relatively few books written on kleptomania, shoplifting addiction, employee theft, or "compulsive stealing" and only a few therapists who specialize in treating these disorders. Treating compulsive stealing continues to be both my bread and butter and my primary expertise and personal passion—I'm a recovering theft addict myself. There are notably more books and therapists dealing with compulsive buying, shopping, or spending. While this field has steadily built legitimacy over the last 20 years, being a shopaholic is still looked at as "the smiled-upon addiction." Hoarding—while traceable to the origins of man—appears to be the most recent disorder to hit the spotlight among the public as well as researchers and clinicians.

I've added a "mini-section" in this book about rule breaking and risk taking. Certainly, people who steal are obvious rule breakers and risk takers—thought they may hide this for decades. Virtually all addicts break rules and take risks; even in recovery, most find it hard to stay within the bounds of the law, guidelines or even follow the suggestions of "the program." Compulsive shoppers and spenders break budgets and—in lying, deceiving, or hiding purchases—commit "financial infidelity." Hoarders break rules of orderliness, cleanliness, and even lawfulness in accumulating things, food, and animals; they often overspend or steal, too.

A glance at the headline news on any given day reveals countless stories, low- and high-profile, on these topics:

Shoplifting: The recession has brought a wave of "retail fraud" (as it's often called)—some of it petty and more of it perpetrated by "professional shoplifters" or rings—(ORT or ORC: organized retail theft or retail crime). Then there's Lindsay Lohan—the Winona Ryder of her day—and the countless other stars, athletes, politicians, and dignitaries who've been arrested for pilfering (Farrah Fawcett, Bess Myerson, Rex Reed, Jennifer Capriati, Reds' pitcher Mike Leake, Caroline Guiliani, Canadian MP Sven Robinson, former Bush aide Claude Allen, and the list goes on). CBC and CNBC recently aired *The Truth about Shoplifting.*

Employee Theft/Credit Card Fraud/Identity Theft: The recession, technology, the Internet, and greed led the FBI to call these three of "the fastest growing crimes in America." What's the difference between the employee who loafs on the job ("time theft") and the CEOs of investment firms and mortgage lenders that nearly brought down the U.S. and world economy? The employee's more likely to get caught, confronted and fired; the CEOs rarely get caught or confronted and, if they do, they get rewarded. *Houston, we have a problem.* TV shows such as *American Greed: Scams, Schemes and Broken Dreams* highlight various growing theft and fraud trends. Shame is getting hard to come by!

Overshopping/Overspending: As our government argues over how to make the smallest dent in our $14 trillion deficit and whether to "raise the debt limit," millions of Americans—and others around the world—suffer financial distress, random as well as self-inflicted from under-saving, overspending, and falling victim to a bad case of "affluenza." Keeping up with the Joneses was never more epic; the new Joneses are the "stars" in the media. But even they fall prey to our culture of excess: Victoria Beckham, Nicolas Cage, Jennifer Hudson, Michael Jackson, Sarah Jessica Parker (who knew Carrie Bradshaw was no acting stretch?), and Newt Gingrich show that men and women alike get hooked. TV shows like *Big Spender*, *Suze Orman*, *Dave Ramsey*, and *Oprah's Debt Diet* have been bellwethers of these crises.

Hoarding: When everyone and his brother bought a home before the housing bubble burst, we had to fill those homes up, didn't we? And if there wasn't enough room in your McMansion, have we got a storage unit for you! Or two, or three or four! The recent popularity of such shows as *Hoarders, Hoarding: Buried Alive,* and *Enough Already!* all prove clutter is king—at least in ratings-land. And for every "packrat" still hidden behind closed doors, more public faces of this disorder are "coming out," including Micahaele Salahi, Heidi Montag and Spencer Pratt, Lisa Kudrow, Mariah Carey, Kevin Federline, Celine Dion, Marie Osmond and Paris Hilton—17 dogs counts as animal hoarding!

Rule Breaking and Risk Taking: Aside from the countless short-cuts and loopholes most of us take from time-to-time, our leaders, role models, and stars can't seem to play by the rules either. Recently, we saw Arnold Schwarzenegger, Lance Armstrong, and Charlie Sheen stoop to new lows— not winning, but losing—public respect and support. When did lying, hubris, and narcissism become the norm? Shows such as *The Real Hustle* and *The Takedown* are merely more direct examples of rule breaking and risk taking than we see from "the good guys" in *24* or any other hero/rescue drama.

What do stealing, spending and hoarding have in common?

Over the last decade, I've counseled nearly 500 clients with various combinations of these disorders. I wrote this book, in part, to better understand and explain the underlying similarities and commonalities between them. All addictions share similar features and consequences but a few things stand out when working with compulsive stealing, spending and hoarding. On first look, all three disorders appear to focus and depend on the acquisition of things. There also seems to be a focus on money—either saving money or having more money through stealing; spending money or even getting a bargain; or hoarding money or avoiding losing money by getting rid of things perceived as valuable. People can steal, buy, or hoard money or objects from stores, work, or others. There also seems to be a preoccupation with time—and time is money: saving time by stealing, saving time by buying, saving time by hoarding and not discarding. The irony, of course, is that people who compulsively steal, spend or hoard spend an inordinate amount of time not only engaged in these activities but in thinking about doing them as well as stopping them.

There appears to be extreme boundary issues for people who compulsively steal, spend or hoard. And while all addictions adversely affect others besides the addict, many addictions (such as overeating, drugging, and drinking) are, in one sense, primarily self-destructive. Stealing requires a victim, a violation of the law, ethics, and actual boundaries. Spending—especially compulsive spending—often requires a victim, too: debts that often can't be repaid (though it may be hard for some to see credit card companies as victims); but also "financial infidelity"—the violation of budgetary agreements with a spouse, family member, friend, or business partner. The compulsive overspender, like the compulsive overeater, can't adhere to the bounds of the bank account (the body) and takes on debt as if calories or pounds. In addition, it's common that persons who overspend are in debt resort to stealing out of desperation. Compulsive hoarders—especially when they don't live alone—crowd out the legitimate living spaces of others, violating their physical and emotional boundaries. Hoarders, too, may overspend, steal, hide, and lie. They may also put others who live with them at risk for disease, accident, fire hazard, or eviction.

These violations of the boundaries of others are anathema to their common traits of codependency and excessive empathy which belie their narcissistic tendencies stemming from beliefs they're inadequate and unlovable. Those who compulsively steal, spend, or hoard do so for themselves but, often steal, spend or hoard for the benefit of others as well: stolen, bought, or hoarded gifts. It's also typical these persons have experienced being victimized in their lives and felt deprived materially and/or emotionally. Thus, they become obsessed with making things right, evening the score, and feel both entitled to their excesses and out of touch with the outrage and negativity their behaviors evoke in others. People who steal, overspend, and hoard are no strangers to legal issues, including criminal or incarceration, financial or bankruptcy, employment or loss of job, divorce or child custody, eviction or foreclosure, or other liability.

Another common feature is a persistent thinking, feeling and attitude of lack, emptiness, scarcity, and inadequacy which they attempt to correct through accumulation of money and/or things. Anxiety is a common feeling for these folks. In short, they tend to feel "I'm not enough... unless I have enough." But, for them, it's never enough. The source of these thoughts, feelings and attitudes may be partly attributed to brain chemistry (nature) but it's safe to say a fair amount of nurture (familial, cultural, and societal) is at play; they seem to be particularly susceptible to attaching their inherent value to money and/or things.

It bears repeating: individual stealing, spending and hoarding mirrors these trends in society; it's chicken-and-egg.

So, we can look at these similarities and commonalities in this chart form—there may be others we haven't yet listed:

STEALING	SPENDING	HOARDING
Thing-oriented	Thing-oriented	Thing-oriented
Money-oriented	Money-oriented	Money-oriented
Time-oriented	Time-oriented	Time-oriented
Boundary issues	Boundary issues	Boundary issues
Narcissistic	Narcissistic	Narcissistic
Shame/Secrecy	Shame/Secrecy	Shame/Secrecy
Anxiety	Anxiety	Anxiety
I'm not enough	I'm not enough	I'm not enough
Legal Troubles	Legal Troubles	Legal Troubles
Society prompts	Society prompts	Society prompts
Bottomless pit	Bottomless pit	Bottomless pit

On a broader scale, the following chart may help you track your own addictions and see any patterns between them

CHEMICALS	FOOD/EATING	BEHAVIORS
Alcohol	Overeating	Gambling
Marijuana	Anorexia	Codependency
Heroin	Bulimia	Shopping
Crystal Meth	Bad carbs	Sex/Porn
Cocaine/Crack	Sugar	Shoplifting
Heroin	Junk Food	Hoarding
LSD/Acid	Fast Food	Employee Theft
Ecstasy	Caffeine	Work
Pain Pills	_____	Religion
Sleeping Pills		Videogames
Sedative Pills		Exercise
Anxiety Pills		Internet/TV

_____   _____

What did you notice or learn?

Note: I'll publish a workbook companion to this book soon.

Introduction

Nobody tries to steal your troubles, and no one can take your good deeds.—Yiddish folk saying

Anyone who lives within their means suffers from a lack of imagination.—Oscar Wilde

Beauty is Nature's coin, must not be hoarded, must be current.—John Milton

Laws bind us. But it's important to remember the law is only what's popular, not what's right or wrong.—Marilyn Manson

As previously mentioned, there's relatively little research or statistics about compulsive stealing, spending or hoarding. Even stats about shoplifting and employee theft in general are hard to come by. But it's safe to say that stealing, overspending and hoarding are growing problems which we as a people are slow to recognize or confront. It's my humble hope that books such as this one help provoke an awareness of and desire to creatively offer solutions for these individual and social problems. ***Consider the following statistics:***

SHOPLIFTING

- Over 10% (30 million) Americans shoplift.—*2011, The Shulman Center estimate*

- Most shoplifters arrested or prosecuted will steal again.—*2011, The Shulman Center estimate*

- There are nearly 300 million shoplifting incidents per year.—*2010, Jack Hayes International survey*

- Shoplifting accounts for 30-40% of retailer's lost profits.—*2010, Jack Hayes & University of Florida*

- In 2009, Retailers lost an estimated $13 billion to shoplifting.—2010, Jack Hayes survey

EMPLOYEE THEFT

- 75% of employees steal from work and most do so repeatedly.—*U.S. Chamber of Commerce*

- 30% of corporate bankruptcies result from employee theft.—*U.S. Chamber of Commerce*

- The FBI calls employee theft one of the fastest growing crimes in America.—*F.B.I.*

- U.S. businesses lose $1 trillion/year to fraud.—*2008, Association of Certified Fraud Examiners*

- Employee theft has risen 50% since the start of the recent recession.—*2010, Fox News Chicago*

- Time theft (loafing) costs U.S. companies $500 Billion/year in lost productivity. *2005, Denver Post*

COMPULSIVE BUYING/SHOPPING/SPENDING

- 6% (17 million) Americans are compulsive buyers.—*2006, Stanford University landmark study*

- Men and women compulsively buy about equally.—*2006, Stanford study*

- 8.9% (25 million) Americans are compulsive buyers. *–2008 Journal of Consumer Research & U-Richmond*

- Arguments over money are the #1 reason for couples' conflict and break-ups. *2008, Psychology Today*

- The average credit *card debt per adult American is about $10,000.—2008, Time and Money magazines*

HOARDING DISORDER

- Hoarding affects an estimated 6-15 million Americans.—*2010, Time magazine*

- There are over 75 National Hoarding Taskforces in the U.S.—*2010, Time magazine*
- Personal consumption expenditures and storage unit rentals increased over 20% since 1980.—*U.S. Chamber of Commerce*

RULE BREAKING

- 59% of American high school students say they cheated on a test in the past year; 21% say they stole from a relative; 80% say they lied to a parent; 92% say they're satisfied with their ethics and character.—*2011, Josephine Institute of Ethics*
- 15% of Americans said they would be likely to cheat on their taxes.—*2010, DBB Worldwide*
- 30% of employers have fired employees for misuse of e-mails or Internet on the job.—*2007, American Management Association on Policy Institute*

It's easy to feel discouraged by the scope and magnitude of the dishonesty and insanity in our midst. One way to stay positive is to remember that sometimes things have to get worse before they get better. Another reason to hold cautious optimism is that the problems of stealing, overspending, and hoarding have been increasingly highlighted as true disorders which can be treated. And just as one person can create a lot of chaos in his own world and the world around him; so, too, can a person who wakes up and finds help similarly create health, hope, and healing.

Terrence Daryl Shulman,
Southfield, Michigan May '11

This book is divided into eight parts:

Part One *highlights shoplifting addiction and the stories of several clients I've treated with this disorder*

Part Two *highlights employee/other theft disorders and the stories of several clients I've treated with these disorders*

Part Three *highlights compulsive shopping/spending and the stories of several clients I've treated with these disorders*

Part Four *highlights hoarding disorder and the stories of several clients I've treated with this disorder as well as the stories of a few others*

Part Five *highlights rule breaking/risk taking and the stories of a few clients I've treated with these disorders*

Part Six *includes interviews with professionals in the field of theory, education and treatment*

Part Seven *highlights relevant research and theory*

Part Eight *includes related topics and appendices*

Part One
Something for Nothing:
Compulsive Shoplifting

There's no such thing as something for nothing.–Napoleon Hill

May 27, 2011. The Daily Mail (excerpt)
Lindsay Lohan began "house arrest" at her luxury beach side home in Venice, California. The actress was fitted with an electronic ankle bracelet during a 5am visit to Lynwood Jail, according to TMZ. She was then sent back to her town house where she is expected to spend around 35 days in confinement. Lohan was ordered to serve time after pleading no contest to stealing a necklace from a Venice jeweler.

Why'd Lindsay do it? Why'd Winona do it? Why do most people shoplift? It isn't about the lack of money. High profile shoplifters typically protest their arrests with initial cries of "I didn't do it," or "It's all a mistake." With the exception of Winona Ryder, who took her case to a jury and was found guilty, virtually every case ends quietly; often, as with Ms. Lohan, with a "no contest" plea. I fantasize that one day a "famous" shoplifter holds a press conference or, at least, releases a statement like: "I'm sorry for my actions; I take full responsibility for them. I offer no excuses but am not entirely sure why I did what I did. I plan to do some soul-searching and get the necessary help. Please don't judge me. I know I'm not alone." We could use a positive poster child.

In 1990, at age 25, it took me six months of working with a PhD psychologist before he and I even began to consider my shoplifting had become addictive; I was his first shoplifter! I must speak with, on average, twenty shoplifters per week who contact me looking for some form of help—people of all backgrounds, most of them fairly intelligent. I'd say 90% have little to no idea why they really shoplift. Equally fascinating, 90%-95% are not ready or willing to work with a specialist like me—even those who have already tried other forms of counseling. According to my recent online survey of 123 respondents who've compulsively stolen, 55% said they were too embarrassed to be honest with a therapist, 53% also said therapy was too expensive. According to the survey, 79% stated shoplifting was their most addictive form of stealing; 24% report they'd stolen over 1,000 times, 21 % over 500 times; 72% cited feeling entitled to get something for nothing as the primary reason they stole while 70% cited depression and 62% cited anger issues.

Most compulsive shoplifters have certain characteristics: they tend to be codependent caretakers or over-givers; have a pervasive sense life is unfair; have unresolved money issues; and have trouble speaking up for or treating themselves. The following are common core beliefs of most shoplifters and others who compulsively steal. I ask each of my clients at the start of treatment to circle and discuss which of these they most relate to; typically, there are at least 5. We go over them at the end of treatment; they've typically softened.

Ten Underlying Core Beliefs of Most Shoplifters
*Life is unfair.
*The world is an unsafe place.
*Nobody will be there to take care of me.
*Nobody's really honest.
*I'm entitled to something extra for my suffering.
*Nice people finish last.
*There's not going to be enough money to live.
*It's a 'dog-eat-dog world' out there.
*No matter how hard I try, things never work out.
*It's not worth my speaking up about anything.

I'm convinced that every boy, in his heart, would rather steal second base than an automobile.—Tom Clark

May 2011Shulman Center Online Theft Survey Results
(Culled from a sample of suspected theft addicts)

1. Number of participants: *111 women / 12 men*
2. Current average age: 41% bet. 40-50 / 32% bet. 50-60
3. 52% married; 22% divorced; 22% single
4. 94% heterosexual
5. 37% some college; 28% college grad; 23% grad degree
6. 42% work full-time; 18% part-time; 17% unemployed
7. 57% work for other; 32% work for self; 12% work both
8. 76% have kids; 43% have two kids
9. 22% household income bet. $50-75k; 18% bet. $30-50k
10. 51% first stole something bet. age 1-10; 40% bet. 11-20
11. 23% stole money; 21 % food; 18% clothes; 38% other
12. 70% first stole from a store; 26% first stole from a person
13. 27% stealing real problem bet age 11-20; 29% bet 21-30;
14. 94% have shoplifted; 70% switch tags; 61% return fraud
15. 74% say shoplifting is biggest problem; 7% from people
16. 81% say shoplifting most addictive; 6% say from people
17. 90% say stealing led to loss of self-esteem; 81% arrested
18. 17% arrested more than 5x; 15% have never been arrested
19. 63% never fired from work for theft; 19% fired once
20. 50% never served 1 day jail; 18% served at least 1 day
21. 52% have served 1-10 days; 17% served 11-30 days
22. 88% have stolen again after arrest or prosecution for theft
23. 32% in counseling more than 3 times; 24% once
24. 72% felt entitled to steal; 70% depressed; 62% angry
25. 24% have stolen over 1,000 times; 21% bet. 500-1,000
26. 55% cite embarrassment/53% cite $ as barriers to therapy
27. 87% sought therapy; 68% books; 52% support groups
28. 38% say therapy most helpful; 25% support groups
29. 20% say 1-2years longest time theft-free; 18% 5+ years
30. 46% say currently theft-free 1-30 days; 13% 6mos–1year
31. 38% also have eating disorders; 30% shopping addiction
32. 69% feel better self-esteem in recovery; 61% more peace
33. 23% go to stores too much / life unfair: relapse triggers
34. 34% say family wants to learn/support my recovery
35. 48% told a few people about their stealing: 18% just God
36. 37% very grateful and very active in recovery

Comparison between Kleptomania/ Addictive-Compulsive Stealing

Kleptomania (DSM-IV Rev.)	Addictive-Compulsive Stealing
*Recurrent failure to resist **impulses** to steal objects **not needed** for personal use/value; **no premeditation**	*Recurrent failure to resist **addictive compulsive** urges to steal objects which **are used/some premeditation**
*Increasing sense of tension **just before** committing the theft	*Generally, **ever-present** tension *well-before theft but increases*
*Pleasure or relief **at the time of theft or** *during* the theft	*Generally, pleasure or relief **shortly after** committing the theft
*The stealing **is not** committed to express anger of vengeance	*Generally, the stealing **is** a means of acting out anger or to make life fair
*The stealing is not due to Conduct Antisocial Personality Disorder	*Same. Generally, most people are honest and law-abiding

Top Ten Reasons People Shoplift
1. Grief and Loss, To Fill the Void
2. Anger/Life is Unfair, To Get Back/Make Life Right
3. Depression, To Get a Lift
4. Anxiety, To Comfort
5. Acceptance/Competition, To Fit in
6. Power/Control, To Counteract Feeling Lost/Powerless
7. Boredom/Excitement, To Live on the Edge
8. Shame/Low self-esteem, To Be Good at Something
9. Entitlement/Reward, To Compensate for Over-giving
10. Rebellion/Initiation, To Break into Own Identity

The Seven Types of Shoplifters (Est. % of Total Shoplifters)
1. The Professionals (Profit/Greed—15%)
2. The Drug, Gambling Addicts (Feed addiction—10%)
3. The Impoverished (Perceived economic need—15%)
4. The Thrill Seekers (Mostly youth—10%)
5. The Absent-Minded (Mostly elderly or rushed—1%)
6. The Kleptomaniacs (Rare—1%)
7. The Addictive Compulsives (Emotion-driven—48%)

20 QUESTION
Assessment for Compulsive Shoplifting

1. Have you ever lost time from work or school due to shoplifting?

2. Has shoplifting created problems in your relationships?

3. Has shoplifting ever affected your reputation or people's opinion of you?

4. Have you ever felt guilt, shame, or remorse after shoplifting?

5. Did you ever shoplift to get money to pay debts or to solve money issues?

6. Did shoplifting ever cause a decrease in your ambition or efficiency?

7. Did you ever experience a "high" or "rush" of excitement when you shoplifted?

8. Have you ever shoplifted to escape worries or troubles?

9. Has shoplifting caused you trouble eating or sleeping?

10. Do arguments, disappointments or frustrations create an urge in you to shoplift?

11. Did you begin to shoplift more frequently over time?

12. Have you ever considered self-destruction or suicide because of your shoplifting?

13. Upon stopping shoplifting, did you continue to be tempted or preoccupied by it?

14. Have you kept your shoplifting a secret from most of those you are close to?

15. Have you ever told yourself "this is my last time" and still shoplifted again?

16. Have you continued to shoplift despite having been confronted or arrested?

17. Do you often feel angry or feel a need for control?

18. Do you have persistent feelings of life being unfair?

19. Do you have persistent feelings of entitlement to get "something for nothing"?

20. Do you have trouble speaking up for yourself, asking for help, or saying "no"?

Most compulsive shoplifters will answer "yes" to *at least* 7 of these questions.

Carly's Story

Carly, 61, is a divorced mother of 3 whose own mother died when she was 2-years old and her father abandoned her. She was raised in Asia but came to the U.S. at age 18 to find her father and to attend college. She began shoplifting shortly after her arrival and has been arrested 14 times—including just prior to contacting me. She had been in therapy numerous times and was wracked with fear and shame.

When Carly contacted me earlier this year to enroll in my 90-day/10-session phone counseling program, I thought I was speaking to a young woman in her 20's. The tenor of her voice was sweet, if a bit squeaky, and her emotional frailty was what misled me. When she told me she was 61, I knew I was dealing with a very vulnerable soul.

Through tears of shame and confusion, Carly shared that she'd been shoplifting since age 19 and had just been arrested for the 14th time—a month ago before Christmas. She'd tried to shoplift some clothes at the Mall. What was even scarier for her was she continued to shoplift up until the time one of her daughters prodded her to call me.

As with all my clients, I do my best to create a safe, non-judgmental space for them to feel whatever they need to feel and share as honestly as possible. They are already beating themselves up when they get to me; Carly was no exception. I asked Carly if she'd looked at my website and knew anything about my background. She had and was relieved to find someone like me—a former shoplifter myself—who might be able to help her understand and stop her shoplifting. She'd been to several therapists previously but none seemed to understand why she stole or how to treat her. Of her 13 prior arrests: *"I always just pled guilty,"* Carly shared sheepishly. *"I always got probation, fines, sometimes community service. I should be grateful I haven't had to go to jail. But I don't feel lucky. Maybe I need to be punished."*

I ask all my clients prior to our treatment: "Why do you think you shoplift?" Carly's answer was typical: *"I don't know."* A significant part of my work is to help enlighten clients about why they do what they do—especially since it's so repetitively destructive. I ask my clients to read my book(s) as quickly and thoroughly as possible. I also ask them to join my private online support group for recovering theft addicts and to consider participating on our weekly phone support groups—since very few states (and even fewer major cities) have live groups that meet. Carly was cooperative, overcame any fear or shame quickly, and found regular structure, support, and friendship in our groups.

The next thing I do is have each client contract with me and their loved ones to stay out of stores. We decide together at a later date if or when it's safe to re-enter them and under what circumstances. Most clients agree to this but most also find avoiding stores is easier said than done. Several things make this difficult: the addictive pull to play with fire; their pride; not wanting to ask for help; and force of habit. Some clients are up front about their resistance. I can't control anyone, so I tell them: "If you go, I want you to be honest with me; I won't yell at you or judge you. I'm trying to help you."

With a safety plan in place to help minimize Carly's acting out her addiction and getting arrested again, I worked to build her trust and asked her to tell me about her life—from the beginning. I'm always looking in the story for the clues: loss, abuse, neglect, deprivation, trauma, betrayal. In short: "What was stolen from them?" Carly's story unfolded...

I was born in Indonesia. My mother died of an illness when I was just two years old. My father was a U.S. serviceman who didn't stick around long enough to see my birth. I was raised by my mother's friend who adopted me. I was raised in poverty but religious. Kids teased me throughout school because I was poor and adopted and I couldn't concentrate in school. I never stole anything though.

In my late teens, I started searching for my father and found out he lived in the U.S. I wrote him and he responded. I was so happy! I felt like I found a piece of myself. I traveled to the U.S. when I was 18 to meet with him. He had remarried and had several young children. He and his family welcomed me at the airport. A local newspaper photographer was there and they ran a story about our reunion. It was wonderful.

I lived with my father and his family. I applied and was accepted to a nursing school nearby. However, things didn't turn out as I had hoped. My father worked a lot, so I rarely saw him; my stepmother was not as welcoming as she was when I'd arrived. I felt like I didn't fit in again. I had a strange accent, weird clothes, and very little money. My Dad took me to the Mall and bought me some shoes. My stepmother got upset, went into my wallet, and took my only twenty dollars. She scolded me for making my Dad buy me shoes. I talked to him later but he didn't stick up for me. She also took the only photograph of my birth mother I had and ripped it up, and yelled: "She's dead!"

The next two years were hell. While I was in school, I had to work and pay rent. My stepmother bought her kids new things but I had to pay for anything I wanted or needed. She once hit me with a broom and a brick for no reason. She and her kids treated me like I was Cinderella. My father continued to work all the time and never took my side. I never got any time alone with him either. I wanted to ask him: Why did he leave? What was my mother like? I was never able to ask him these questions.

I was 19 when I first shoplifted a pretty yellow sweater. Winter was coming and I went with a friend to a store. I didn't plan to steal—but when my friend walked away to look at something—I got an urge and just put the sweater under my jacket. I felt guilty and started to pray to God to forgive me, yet I felt relieved when I didn't get caught. I hid my sweater from my stepmother so she wouldn't find it and throw it away. I knew I had done wrong but I felt I deserved it because life was so hard and I didn't have nice clothes.

I shoplifted a few more times over the next year or so until I graduated from nursing school. Then I started making money and moved in with a man I'd been dating. We broke up and I dated another man who I soon married. I stopped working and naively hoped he'd take care of me. I quickly discovered he was very abusive and controlling. Several months into the marriage, I was pregnant and found out he was having an affair. I felt trapped. I got caught shoplifting nail polish.

We had three children together over the next several years. I was shoplifting more and more because he controlled the money and I wanted my kids to have the things I didn't have, normal things any child should have. I was arrested several times during this period, sometimes while my kids were with me. I was terrified and ashamed. My husband just humiliated me. He never once thought to ask me what was wrong. Even if he had, I wouldn't have known what to say. He wouldn't have understood; I didn't understand. I thought I was a bad person and felt I deserved my husband's scorn.

Several years later, things got even worse when my fourth child died two weeks after his birth. I was angry at God but felt he was punishing me for my shoplifting. I fell into a three month depression. I knew my husband was cheating on me during this time and that hurt even more. When my depression lifted, I started to shoplift and was arrested again. I thought about taking my life but I couldn't leave my children like my parents had left me. Eventually, I left my husband; I couldn't take it anymore. I took the kids, got my own place, and went back to work as a nurse.

But as time wore on, I kept having nightmares and anxiety attacks. I felt haunted by my past. Then, my oldest daughter had a miscarriage. It must have triggered something in me because I started shoplifting and was arrested again. I've never been a very good thief. It's like I want to get caught. My kids found out and were very concerned about me. They asked why I did it but I didn't know. I stopped for a short time but was re-arrested after finding out my son was HIV positive. I almost lost my nursing license. I finally went to a counselor but she didn't seem to know how to help me.

A few years later, in 2008, my father died. We'd drifted apart over the years but I was still very sad. I shoplifted and got arrested immediately—again, for a stupid little thing I could have easily afforded. This time, I lost my nursing license. I felt terrible. I hoped to work 10 more years. I fell into a depression again and hardly left the home. My kids were really concerned about me but they didn't know what to do. My last arrest was in December 2010. One of my daughters found me the help I needed all along. I don't know if I'd have been ready for it earlier, but I finally feel like I'm not alone...

Over the next three months, Carly and I had sessions weekly; one of her daughters joined us twice as well. Carly finally connected the dots: she realized her shoplifting was a cry for help and she had to express her pain openly with me and others until she felt some true relief. She did that more than once. A good sign was when she attended a local grief and loss support group and could identify with the pain others in the group expressed and also report that she felt she'd unloaded so much pain and grief in our therapy that she didn't feel the need to rehash her story. She felt peace.

Post-script: When Carly went to court—despite her lengthy history of convictions—the judge showed compassion, acknowledging Carly's efforts to find the right treatment. The judge told her: *"I don't think jail will help you. But, for your sake, I hope you never have to find that out."*

Patrick's Story

Patrick, 50, is a well-respected African-American pastor and community organizer in a major U.S. city. He had been shoplifting and breaking other rules since he was a kid. But his shoplifting began to spiral out of control several years ago when his wife developed cancer, recently died and left him to raise their young child alone. He managed to keep his addiction and arrests secret. He was arrested a third time prior to contacting me and felt great shame and terror about losing his job, his reputation, his freedom, and his child.

No one should be surprised when clergy or religious people "sin." We've heard of child sexual abuse scandals, ministers caught in heterosexual or homosexual affairs, and financial fraud and theft in every religious institution. Still, when Patrick contacted me after his third arrest for shoplifting and told me his vocation, my role as therapist took an added tone of ministry to his tender, tortured soul. Patrick had recently tried to shoplift a small, inexpensive item. *"I had $3,000 on me at the time,"* he sighed. Patrick "confessed" he'd shoplifted since he was a kid but it escalated over the last six years since his wife had been diagnosed with cancer. (A few studies have shown a correlation between cancer and the onset of shoplifting). Patrick's wife succumbed to her cancer six months prior to his contacting me. He was left to raise their son; his mother also passed while his wife was sick.

I created a safety plan with Patrick, mailed him my book, and promptly added him to my private online support group. He contacted his attorney about his most recent arrest. Patrick received only minor consequences in the past and, by chance, his arrests had stayed out of the local papers; he was able to keep his job as pastor. This time, he was convinced his luck had run out, that his arrest would go public. Over the course of several sessions, I asked Patrick why he began shoplifting at a young age, how he'd met his wife, why he'd gone into ministry. He recounted his journey…

I was about 10-years old when my shoplifting started. My father was in the Vietnam War at this time. He was wounded severely and was in an out of military hospitals. My Mom was a mess, so she took me and my sister to live with relatives out of state for a few months. That family was full of alcoholics and thieves who stole regularly to make ends meet as well as for profit. I felt abandoned. We eventually went back to live with our mother. Our relatives visited now and then and brought things like dresses and steaks to sell to my Mom dirt cheap. She knew they were "hot" but she liked getting a good deal and helping them out, too. Mom was a school teacher; we had the bare essentials but few luxuries.

Sometimes, my cousins—who were a few years older—stayed in town for a while. I hung out with them and they taught me how to steal. We felt we were getting back at the system, especially because we'd experienced racism on a fairly routine basis. But my sister knew what was going on and she never stole. Shortly after my shoplifting adventures began, I got caught. My Mom found out and whipped the hell out of me! I felt ashamed but I was upset she reacted so strongly; she'd never tried to dissuade her people from stealing. It had some effect on me, though, because I didn't steal for a while.

I did pretty well in school and well enough to go to a decent college. Somehow, though, the stealing bug reemerged. At first, I paid a couple of friends to steal a few things for me, like this figurine I gave to a girlfriend. We broke up. After graduating, I bounced from job to job and always seemed to take little things from work or break rules here and there. A couple times, I was confronted and warned, which was embarrassing. I'd always tell myself to cut it out but it never seemed to last very long. I had a hard time being honest in my relationships, too. I fell in love with this woman but I didn't tell her about my stealing or my occasional romantic wanderings. She found out and broke up with me on the spot. It took me a long time to get over that.

After several years of drifting, I became interested in attending the seminary. I was in a lot of pain and felt conflicted about my stealing and dishonesty. I thought the structure and discipline of the seminary would help heal me or set me on a better path. I enrolled in their 3-year program. It was a good move for me. I began to reconnect to God and reconnected with my father who was still in the hospital. He told me he was proud of me. That meant a lot.

My older sister got married just before I graduated. My Dad gave her the money for the wedding but then she and my Mom had mixed feelings about inviting him. They said it was because it was too hard to transport him because of his condition and he lived in another state. I got so mad! I flew to his state and flew him back and drove him to the wedding. It was the last time I saw him; he died two months later. He didn't get to see me graduate. I still regret this.

After my father's death, I relied on my faith but it was hard. Then, I graduated and started dating a white woman, which caused a civil war in my family. I could never make everybody happy. I started to shoplift again. I married an African-American woman shortly afterwards. I never should have gotten married. I didn't really love her, I didn't tell her anything about my stealing, and I was still grieving my father's death. She wasn't the most honest person either. We divorced after a couple of years. I started work as a pastor but still shoplifted on occasion. It was stressful, living this secret life and feeling like a hypocrite preaching about the Ten Commandments and how to live a righteous life.

Then, I met the love of my life. This was about 11 years ago. We got married quickly. Unfortunately, good times didn't last long. She had a miscarriage a year after we married which threw her into a depression. I felt helpless. She became pregnant again and it was a tough pregnancy. We were so afraid of losing our child again but were blessed with a healthy baby. But a few months later, my wife was diagnosed with cancer. I was caring for my wife, my son, my congregation, and my mother who was sick, too. I felt like Job; but my faith was shaken and I started shoplifting again.

My mother died two years later, in 2004. My wife's cancer returned despite aggressive treatment. I felt so much pressure. People think I don't care enough but I care too much. I confided in a mentor within the church; all he told me was that I had big shoulders and people were counting on me. Shortly after our conversation, I had my first shoplifting arrest. It was humiliating. I kept it secret and got through the court proceedings with a slap on the wrist. I told myself: I'm never going to steal again. And I believed this.

Then Hurricane Katrina hit. The magnitude of Mother Nature and governmental failures brought up all my doubts about God and justice. I didn't know who to turn to. I had one long "dark night of the soul." My shoplifting started to increase and, two years after my first arrest, I was arrested again. I went to a local counselor and got on anti-depressants. I didn't mention anything about stealing or being a pastor—just that my wife had cancer and I had stress on the job and raising my child. It helped a little. I managed to put together a good two years of not shoplifting.

But, about a year ago, my wife finally passed away. I felt relief but all the grief I was holding back finally rushed forth. I turned to shoplifting and I knew it was only a matter of time before I got caught again. So, here I am. I need help.

My work with Patrick was complex and grueling at times. My first goal was to help him feel safe and find safe people he could trust to unload his "secrets." *"We're only as sick as our secrets,"* I told him. Patrick felt understandably skittish and dragged his feet sharing on the online support group as well as connecting with recovering shoplifters near his city. We made a great deal of progress connecting the dots about the origins of his stealing, linking it to his early feelings of loss and abandonment, his exposure to stealing at an early age, his exposure to the inherent injustices of racism and discrimination, and his tendency to "care too much" and do too much for others at the cost of self-neglect. I told him: *"we in the helping professions (clergy, therapists, doctors, lawyers) are both blessed and cursed by our desire to help."*

Therapy provided Patrick the forum to share his grief over the deaths of his wife, his mother, and his father. He improved his self-care (diet, exercise, reading), set better boundaries, asked for help, and accepted his own imperfections and mistakes with more grace. After 3 months of therapy, he'd progressed but I still had concerns. I suggested he continue therapy, but when his court case resolved favorably again, he assured me he had the insight and the tools to stay on this side of the law.

Three months later, however, Patrick was arrested again. He'd fallen into the same cycle: overworking, not taking care of himself, and not making his recovery program a daily priority. He resumed therapy with me. This time he shared with the online support group, confided in some local friends, and made his recovery a true priority.

Post-script: A month after Patrick took another break from therapy, he e-mailed me. Remarkably, he decided to deliver a sermon at his church where he "confessed" to his congregation about his shoplifting arrests and his "primary sin" of pride: not being able to admit his weaknesses, ask for help, or trust that others would still accept him. Many in his parish were shocked! But he received hugs and words of admiration and support for his openness and courage. I haven't connected with Patrick in about a year. I hope he's still doing well.

Julianne's Story

Julianne, 45, is a successful psychotherapist in a major east coast city. No stranger to treating addictions herself, she'd suffered from eating disorders and compulsive spending for many years, as well as occasional stealing. Her shoplifting, however, escalated in the last year after two of her clinic workers stole $10,000 from her. Recently divorced and remarried with a teenage child, she was arrested for petty theft; her marriage and career teetered. She was on the verge of a nervous breakdown when she contacted me.

As a therapist who's been in therapy several times over the last 15 years of my career, it's a humbling feeling to be the helper seeking help. It was no exception for Julianne. Here was a therapist who'd been in the field as long as I had and who'd also carved out a successful niche treating addictive disorders. She had a myriad of issues which had chipped away at the foundation of her personal and professional well-being. She was a self-admitted workaholic and a long-time shopaholic. But what caused her the most anguish was her recent first arrest for shoplifting a few hundred dollars worth of clothing from a department store. *"When I got caught, it was like I didn't even care; I knew I was being watched, too."* She called her husband to bail her out after spending the night in jail. *"I've never felt more ashamed in my life."*

Julianne had been stealing—mostly shoplifting—on and off most of her life. She'd been honest for several years until she recently discovered her bookkeeper and a fellow therapist had embezzled and defrauded her of nearly $10,000 over a two-year period. This traumatic betrayal triggered Julianne's shoplifting and, as happens so often and tragically, led to a betrayal of herself, her husband, and left her in pieces.

I worked to help Julianne overcome some of her initial shame and anxiety. She felt alone: she'd never met a shoplifter, though she'd sometimes counseled clients who mentioned shoplifting behavior in passing. She had no knowledge how the legal system worked as this was her first arrest. She was terrified her name would end up in the news or, worse, online; her reputation would be ruined. Further, she feared spending anymore time in jail—*"one night was just pure hell!"* she exclaimed.

I had to find a way to treat Julianne as an equal—as I do with all my clients—yet, make sure I maintained some authority to guide her. Therapists often make the worst patients; they know too much about the therapeutic process which can impede them from following suggestions. But Julianne's vulnerability worked in her favor. After creating a safety plan with her, she began to share her story...

I'm divorced and have a teenage son. My first husband was verbally and emotionally abusive and I finally left. I just got married a year ago. My husband is a psychiatrist. We've had conflicts during the last few months over money, our work schedules—it's been tough. And now this! He's in shock; he doesn't know what to think. He thinks it has to do with the money that was stolen from me. But it's more than that.

Do you think you were trying to take back—even symbolically—what was taken from you?

I'm sure that's part of it. But my stealing goes way back. My husband asked if this was my first time shoplifting. I said "no" but I don't know how much to tell him. He's been supportive so far but I fear he's going to use it against me. My first memory of stealing was actually seeing another kid shoplift when I was about 7 or 8-years old. It was traumatic for me. I remember feeling guilty and scared, like I was the one who had stolen. It's no wonder I became a therapist—I have an overactive ability to empathize with others.

17

What else was going on in your life about this time?

Well, there was this other trauma that I thought I'd worked through. There was this old man in our neighborhood who was always hanging around the kids, giving us candy and toys. He invited me and a couple of my girlfriends over to his house. He made us undress and then he exposed himself to us and made us touch him. I got so freaked out I ran into a bathroom and locked myself in. I was terrified. I felt guilty I'd left my two friends in there with him. I don't know if anything more happened between them. Eventually, he persuaded me to come out and play with some toys—there was a toy I was fixated on but I can't remember what it was. Somehow, I got out of there and ran home.

The following day, my father angrily asked me where I was the day before and what I was doing. I was shaking and couldn't speak. He called my friends' parents and we all went to the police station. I was so confused—I thought I was in trouble, like I was being arrested. I'm not sure what happened to the old man, but my parents punished me. My mother told everyone about it but I'm not even sure what she told them. I was on my own emotionally.

I began shoplifting things shortly afterwards. When my folks caught on that I was taking things, they yelled at me and told me I was "bad." Folks from their generation rarely took their kids to therapists but I needed help. I remember in 9th grade I confided in a teacher; I trusted him and he ended up coming on to me. I freaked out again. I remember trying to talk to my Mom about my feelings of being "violated." But she just expressed pity for these men and told me I should, too. It's the story of my life—nobody really gets me. My first husband certainly didn't. He cheated on me and blamed me for his infidelity. A couple years later, I found out my father was arrested for soliciting prostitutes. He and my mother stayed together but this just confirmed how dysfunctional their marriage was; it prompted me to leave my husband.

18

So, do you feel you were stolen from—the sexual abuse, your parents' lack of nurturing, your husband's infidelity?

Yes, I've felt symbolically stolen from but my co-workers actually stole from me. I had a psycho ex-boyfriend who stole money from me. But worst of all is my own mother stole from me but she'd never admit it. She stole money, clothes, food, and other things from me. My brother and sister actually joke about it. My Mom's mother stole from her, too. She's always felt deprived—materially and emotionally.

I shoplifted little things during my teens—especially cosmetics and food. My mother was hard on my father for being overweight and she didn't allow me to have any junk food. So, I stole food from stores and even from our own home—my mother tried to hide it. I also have this memory of shopping with my father and the sales clerk rang the jacket up for $100 less; instead of telling her she made an error, he was happy she made a mistake. I felt that was wrong; and I felt guilty—just like the first time I saw that kid shoplift.

I've always been the kind of person who puts other people ahead of myself. I think my shopping—and even my shoplifting—have been ways of rewarding myself. I see now, I have to get a handle on this. I've had my head in the sand— that's how I missed my employees' stealing from me. My accountant actually caught it or it might've gone on longer.

Over the next two months, I encouraged Julianne to get involved in the day-to-day finances of her business and personal finances. She also had to cut back her work schedule. She decided to take a week off work. I encouraged her to seek support from family and friends. It was high time the helper asked for help. She hired an attorney. She came clean with her parents and sister about her problems and was surprised they were so supportive; her husband was a different story. He was stressed, working long hours, and remained angry and suspicious of her. She understood this but had to learn how to stick up for herself and express her own feelings, including anger—a vital sign of growth.

Julianne and her husband had a rough time. He interpreted her new-found assertiveness as part of her pathology. They had a phone session with me and I explained to him that Julianne's anger and rage was ancient and had to come out to be healed. She'd always felt neglected and misunderstood. Their marriage continued to unravel. They saw a marital counselor but to no avail. I suggested another couples' session but he was convinced I wasn't helping her. It's sad when I encounter these situations. Addictions, and the lying which goes along with them, take a toll on intimate relationships; theft addictions often are harder to understand and forgive. Eventually, Julianne and her husband separated.

As I continued to work with Julianne, I admired her strength to get through very tough times. She felt hurt by her husband's unwillingness to give her another chance and not seeing her shoplifting as a cry for help that could be healed. Julianne's legal issue resolved favorably: she pled guilty and received one year's probation, some fines, and community service. She hired a new office manager and became more involved in overseeing the finances. She stopped working on Saturdays and let go of some patients she'd been seeing for free. She reconnected with friends, avoided stores, and reported very few urges to shop, much less shoplift. She also found healthy ways to manage stress and to reward herself. As for Julianne's broken marriage, she was philosophical…

I don't know if we'll get divorced or try to work things out. Time will tell. I'm okay with being single. I have a full life: work, family, friends, a teenage son. I think this all happened for a reason. I still have so much to heal. I get tired and discouraged sometimes. Shame is so ingrained in my being. I have to confront it. I can't let people walk all over me anymore. If I don't stick up for myself, nobody will.

Dr. Chinh's Story

Chinh, 40, is a well-respected doctor in a major U.S. city. He was born in Vietnam and moved to the U.S. with his family in 1975 after the war. He was in the U.S. military but was discharged for shoplifting. He is married with four children. He acknowledged issues with anger and risk taking— including driving recklessly and using Internet pornography. He was arrested for shoplifting prior to contacting me and finally told his wife about his problems. She didn't understand why he would steal and risk so much. He worries he'll lose his job, his home, and his family.

A couple years ago, I got a phone call from a soft-spoken man named Chinh. He'd been referred to me by a local attorney in his state. Chinh was born in Vietnam and had lived in the U.S. most of his life—he even served in our military. I sensed a great deal of shame and fear in his voice. I told him I've counseled shoplifters of all backgrounds and most, like him, were smart, hard-working, otherwise law-abiding people. He'd never had any kind of therapy before. He'd just been arrested for shoplifting and he feared losing his medical license. He'd told his wife about his arrest and, with my urging, that he'd been shoplifting for 30 years. *"She didn't know what to think,"* he told me.

Chinh also shared that he had a history of thrill-seeking and risk-taking (such as driving fast and recklessly) and a short and explosive temper. He also acknowledged some problems with Internet pornography. After a few sessions, Chinh's story began to emerge...

I recently was arrested for shoplifting while I was out of town for a doctors' conference. After the conference, I went to a store and tried to steal 4 DVDs—worth about $60. They *were all war or police movies. I'm not sure why I wanted them. I had to tell my wife. She's confused. She asked me why I did this. I told her: "I don't know."*

I was born in Vietnam as the war was in full-swing. My family and I moved to the U.S., after the war ended, I was about 8. My Dad had been in the Vietnamese army and was shot but recovered. I admired him and wanted to be like him. I never stole anything before we moved. It was a difficult adjustment for me here. I didn't speak English and it was hard fitting in. My parents were honest, hard-working, religious people. They taught me and my sisters the importance of honesty and hard work. I remember my sister got caught stealing and they spanked and grounded her.

Around age 9, I remember walking in the woods and finding some girlie magazines. It was exciting and I hid them out there but when I went back a few days later, they were gone. I don't know if this made me shoplift but I went to a convenience store and stole some candy. I don't know why I did it; maybe it was because I didn't have any money and whenever I asked my parents to buy me candy they'd say no. They'd buy me other things, though. Eventually, I got caught stealing candy and the manager told me not to come back. I stopped stealing for a while after that. There wasn't anything significant about this time other than my adjustment issues.

During my teen years, I did okay in school but I didn't like rules too much. I remember taking my parents' car out before I had a license. I got a couple of tickets and my parents punished me and made me pay them myself. In high school, I got into a few fights and cheated on several exams. I got caught one time and was suspended for a day. That didn't feel very good. My parents were really upset. I became sexually active but kept this a secret. My parents wouldn't have been happy. They found some of my girlie magazines and punished me.

My parents had a pretty low tolerance for making mistakes or breaking rules; so do I. I'm a Type A personality and a bit of a control freak. I know shoplifting is a mistake, I know it's wrong but I get this big rush from it—I always beat myself up afterwards. I'm a big time perfectionist. When I was young, I tried to be better than my sister at everything. I think this is partly what drove me to want to be a doctor. I wanted to be successful and be admired. If my parents knew about my shoplifting, they'd be very disappointed. If I lose my job, I'll have to make up a story about why.

Speaking of mistakes, I joined the military because I knew they'd paid for my college. But I hated it. I was bored and all the rules and structure really wore on me. I joined when I was 21 and served active duty stateside as a doctor from 30-34 until I was discharged under an Article 15. I got caught shoplifting some video game software at the local PX. I felt the punishment didn't fit the crime. I lost my benefits, too.

I met my wife during medical school and, when I was discharged from the military, we already had two kids. I made up some story about what happened. I told my wife and my parents that it was a mistake, a misunderstanding. I could tell they didn't fully believe me but what could they say? I didn't shoplift for about a year. I focused on finding a full-time job as a doctor and was fortunate to do so.

I like being a doctor but it's stressful. I started shoplifting again—usually after work. It seemed like a quick and easy way to relieve stress. I probably shoplifted several hundred times between 2005 and 2010. Sometimes, it was spur of the moment but 90% of the time it was planned. Usually, I shoplifted things for myself like CDs, DVDs, or videogames. I rarely used the stuff I stole; I just didn't have much free time. When I get home, I have to help my kids with their homework; then I have to study or catch up on office work.

I asked Chinh what he did for fun and if he had any hobbies.

I've had several hobbies like playing golf, playing the violin, and collecting and working on antique cars. But I don't seem to have time for these things. Besides, my wife used to tell me my hobbies take up too much time and are too expensive. She's pretty frugal; I tend to be freer with my money.

I asked: Do you feel restricted by or angry with your wife? Has shoplifting been a means for you to have things without your wife knowing you bought them?

I do feel angry at her sometimes. But if I raise my voice at her or the kids, she doesn't take well to this. She's the tender type. I don't think she'd even approve of my buying all these CDs, DVDs and videogames. She's very specific about what she wants—but so am I. I have a lot of pressure at work. I do surgery. I yelled at a nurse just the other day for giving me the wrong instrument. If there's a mistake, I'm the one who's going to be sued. I was sued once—it was a totally frivolous case and we settled it—but I don't want to go through that again. Doctors aren't supposed to make mistakes.

It felt it was necessary to schedule a couple's session with Chinh and his wife. There were too many power struggles. He needed to see her as his partner, not his parent. During the session, I helped Chinh articulate what he'd learned in therapy with me so far and to come clean about the extent of his shoplifting. To our surprise, his wife was attentive and appreciative that he was finally opening up with her. We discussed Chinh's stress level at work. I explained to his wife how important it was that he deserved to spend some of his hard-earned money the way he wanted to; in addition, he deserved to enjoy hobbies which bring him joy and kept him out of trouble. "Otherwise," I warned, "Chinh is going to keep stealing… or worse."

Chinh's wife was able to hear this. The only question was: would it translate into real change in their relationship? Fortunately, it did. Chinh agreed to make sure he came right home from work each day and spend a few minutes before dinner talking to his wife about his day and asking her about hers. While Chinh's wife certainly deserved a break from the kids upon his return from work, he also needed some down time. They agreed to work this out.

Over the next two months, Chinh reported progress. He came right home after work, got back into some hobbies, enjoyed more leisure time with his kids like taking walks with them and their dogs. Chinh shared how he and his wife felt more connected. They both enjoyed discussing their days with each other. He also reported less impatience with his staff.

I'd always wondered if young Chinh had any residual trauma about the Vietnam War that may have played a part in his shoplifting. I waited until we'd built a rapport and touched on some more current stressors in his life. I asked him: Did you witness any violence during the war? Do you think the war scarred you in any way? Whether true or not, he didn't seem to want to go there: *"I'm at peace with the war,"* he declared. I wasn't sure if he meant the Vietnam War or the war within himself.

Post-script: Despite Chinh's stellar record as a doctor, a very supportive letter from me, and good representation by his attorney, Chinh was not able to get his theft charge lowered. In his state, even a misdemeanor conviction resulted in the short-term suspension of his medical license—thus, he was forced to close his office and lay off his staff. Again, he felt the punishment didn't fit the crime, though he took full responsibility for his actions and the consequences. He surmised that since he'd gotten away with shoplifting hundreds of times, he had to accept his karma. When we completed our therapy, Chinh was trying to sell his home as well. I felt bad for his family being uprooted because of his actions. I hope he and his wife stay resolved and he continues to work a recovery program which keeps him from shoplifting and other risky, destructive behaviors.

JoAnn's Story

JoAnn, 55, is a divorced mother of three who has worked in finance and accounting at a Fortune 400 company for nearly 25 years. Her shoplifting began about 15 years ago after a messy divorce and after entering recovery for alcoholism. She's been arrested several times and was arrested again recently prior to contacting me. This time, she was charged with a felony and was facing jail time and the loss of her job.

I've been in finance at a major company for 25 years. I've been shoplifting for about 15 years and have been caught several times but managed to dodge the bullet. I never went to jail time so I never missed work and my job never found out. If my job did a background check today, I'd be screwed. I've never had any problem with employee theft, just shoplifting. I know I need help no mater what happens in court or with my job. I can't live this double-life anymore.

I think I shoplift because of stress—I have a very stressful job—but also because of anger. I have a lot of authority issues. Fortunately, most of my work doesn't require much supervision. I'm also a recovering alcoholic and maybe I switched addictions along the way. My parents were both alcoholics: that probably says a lot right there. I have two siblings but they're much older and left the home when my parents' drinking and fighting was its worst. In essence, I was an only child and felt abandoned and alone.

My drinking got out of control in my 20s. I went to treatment and got help. Then my father and mother died within a few years of each other, so that was difficult. I was always close to my Dad but my Mom and I were just starting to get close, too. I spent as much time as I could, helping take care of them in their final years. I resented my older sister who always seemed to have life easy. She didn't help much with the folks. She retired early and traveled the world.

After their deaths, I met a man and got married. I think I was trying to fill the void left by their deaths. My husband was much older; I think I was looking for a father figure, too. We met while we were both employed by the government doing secret work. I saw a very seedy and dishonest side of things. After a few years, I stopped working when we had three kids in quick succession. Shortly after having my third child, I found out my husband was having an affair with a co-worker; he left me for her. I was devastated. Here I am with three young kids and no job and no husband. I just fell off the wagon and started drinking again; then, I started having affairs with married men as well. I was out of control.

My ex- and I had a messy divorce and, because of my drinking, he got custody of our three kids. I had to sign them over to him. I didn't even realize what I was doing; I thought he was just taking them for the summer. I eventually got into treatment again. When I got out, miraculously, I found work at my current company. Anyway, the next several years were tough, living without my children. Then, my ex-husband married a younger woman—a doctor, no less—and because he wasn't working at the time and I was, I had to pay him child support. I just about lost it! It was around this time, about 15 years ago, that I started to shoplift. It started impulsively, out of sheer desperation. I stole food—I simply couldn't afford it. I felt guilty but, within a month or so, it became like a habit. I shoplifted about 30 times before I was arrested the first time trying to steal some clothes at a clothing store. It was a terrible feeling. I thought I was going to die. I kept it secret and had an attorney handle it. I thought I'd never do it again, but I did—a few months later.

I've been arrested at least five times since then. It's always little things, inexpensive things: food, clothing, knick-knacks. I seem to get arrested about every couple of years. But after my first arrest, every time I've been arrested I just feel numb—like I don't really care what happens to me, like I deserve it; whatever happens, happens. I was arrested just over a year ago for taking food from a grocery store after I'd relapsed with alcohol. I finally got on anti-depressants. They've helped a bit but, obviously, I still have problems. I just got caught again for taking a few pairs of shoes. This is my bottom; I'm just ready for help with this. My attorney thinks it's an illness but it's hard to convince the courts. They sense something's wrong with me—I've got a good job so it's not been about the money. I'm worried about jail.

I have so much anger and regret in life—I think that's my biggest problem. I lost my children. I lost time with them and I lost their respect due to my drinking even though they know it's a disease. We've slowly been reconnecting over the years. One of my daughters is a shopaholic and I feel responsible for this. My youngest daughter moved in with me recently because they found a lump in her breast. I'm trying to be there for her but I get angry at her for being lazy— she's not working and she knows how to play the guilt-card with me. I'm stressed financially because of my legal issues. I asked her to pay rent if she's going to be here much longer. My kids don't seem to have any idea of the stress I'm under—even if most of it's of my own making. I've wanted to just tell them the truth about my stealing but I'm afraid. But, if I go to jail, I don't want them to find out that way.

I worked with JoAnn to sew together the various threads of her life as they related to her alcoholism and, more specifically, her shoplifting addiction. Her parents' alcoholism and neglect left her feeling ashamed, helpless and abandoned. Her marriage was like a bad replay. These betrayals contributed to JoAnn's deep rage and chronic disrespect for authority and rules. It was amazing she functioned honestly in her work. She used alcohol and shoplifting to douse her flames of rage but it was like pouring gasoline on the fire. We worked to help her find a path

28

toward forgiving herself for giving up her kids and not being there for them. She knew all too well the effects of addiction on children. In addition, JoAnn still needed to grieve her parents' deaths because she hasn't been sober long.

Eventually, JoAnn found the courage to tell her kids about her shoplifting addiction and her pending court date. First, she told her oldest daughter, then her son and, next, her daughter who lived with her. *It was such a relief. They were all so wonderful about it. I don't know why I was so afraid all these years. My oldest daughter said she was glad I was getting help and shared for the first time about her shopping problem; she wants to seek help, too. Now I think my youngest daughter understands the stress I'm under and I'm hoping it will help her be a little less self-centered. But I think the most powerful reaction was my son's. He told me he was proud I sought treatment; he'd got treatment for alcoholism, too. He told me: "Mom, you've always been there for us." I was crying and told him I didn't feel like I was there for them. He just reached out his hand and we walked together for three miles. Maybe, all this had to happen so I could get finally get real with them.*

Post-script: As JoAnn reached the three-month mark of counseling, she headed to court, with the support of her three children. Three months later, I got this letter from her:

Dear Terry,
I just got out off jail. I served 60 days and lost my job. I am now working on my resume and trying to come to terms with all that has happened. I am reaching out to some new friends in recovery and will send something out to the entire CASA online group soon. I'm meeting with my former work manager to clean out my office and she said she has some contacts for employment. My daughter is going with me to clean out my office—a big job after working there 25 years. I'm staying out of stores as, I know, this is a stressful time for me and I'm vulnerable. Thanks for all your help, JoAnn

Marie's Story

Marie, now 50, was one of my first telephone counseling clients when she called me back in late 2003. She was 42 at the time, and still lives on the west coast. She was facing deportation after her 5th shoplifting arrest—this time, a felony. Originally from Asia, Marie had been living in the U.S. for 20 years but couldn't become a citizen due to her criminal history. She served a year in prison on one case. She'd been in recovery for another addiction and wanted help to understand and treat her shoplifting addiction.

Marie grew up in Asia and was repeatedly physically and sexually abused by her father and an uncle when she was 8-10 years old. *"One time, my father almost beat me to death."* She had several brothers and sisters; her family was impoverished. Her paternal grandmother taught her how to steal. *"It was a matter of survival,"* she said matter-of-factly. *When I was caught stealing, my grandmother slapped me! She had to save face. Later, my father kicked my mother out of the house when she got sick. I became a surrogate wife for my father and a surrogate mother to my siblings...*

When I turned 13, my mother suggested I become a prostitute. I had few options, so I took my mother's advice and worked as a prostitute for several years. It was good money. I enjoyed the power I felt but I felt sickened at times. Eventually, I quit and found a clerical job: that's how I met my first husband, an American businessman traveling in Asia. I was in my early 20's. He helped me come to America to be with him. We got married so I could stay in the country.

Soon after their marriage, Marie's husband turned from Jekyll to Hyde: he physically and verbally abused her. *"It was like my childhood all over again."* She stumbled into several addictive behaviors, including shoplifting when she felt angry and powerless. *"I felt like I deserved it."* She had a penchant for pilfering herbs and minerals from Asian health and grocery stores. *"They must have reminded me of my upbringing and we didn't buy herbs or minerals—they were too expensive. I always felt deprived—not just materially but emotionally. I also was angry at God for not protecting me."*

Marie divorced her first husband but managed to stay in the U.S. on an extended work visa. *"But I continued to be attracted to "geographically and/or emotionally unavailable men."* She continued shoplifting and her subsequent arrests kept her life in turmoil. She suffered depression and anxiety and eventually went on medications which helped a little.

In counseling, I educated Marie about shoplifting's addictive aspects, added her to my online support group, and we discussed my book *Something for Nothing*. She was sharp and inquisitive and related to many things shared in the group and in my book. She understood her shoplifting was a "cry for help." Because of her earlier victimizations, shoplifting made her feel she was getting her power back; but like the power she felt prostituting herself, it didn't last long and a made her sick to her stomach. She knew there had to be a better way to find power and peace.

Marie and I also processed her guilt over leaving her family in Asia—particularly her disabled sister—by coming to the U.S. to live her own life. Much like "survivor's guilt," Marie came to realize she stole things that reminded her of home and, by getting arrested, was unconsciously punishing herself for leaving her family. *"I don't know if I deserve to be free or happy so I need a way to sabotage this."*

Marie received a positive legal outcome—she avoided jail and deportation and was put on probation; my letter certainly helped. She spent the next year counseling with me once or twice a month. She had trouble staying out of relationships, though each new relationship she got into was less abusive and controlling. As she worked through her core issues, she felt less driven to act out and became more involved in recovery groups, her work, friendships, and hobbies; yet, she felt called to do something significant with her life. She told me: *"I want to help people. I could sit on my pity pot or I can make amends by giving back to society."* Little did she know what opportunity would come...

Post-script: Marie called me in 2008, in tears. She'd recently been caught shoplifting again, after nearly four years of solid recovery. Prior to leaving to visit her family in Asia in late 2007, she'd broken up with one man and was dating a new one; she had mixed feelings about this and about visiting her family. Her trip stirred up deep emotions: seeing her country's poverty and her disabled sister's mistreatment by her family left Marie feeling guilty, helplessness, angry, and sad. She fell back into her role of caretaker, overextending herself financially and emotionally.

When she returned to the U.S., she was arrested for stealing groceries from an Asian store. I helped her unpack the feelings her family trip had stirred up. Her trip also triggered memories of her childhood abuse. She'd underestimated the power of the past and was ill-prepared to process her emotions; she acted them out in familiar fashion: shoplifting.

Marie felt understandably nervous about her impending court date; after all, she'd just narrowly escaped deportation proceedings four years earlier. She worried this was the end of her luck. But, by some miracle, the judge placed Marie on a lengthy probation. The judge took Marie up on her offer to start a local C.A.S.A. group to help fellow shoplifters. Marie started the group a month later; it's been meeting over three years and has 20-30 members at each weekly meeting. Marie reports periodically to the judge who sentenced her. I've visited Marie and C.A.S.A. several times and am proud to call them fellow sisters and brothers in recovery.

Gina's Story

Gina, 41, is a divorced mother of 3 young girls. She's had a long history of lying, shoplifting, employee theft, and rule-breaking behaviors. She's been arrested numerous times which has severely impacted her life. She's a dynamic, open-hearted soul who's struggled with the pain and shame of her actions; but her greatest heartache comes from the judgment and ostracism by her "religious" family. She focuses on her relationship with her girls, her soon-to-be husband, and her own recovery; but she knows she has to be careful every day.

Hello, my name is Gina. I'm a busy mom of 3 and have been a small business owner for the past 9 years. Before that, I worked as a pharmacy professional for 15 years and have a background in science from a respected university. I grew up the youngest of 6 children in what most would call an ideal middle-class home. My father was a hard-working tradesman and my mother was a school teacher. We went to mass every Sunday and enjoyed frequent family events together. But behind closed doors, I felt lost and insignificant among my family members. Blame always seemed to fall on my shoulders. The lack of validation and encouragement from those around me caused my self-esteem to erode. My parents often filled my life with material things instead of affection. Early on, I equated "things" with self-worth and love. I was perceptive, even as a child. It was all too apparent my existence was tolerated at best; never appreciated. This black void, this lack of belonging, would shape my entire life. Since childhood, I've suffered from bipolar disorder and depression, but my family never acknowledged my illnesses. My Mom often told me I was "impossible to love." I asked about seeing a therapist but therapy was viewed as ridiculous and a sign of weakness.

When I was 6, my neighbor molested me—luring me into many violating acts short of intercourse. A few years later, one of my brothers coerced me into oral acts on him. I was too young to know better, but I knew I didn't like it and it stopped. I'd held these secrets locked for years. When I finally told my mother about the neighbor, she didn't say a word. She didn't trust me—I'd lied before for attention—so I blamed myself for her lack of comfort. I wondered if she'd ever told tell my father, but nothing was ever said. No one seemed to care. So, I never told anyone about my brother.

I started shoplifting shortly after the abuses. I had no healthy relationships to guide me on the right path. I did what I wanted and was often unsupervised. I felt life had cheated me, that I deserved more. Shoplifting offered an escape from my pain, my reality; it took me to a place where I could reward myself when I felt worthless. It was my drug... and I was addicted. I was 12 when I was first arrested for shoplifting. My parents did little to address it. I continued to steal on and off. My second arrest came 7 years later, at age 19, when I was in a destructive relationship and my depression worsened. I felt such shame and remorse. I told the police officer I wanted to stop; all he said was: "just stop." Throughout my 20s, I was fired from 6 jobs for employee theft and deceit. I was arrested a third time in 1994. I tried confiding in my parents, but they told me I was stupid for stealing and I should just cut it out. They seemed to have no interest in understanding or helping me.

A few years later, I stumbled into marriage and started a family. I now realize I rushed into all this—longing for a family to call my own. But it was doomed from the start. My stealing continued and I was arrested a fourth time, in 2004, as my marriage began to crumble. I was re-arrested in 2005 and again in 2006; a total of six times. Each arrest resulted in probation. Counseling was never offered or mandated for my shoplifting "problem." I finally sought help and found Terry Shulman and the C.A.S.A. support groups. It was

2006; I was 36. It's difficult to ask for help when you're not used to getting it. I read Terry's book, Something for Nothing, and will never forget how I felt learning I wasn't alone. I thought no one could ever possibly understand my behavior. For the first time, I had hope; but not for my marriage—that was over. I tried confiding in my husband but he always "looked the other way" and blamed all our problems on me. I had to change my situation for me and my kids. I got divorced in 2007. Since then, I've gone through intensive therapy with Terry; this, along with my involvement in C.A.S.A., has been crucial to my continued recovery. I'd been to psychiatrists, tried medications, and found periods of relief from depression; but nothing really helped until I found Terry and C.A.S.A. I'm a loving, giving, smart woman who desperately wants to be an honest, solid asset to society.

I lost a lot. My criminal record prevents me from pursuing my medical career. I've been estranged from my parents and siblings for several years. I have to stay away for the sake of my recovery. Most of them are judgmental and are too closed-minded to understand addiction or mental illness. This is the most painful experience I've ever endured. The lack of support from those who are supposed to love you is immeasurably hurtful. They see me as someone looking for an easy road through life—a liar and a cheat. But that wasn't who I wanted to be. Several members even aided my ex-husband through the divorce proceedings, going as far as attempting to have my children taken from me saying I was unfit. I cannot begin to describe the utter devastation I felt when my own family turned on me.

But these days, I have a concrete faith in God, and in myself; and I believe our sole purpose here is to help one another. I'm no expert at life or recovery, but I'm an expert at my own story. I take full responsibility for my past and I try to forgive those who've wronged me. I've been on the path toward recovery for almost 5 years now. I've gone as long as a year without stealing but have relapsed. Each time, I get back up and re-commit. It's been a year since I've stolen. C.A.S.A. meetings are a safe place to share with other good, but wounded souls. Because of C.A.S.A., I'm able to find strength one day at a time. If my experiences can help someone else find the path toward recovery, we all grow. In October 2010, with Terry's help, I started a local C.A.S.A. group near me. My church granted us the space and we met there weekly. Things were going well for several months. Then, in 2011, a local newspaper ran an article about our group. Some church members complained, upset about our group meeting there. I got a call from the church: our group was no longer welcome—we'd made members feel "uncomfortable." I was heartbroken. This was not only my C.A.S.A. home, but also my worship home. Our group hasn't met there since and I've not heard from the pastor despite several attempts. I can understand the members' reactions, but a pastor? My faith in him was broken. This triggered many painful memories of how my family disappointed me when I needed them most; first my family, then my church.

People and events can be so unpredictable. The article was meant to educate and help others; instead it brought judgment and hypocrisy. The "silver lining" is the pride I have for how I dealt with the disappointment. I didn't go out and steal; I let my feelings be felt, talked with those I trust, and walked away from the negative ideology. I've made wonderful friendships with the local members and I hold my desire to spread awareness about this addiction very dear. I'll continue to move forward with optimism. I'm strengthened by my life lessons and have become the mother I always knew I could be. I am proud of who I've become and am no longer filled with shame. Along with my commitment to my own recovery, the love and support from my fiancé, my children, Terry and my C.A.S.A family, I know our group will find a new home.

"Our greatest victory isn't never falling, but in getting up every time we do." Thank you, Gina.

Notes & Reflections:

Part Two
Biting The Hand That Feeds:
Employee Theft and Other Theft

Crime is contagious. If the government becomes a lawbreaker, it breeds contempt for law; it invites every man to become a law unto himself; it invites anarchy. – Louis D. Brandeis

It's universally wrong to steal from your neighbor, but once you get beyond this one-to-one level and pit the individual against the multinational conglomerate, the federal bureaucracy . . . or the utility company, it becomes strictly a value judgment to decide who exactly is stealing from whom. One person's crime is another person's profit.—Abbie Hoffman

U.S. Government Sues Goldman Sachs for Fraud (excerpt)

Open Secrets, April 16, 2010 by Michael Bechtel
Securities and Exchange Commission today filed a civil lawsuit against financial giant Goldman Sachs and one of its vice presidents, alleging the company defrauded investors by "misstating and omitting key facts about a financial product tied to subprime mortgages as the U.S. housing market was beginning to falter." By doing so, the government has set its sights on one of the largest wielders of political clout, which has denied any wrongdoing in this case...

Employee theft and various corporate fraud are the most pervasive and severe problems in this book. Yet, from my research, these problems prompt the least amount of inquiry into why people steal from work or commit fraud; they're typically treated primarily as legal, moral, or financial issues. Shoplifting has been highlighted much more in the media and has been investigated as a likely addiction. Compulsive spending and hoarding, while not illegal per se, have drawn even more attention, research and treatment options.

Judge's Attendance Reviewed after Reports of Slacking (excerpt)
Detroit Free Press, May 19, 2011 by L.L. Brasier

Oakland County's Chief Judge said that she is reviewing the attendance records of fellow Judge Rae Lee Chabot after a TV camera crew caught Chabot working short days and in some cases not coming to work at all. "If what they reported was accurate, I will certainly be taking it up with Judge Chabot," said Chief Judge Nanci Grant.

A WXYZ-TV news team, which trailed Chabot for five weeks in March and April, caught her leaving work at noon, taking 3-hour lunch breaks and, at times, not coming to work at all.

County Commissioner James Runestad, said he was reserving judgment until he had more facts, but said he'd received numerous phone calls about the story. "I'm absolutely going to look into it," said Runestad. "Somebody's got to raise some hell. It's outrageous if someone is paying for their day in court and the judge isn't there." Chabot, 62, has been a judge 10 years and earns $140,000 a year.

If true, was what Judge Chabot did theft or stealing?

How do you define employee theft? Have you ever:
*Fudged your time card?
*Padded an expense account or report?
*Made personal phone calls on company time?
*Used company postage?
*Used office supplies for personal use?
*Took office items home?
*Borrowed funds for personal use?
*Made personal copies on the copier?
*Failed to report accounting/payment errors in your favor?
*Used the company car for personal business?
*Ran errands on company time?
*Abused the Internet?

Top Seven Reasons People Commit Employee Theft
1. Greed
2. Perceived economic need;
3. To support an underlying addiction (drugs, gambling, etc)
4. Work-related revenge/justification;
5. Attitudinal ("It's not stealing")
6. Opportunistic temptation;
7. Other emotional/life stress issues (the largest group)

We're living in a changing world, especially when it comes to work and the workplace. Note these trends:

-weakened unions
-downsizing and outsourcing
-fewer if no benefit packages
-working harder with less time and less support

Only 46% of employees have ever asked for or negotiated a pay raise.—Accenture survey of 3,400 executives

Is it any wonder most employees feel: "They owe me!"

A recent study reveals what HR and benefits pros are thinking and doing. It's no secret that the recession has killed employee job satisfaction and productivity. The No. 1 reason: payroll budgets have dropped off a cliff. But employers are determined to find ways to keep talented employees happy and working hard, without increasing payroll, a 2010 CareerBuilder survey found. What did the survey of more than 2,700 employers uncover? Pay worries. Employers' top five concerns are:

1. Providing competitive compensation (34%)
2. Maintaining productivity levels (33%)
3. Retaining top talent (31%)
4. Worker burnout (30%), and
5. Providing employees opportunities for advancement (25%)

A 2008 LabManager survey of employees lists the following
Top 10 concerns of employees:

1. Higher salaries and compensation
2. Benefits programs
3. Pay increase guidelines
4. Favoritism
5. Pay equity
6. Human Resources Department
7. Excessive Management
8. Inadequate communication
9. Over-work
10. Workplace conditions and cleanliness

It's been said that happy employees make for more honest
employees. This doesn't mean that your star employee won't
one day be led out in handcuffs. But there are many
companies who continue to rank high in employee
satisfaction and make the "best companies to work for" lists.
As with any relationships, work relationships need nurturing,
too. Here's a short-list of some tips that improve morale.

1. Recognize birthdays and personal accomplishments.
2. Treat them with respect.
3. Establish an employee-recognition program.
4. Back them up.
5. Keep training them.
6. Get to know them.
7. Avoid layoffs and cutbacks.
8. Throw a party, treat them to lunch.
9. Organize employee community projects
10 Offer financial rewards.
11. Conduct employee-satisfaction surveys.

*Charles Schwab & Co. has scrapped its employee-of-the-month
awards. Some managers felt obligated to honor each employee,
devaluing the award. Other managers rewarded only their
favorites, sowing resentment.*—Bloomberg Businessweek, 2011

20 QUESTION
Assessment for Compulsive Employee Theft

1. Have you often lost time from work by loafing or not working your full hours?

2 Has employee theft caused problems in your relationships?

3. Has employee theft ever affected your reputation or people's opinion of you?

4. Have you ever felt guilt, shame, or remorse after committing employee theft?

5. Did you ever steal from work to get money to pay debts or ease financial distress?

6. Did employee theft ever cause a decrease in your ambition or efficiency?

7. Did you ever feel a "high" or "rush" of excitement when you stole from work?

8. Have you stolen from work to escape worries or troubles?

9. Has employee theft caused you trouble eating or sleeping?

10. Did arguments, disappointments or frustrations create an urge to steal from work?

11. Have you noticed you began stealing from work more frequently over time?

12. Have you ever considered self-destruction or suicide as a result of employee theft?

13. Upon stopping employee theft, were you still tempted or preoccupied by it?

14. Have you kept your employee theft a secret from most of those you are close to?

15. Do you have trouble with authority or following rules?

16. Have you continued to steal from work despite having been confronted or fired?

17. Do you often feel angry or feel a need for control?

18. Do you have trouble taking criticism?

19. Do you have persistent feelings of entitlement to get "something for nothing"?

20. Do you have trouble speaking up for yourself, asking for help, or saying "no"?

Most persons with employee theft issues will answer yes to *at least 7* of these questions

Tami's Story

Tami, 53, is a recovering alcoholic and divorced mother of a teenager. Naturally good with numbers, she had no college education but lied on her resume many years ago and got a job as an office manager for a large medical group. Over several years she embezzled hundreds of thousands of dollars to assist various family members and to build a lavish lifestyle, in part, to appear more successful. When she contacted me, she anticipated being confronted and fired, started drinking again and was terrified of losing everything.

I received a frantic phone call in early 2007 from a 53-year old Florida woman who's world was about to unravel. Tami was being investigated by the IRS and other fraud examiners for grand-scale embezzlement from the medical group where she'd worked for nearly twenty years. She was divorced and lived with her teenage son; she worried more about his future than her own. Tami enrolled in my 90-day phone counseling program, stating: *"I've had a problem for a long time. No matter what happens, I know I need help."* Coincidentally, I was headed to Florida in a few days for vacation with my wife. I arranged to meet Tami at an outdoor café for our second session. I gave her my book *Biting The Hand That Feeds* and listened intently as her story unfolded...

I've been stealing my whole life. I'm also a recovering alcoholic. My older sister was a drug user and drug dealer. Around age 13, I remember stealing some money from her stash. My parents' divorced around the time I left home when I was 15. I dropped out of high school, and then started drinking and abusing drugs. I drifted and found odd jobs like working as a cashier at a convenience store. I stole money from the drawer a few times and was caught and fired. Any money I got, I spent. I'm still this way.

43

I started dating this guy. We were really getting close when he was murdered in a drug-related incident. I was heart-broken. About a year later, just after I turned 17, my Mom was murdered by her abusive boyfriend who then took his own life. What can I tell you: I went off the deep-end. My drinking and drugging escalated but that's also when I started becoming the caretaker of my siblings and my father.

Within a few years, I managed to complete my GED, took a few college courses, and taught myself accounting. I lied about my credentials and got my first accounting and bookkeeping jobs. I began skimming money and writing checks to fake vendors and then cashed them. I didn't use much of the money myself; I used most of it to help my sister, brother, and my father. They didn't ask any questions. I started dating another man and married him. He turned out to be a pedophile and I left him soon after.

I guess I have a lot of trust issues. It's ironic that I come off as trustworthy to most people—especially my employers—but I'm really just a big fraud, a thief. Over the next 10 years I lived a secret life, stealing relatively small amounts of money from various jobs. It's a miracle I was never caught. I'd quit and move from city to city if I thought people at work were getting too suspicious. I held low level accounting jobs at first, including for a construction company and a "count room" in Vegas—there was a lot of employee theft going on at that job. I felt guilt and stress all the time but the way I looked at it was, my life was already a fraud—I was lying about my credentials—what's the difference? My drinking kept me in a fog and my codependency drove me to rescue everyone. I wonder if anyone will be there for me.

In 1989, I landed this job with a really good company—a medical group of various doctors and surgeons. They were really good to me, paid me well, and treated me like family. As I steadily worked my way up the ladder, I had more access to money, checks and credit lines. I had periodic urges to steal but resisted them. A few years later, I wanted to adopt a child. Even though I was single, within a year, I was able to do so. I was so happy, but now that I look back on it, I see how obsessed I was with giving him the best of everything. I bought my first home which was great but kind of scary. I began embezzling money from work. I spread it out and there was no real oversight: everybody trusted me.

Then, my brother got a DUI and I bailed him out by hiring an attorney for him. I also helped him with a down payment for his home. As my son grew up, I bought him the best of everything—clothes, toys, you name it. A few years later my sister started having trouble with her kids. Her daughter died of a drug overdose and she was afraid her teenage son would, too. I started embezzling more money and gave my sister $50,000 to send her son to an out of state drug treatment program. Once I'd crossed that line, something seemed to take over. As fate would have it, the company was sold—I even helped negotiate the sale price—but they didn't keep me on. I wondered if they suspected me of stealing. I felt rejected and abandoned. I felt angry; it was unfair. I know it's crazy but that's how I felt.

Over the next few years, I found sporadic employment, sold my home, and moved to another part of the state. I needed to get away from my family and wanted to turn over a new leaf. I went about a year without stealing. I had a little savings from the sale of my home but began living off my credit cards when I wasn't working. I started drinking more due to the loss of structure. I'm easily bored and restless.

After about five years since leaving my job with the medical group, they tracked me down and called me. I was terrified they'd finally discovered my secret. Instead, they actually called me to ask if I wanted to come back to work for them. I couldn't believe it; first, I thought it might be a trap or something. I was torn: I liked where I lived and was trying to stay on the straight and narrow. I was flattered they still wanted me. I also needed the money. I knew there'd be a chance I'd steal again but I decided to accept their offer. I thought I'd be able to be honest this time.

I sold my home and moved back downstate with my son. It didn't take long for my brother and sister to come calling, asking for—expecting—one thing or another. I don't know why I couldn't say no. Within a few months, I started embezzling again. I put my heart and soul into that job—they were paying me $200,000 a year—but it never seemed like I had any money to save. I was overstretched. I was always working, spending, stealing, or helping my family. I didn't even have much time or energy for my son. I fell into the trap of buying him all this stuff to compensate for my not being there. He didn't ask for much; I knew he'd rather just have time with me. I don't even have time for myself. I don't have any hobbies. If I had my way, I'd be an interior designer. Soon I may be decorating my own prison cell...

As Tami continued therapy, I added her to my private online group and she connected locally with a few group members who lived in her area. It was amazing her employer never discovered her early stealing, rehired her, and kept her employed with access to financial information and assets while IRS and fraud investigations continued. I encouraged her to take a vacation but she thought that might bring more suspicion to her. I asked if she was still tempted to embezzle and she said "yes." Tami's drinking continued and interfered with our therapy. I told her to get into treatment immediately. She knew she needed help but didn't know who'd watch her son. I persuaded to talk with her father who'd been sober for several years. He was shocked about her stealing but agreed to watch her son while she got help.

"Are there any inpatient treatment centers for people with theft problems?" Tami asked me. None that I know of, I said.

Tami ended up finding an inpatient program that could take

her in a week. Within days of telling her employer she'd be checking into alcohol treatment, she embezzled $6,000 by writing a company check to herself—blatant and sloppy. She had spiraled out of control. She began a 90 day treatment program covered in part by insurance and part out-of-pocket.

When we resumed our treatment by phone, Tami sounded completely different. She "confessed" something she said she'd never shared before which she got in touch with and shared about in treatment: *I started being molested by a pedophile at age 13. I had to go to work at this age to help my Mom pay our bills and that's where I met him. He's the one I married. I was just 16-years old. My Mom had to sign papers. Why didn't she protect me? (Tears...) It was all about my working and giving my money to my Mom.*

Over the next couple of months, Tami and I had weekly sessions. She also had a local therapist and psychiatrist, attended A.A. regularly, and participated on our online support group. She never returned to her former job which eventually found proof of her ongoing embezzlement and went to the police. By year's end, Tami was indicted for embezzling over $500,000 during a ten-year period. Tami sold her home and many of her possessions and moved into a small apartment with her son—then 18—and hired an attorney for $50,000 to represent her. She continued to work her recovery programs for both alcohol and stealing. I encouraged her to come clean with her son, who was smart and knew something was going on anyway—besides just her alcohol problem. I'm not certain she ever did so. She still wanted so badly for him to see her as she wanted to be seen.

Post-script: I wrote a letter on Tami's behalf but she fell out of contact with me and the online group soon afterwards. I wondered what became of her. Then, about a year ago, I received an e-mail from a friend of hers. Tami's case had been delayed for two years but she finally pled guilty to embezzlement. She was sentenced to 10 years in prison.

Randi's Story

Randi, 35, married with no kids, contacted me after having been forced to resign from a 10-year job at a prestigious university. She'd worked in purchasing and, during the last five years, fraudulently ordered various supplies and electronics for her own personal use, as gifts, and to sell. Over time, she became more brazen and knew she'd be caught but couldn't stop. She also began shoplifting 15 years ago. While unlikely to be prosecuted, she knew she needed help. She came clean with her husband but not her family. She wanted to know what drove her to steal and how to stop.

I feel really embarrassed about living a lie for so many years. I feel like a phony. My husband is one of the most honest people I've ever met. I don't want to lose him. I know this is a turning point in my life. I'm relieved to find help. I've been stealing half my life and I know I need to change. My husband and I have been married about 7 years but we've known each other since we were teenagers. I'm a smart person—I've got a graduate degree—but I've been stuck. I think that's partly why I've been stealing. I've been confused about my next step; stealing distracted me but just made me more stuck. It took a lot of my energy and further undermined my self-esteem and self-confidence.

My stealing from work really escalated about three years ago when my husband stopped working and went to graduate school. I started to worry more about our financial situation. His parents are pretty wealthy and were paying for his school but still... I feel like they have a lot of say-so in what we do; I'm not used to that. My folks were always really bad with money. I basically had to learn how to support myself at an early age. I've always felt this pressure and resentment. I guess you could say I felt it was unfair.

48

I worked at a major university and had access to information about everyone's salaries. I guess I felt underpaid and envious. I didn't ask for a raise but should have but I felt I didn't deserve one—especially because I was stealing. I was really close to my boss. When she finally found out about my stealing, she asked me: "Why didn't you ask for help?" There were many times I wanted to but I've always had a hard time asking for help. Even when I tried to talk to my husband about some of my pressures and concerns, he didn't really understand; he's less of a worrier than I am.

I grew up in the south. My Dad was an alcoholic. He'd work, come home, drink and fall asleep. He wasn't really there for me. My Mom is a total narcissist. Even my older sister would agree. She bounced checks and we never had any money. She used mine and my sister's social security numbers to get credit cards in her name. I wanted to get away from her. My sister always had fights with her but I never show my anger; I'm the peacemaker. When I tell my sister about getting fired from my job and about my stealing, I know she'll blame it all on my Mom. I think there's a connection there but I know I need to take responsibility for my actions.

I grew up with both material and emotional deprivation. My folks never talked about anything real. I guess I inherited that trait. I didn't want to bother anybody. Sometimes I stayed with friends so I could be around normal families. After high school, I started shoplifting. I got caught with a friend during college and was suspended for a while. My parents knew about this but acted like it never happened— they never even asked me if anything was wrong. I quit shoplifting and took a few jobs—I was a nanny for a while— but I didn't steal even though I had some thoughts about it.

I started dating my future husband shortly after graduating college. I remember one time when we were going through a rough period. He moved away and I happened to be working at a shoe store. I worked the cash register and didn't ring up some of the cash sales; I pocketed the money. Somehow, it comforted me. It seems like when things are in transition in my life or I feel lost or alone, I have more urges to take things. It reminds me of the feelings of loneliness I used to have growing up in my family. I think I felt entitled to steal.

My husband moved back and I took the job at the university. It surprised me they didn't have very many oversight systems to track theft or fraud. Some people got caught, however, and they were fired. I tried to think about this but I started to test the system here and there by ordering little things, inexpensive things—sometimes I'd just give them away to people. Then, about five years into my job, I got married—I think this transition caused me to start stealing. I felt responsible for the marriage just like I felt responsible for everyone in my family growing up. I didn't want to be like my Mom—irresponsible—but I went too far the other way.

Another factor that drove me to steal was the financial and emotional stress I was feeling as I tried to get pregnant. We didn't tell our parents anything about this. We had several fertility treatments—$5,000 each—but they didn't work. I felt helpless and frustrated. I think this drove me over the edge.. Stealing was my way of helping defray some of the costs. I started selling items I was ordering at work, like digital cameras. But, even more, stealing seemed to help me feel like I had some power or control over things

As Randi and I continued our sessions, she identified with many of the stories in my books and with the stories of those on my online group and some weekly phone support groups. She had most of the hallmarks of so many people who develop theft disorders: she felt "on her own" from an early age; she stuffed her anger and rarely spoke her truth; she played peacemaker and caretaker; she grew up too quickly and had an exaggerated sense of responsibility; she found it hard to ask for help; and she felt entitled to steal based on the unfairness of her life, her suffering, and her sacrifices.

It was very hard for Randi to be out of work for a while but it forced her to take care of herself and allow herself to be taken care of. We had a session with her husband that helped him understand the origins of her stealing and how he could assist her in recovery. Randi was grateful he was so supportive and promised not to leave her. They both decided not to tell their parents why Randi was fired—at least for now.

Randi completed most of the exercises in my books. This helped structure some of her time. She especially got value from doing my "life is unfair" and "lucky gratitude" lists; she had to get in touch with and unload a lot of grievances before she could get to the good stuff she had going for her. Randi eventually wrote an apology letter to her former boss which she e-mailed and read to me. She set some boundaries with her parents and reconnected with some old friends. She'd made it through the holiday season and had just begun applying for new jobs when our treatment came to a close.

Post-script: Several months after completing my counseling program, Randi contacted me to schedule a follow-up session. She sounded great! She'd found new work and recognized she'd still have to watch temptations, but she and her husband were getting along better than ever. *"Oh, and one more thing,"* she added. *"We're pregnant!"*

Shane's Story

Shane is married, in his mid-30's, and has a newborn. He was raised very religious and has always been concerned about his image and impressing people. He's had problems with lying and stealing since his teens and was arrested for shoplifting about ten years ago. A few years ago, he was confronted and fired from a job for taking office equipment home. He told his wife but downplayed the details as well as his history. Recently, however, his father-in-law confronted him about some missing belongings and Shane's wife gave him an ultimatum: Get help or get out!

Shane's wife initially contacted me very concerned about her husband's history of employee theft and, more recently, his taking things from her father who confronted him, more concerned than angry. Shane felt extremely embarrassed. He'd never had counseling before and was somewhat reluctant. But his wife used some tough love. With a new baby, Shane realized he had to get help. Over the next three months, we had phone sessions weekly. His story unfolded...

Nobody in my family knows about any of my stealing—just my wife and her family. Fortunately, she comes from a family that's not as judgmental as mine. I'm embarrassed about my behavior. It's my worst nightmare come true: I've always tried to make sure people have a good impression of me. I'm not sure why I steal, maybe it's related to this need to make people think I'm better than I actually am.

I grew up in the southwest but my family moved a couple of times and they live in the Midwest now. I'm the oldest of four. I was brought up pretty religious. Stealing and lying were always frowned upon. I think my parents—and probably my younger siblings—would be disappointed in me.

It's strange, though, because I'm actually honest in all other areas of my life. I didn't have a bad childhood. I've always been quiet in my family—they can be a little sarcastic and so can I—but when I visited friends' families, I was always talkative and outgoing.

We grew up middle-class. I don't recall ever wanting anything. My folks had pretty normal rules and expectations. They were pretty careful with their money. If anything, maybe they seemed a little more generous and attentive to my younger sisters; I just figured it was because they were girls. As I got older, I took an interest in business—I've always been good with numbers—and I remember wanting to make money. I like material things but I also wanted to make money for security and to be able to take good care of a family when I was ready to start one.

When I got married six years ago, I started to worry more about not having enough money. I'm not sure where that comes from—maybe it's just the culture—but I think this worrying played a part in my stealing. But even before stealing, I'd tell white lies here and there to make myself look better. I also cheated on a few tests in school. I went through a dark period during high school. I had a bad case of acne and didn't feel like I fit in sometimes. I remember feeling there was no real justice in the world: the jerks got the girls and some athletes got more playing time than I did if the coaches liked them, even though I was better.

When I went to college, my parents paid for half but I had to pay the other half. I had mixed feelings about this; I'm pretty sure most of my friends didn't have to pay for their school. I guess this reinforced my anxiety about money—like I'd better make enough so I don't have to worry about it. So, just before graduating college, I started a small software company. It had its ups and downs. I invested any money I earned or saved into that company. I also invested $5,000 in a friend's business. After about a year, he told me he'd lost *all the money. When I looked into it, I found out he'd lied to me and had actually invested it in an illegal scheme. I felt like a fool for trusting him—plus I lost a friend. I never told anyone—certainly not my folks—because I was too embarrassed. Around this time, I started to shoplift little things here and there. I felt like $5,000 had been stolen from me and I was trying to even things up.*

I worked some part-time jobs but kept investing a lot of time and money into my software business, hoping it would take off. I was struggling financially but didn't want to let anyone know this. When I finally gave up and sold my company after five years, I barely made much. I lied about that to my friends and family. Then I was arrested at Costco for shoplifting several items. I didn't tell anyone. I went through the legal system, pled guilty, and got it off my record later.

Then I met my wife and we started dating. I didn't tell her anything about my stealing. I thought it was behind me. But shortly before we got married, she received an anonymous phone call from someone telling her not to marry me because I was a thief. It rattled both of us. I have no idea to this day who made that call. She confronted me about it. I told her I'd had a few problems in the past but it was no big deal. She pressed me a bit more but eventually accepted my answer. But I always felt she was suspicious of me from that point on. I guess I should have sought out counseling at that point but who thinks to go to counseling for stealing?

Then I worked as an assistant manager at a golf equipment store for five years. About a year after getting married, I started stealing stuff from that job—mostly clothes. Some things I stole I gave as gifts. I think I felt entitled on some level, partly because I knew other co-workers were stealing, but also because I felt I worked harder than most people. My wife questioned me a couple of times about things I brought home. I lied to her and told her that the golf industry gave away lots of free stuff.

54

Eventually, I left this job to go back to school full-time for 2 years. I kept my nose to the grindstone and didn't steal much except for a few stupid things while doing an internship at a cable TV company. I graduated in 2009 and my wife and I moved to the east coast where I'd landed a job as an office manager for a business. This was around the time my son was born. Maybe I was stressed or nervous about being a good enough father. I didn't steal right away but one night I took some video equipment home with me. I had been looking at it for some time, so it was planned. I knew the office had security cameras but I didn't think they'd even miss it. But they did. They got me on camera. When confronted, I should have told the truth—I think they would have just given me a warning. But I tried to lie about it and that made it worse. They not only fired me but prosecuted me, too. I told my wife I'd taken the stuff—but I didn't tell her I'd also denied it. She asked me why I did it; I didn't have a good answer myself, let alone for her.

I thought our marriage was over—that her suspicions about me had been confirmed. Maybe because we had a child together, she stayed with me. We ended up moving back out west. She told her father what happened. I was embarrassed. But he seemed to want to help me. A couple weeks later, he asked me to help him with a small construction project. I ended up taking some tools at the job site. Some people asked my father-in-law about this. He told my wife and then they confronted me. I confessed. They told me to get help. But I started a new job a few months ago in another state— I'm temporarily separated from my wife and son—so my wife went on the Internet to find help. I was up front with my current employer about why I was fired from my last job. I'm amazed they hired me. I'm not working around money or equipment but I still get tempted to take things here or there. I know I need help. I don't want to lose my family...

Shane and I worked together weekly for three months. For never having had counseling, he did connect some dots and was probably as honest with me as he'd been with anyone. His wife joined in on a session. She shared that, even though they'd been communicating by phone, Shane seemed much more open and relaxed. He shared things we discussed in therapy with his wife which helped her understand how his lying and stealing developed. She asked him if there was anything else he was not telling her. He said "no" but admitted he didn't tell her every detail of every time he stole. I reassured her, noting how it's not always best for someone who's had an affair to recount every detail. She reminded Shane: *"I didn't fall in love with and marry you because I thought you were perfect. I know you're not perfect. I love your quirks but I want you to be honest with me. I want to feel close to you."* Shane seemed to take it in.

As Shane created some space between him and his family and did some more reflecting and soul-searching, he saw more clearly some dysfunctional family dynamics. He refocused on the important things in life—not money or stuff, but relationships, peace of mind, and spirituality. He wanted to teach his son the importance of integrity and self-acceptance. He wanted to be the best father he could be. Along the way, he learned that "best never means perfect."

Post-script: As Shane reached the 3-month mark of our work together, he and his wife and son were about to be reunited under one roof; perhaps the time away from them helped Shane appreciate his wife and his life even more. I only hope Shane continues his therapy and recovery journey. He has a long way to go…

Bristol's Story

Bristol is the 18-year old youngest daughter of very wealthy parents in a very affluent part of the country. Her father is a self-described shopaholic and her mother may be a closet shopaholic. Bristol had a strained relationship with them. Her parents contacted me after discovering she had fraudulently charged $30,000 worth of clothing and goods on their credit cards. They arranged for me to fly to their state to work with Bristol over three days in their home.

Two years ago, a mother called frantically—convinced her daughter was a shopaholic. "How do you know?" I asked.

She replied: *"Because she recently charged over $30,000 worth of clothes on my husband's and my credit cards without our permission!"*

Me: Do you know why she did this?

Mother: She's got a lot of issues. Mostly, I think she's a spoiled brat and thinks money grows on trees. She probably gets this from her father. He's a shopaholic, too; he admits it. I see you offer a 3-day program? Is there anyway you can come to us? She can't go to college until she gets help.

Me: Well, that's possible. I'll have to check my schedule. I'd have to charge a premium to travel to you and you'd have to cover my airfare and lodging. Don't worry, I don't have to fly first-class or stay at The Ritz.

Mother: We've got money. Let us know when you're available. This is an emergency!

Me: Can I ask you a couple more questions? Is your daughter in therapy or on medication? Does she want help? I'll need to talk to her first to assess her readiness and willingness for help. I don't want to waste your time and money.

Mother: She's been in therapy for several years but it's not working, obviously. I think she needs specialized help for her shopping problem. That's why I contacted you. We haven't been able to find help locally. Yes, she's on meds—anti-depressants. What else? Oh, does she want help? It doesn't matter if she wants help, she needs help. But if you need to talk to her, I can put her on the phone... BRISTOL?!... BRISTOL?! Pick up the phone! It's the therapist I told you I was going to call! He wants to talk to you!

Me: (Hmmm... what am I getting myself into here?)...

Bristol: Hello?

Me: Hello Bristol? This is Terry Shulman. I'm a therapist in the Detroit area. Your mother called me and wanted to talk to me about something that happened recently with you. She found me on the Internet because I specialize in working with issues related to shopping and stealing—

Bristol: Uh-huh...

Me: Can you speak freely for a few minutes or is there someone there with you?

Bristol: No, I can talk. I don't really care if anybody listens. Nobody listens to me anyway.

Me: Okay, well, was there an incident recently where you used your parents' credit card without permission?

Bristol: Yeah. I did that. I guess I got their attention.

Me: Did you charge something like $30,000 on it?

Bristol: I don't know how much I charged. I wasn't counting. That's what they said it was. I guess that's what it was.

Me: Do you think you have a problem with shopping? What did you charge, clothes? Do you have your own credit card?

Bristol: They think I have a problem with shopping but they're the ones who have the problem. I have my own credit card but they make me pay for everything myself anyway.

Me: It sounds like you're angry at your folks. Are you?

Bristol: I don't know if I'm angry. I'd say I'm more sad; frustrated, maybe.

Me: Is this the first time you've stolen or charged something without their permission?

Bristol: Yeah, I guess. But they steal from me all the time.

Me: What do you mean, they steal from you?

Bristol: My grandfather left me a trust fund and they use it like their piggy bank. Anything I want or need, they take it

*out of that fund. I don't even know how much is in it but I'll
be lucky if I have anything left.*
Me: Well, it sounds like there're a lot of issues going on
besides the recent credit card charges. Your mother says
you're in therapy. Did you talk to him or her about all this?
*Bristol: Him and her. I have two therapists. I've been going
to them forever. It's the same old story.*
Me: Well, I don't know if I can help you. Have you looked at
my website? Maybe you'd like to read a little bit about me
and make up your mind. I guess your folks are willing to fly
me out to work with you for 3 days. We'll probably get them
involved after we've had some time to work together.
*Bristol: I've looked at your website Mr. Shulman. I don't
know if you can help but I'm willing to meet with you.*
Me: Call me Terry.

One week later, I flew out to the west coast, and took a
shuttle from the airport to a quaint little hotel in a tony town.
Around mid-afternoon, a friendly, lithe young woman in a
blue convertible BMW picked me up. She was Bristol's
attendant, aide—I don't know what you'd call her. She said:
"You've got your work cut out for you," she said. "With
Bristol?" I asked. *"No, with her parents."*

The car wound up through the mountains and, a few minutes
later, stopped at the gates of a very exclusive community.
The gates opened mysteriously and we drove past one
mansion after another. We came to another gate. (You've got
to be kidding me, I thought). Again, the gates slowly parted
and we drove up a hill past even larger mansions until we
arrived at the top and pulled into a driveway next to a white
Mercedes SUV and a jet black Range Rover. I stepped out
and looked in awe at the view of the valley below.

I was escorted through huge wooden doors into the estate.
The architecture and design of this house were breath-taking.
I did my best to stay centered and unimpressed as I heard the
quick clack of high heels on stone floor get louder, closer.

"Hello Terrence. Welcome." Bristol's mother was a striking and formidable woman, self-assured and a bit intimidating. She told me to have a seat and asked if I'd like some lunch. I obliged and sat in a screened in porch where Bristol and I would spend much of the next three days together. Bristol's mother used an intercom to summon her for lunch. I felt like I was in *Citizen Kane's Xanadu.*

In walked Bristol—more petite and meek than she sounded on the phone—dressed in Goth black. We said hello and shook hands. I sensed both a great vulnerability and an immense strength. We dined on sandwiches and sodas. Her mother treated Bristol with measured caring. Was this the same mother I spoke with a week ago who seemed to want to eat her young? Maybe we were all just on our best behavior?

On Day 1, I worked to gain Bristol's trust. I also had a lot to learn about her life and her concerns in order to formulate a plan to help her. Bristol showed me her journals of poems and short stories. She planned on going to a liberal arts college in the fall. I shared that I'd also done some writing and had once planned to be and English teacher. Slowly, a picture emerged of Bristol as the go-between, the shock absorber between her parents' troubled marriage. Her two older sisters had already left for college and Bristol said they had issues with Mom and Dad, too. But Bristol was left alone to fend for herself. She painted her story like this…

My Mom was raised poor and is a closet shopaholic—she acts like she's frugal but she hides bags and other purchases. She's also a control freak and is obsessed with her looks. I'm not really into superficial stuff and she knows it. My Dad is a workaholic. He inherited his father's business and took it to the next level. This home is his monument to his own ego. My sisters were already gone by the time we moved in a year ago. I'm leaving soon, too. My Dad is the trustee of a fund my grandfather left for me—he left trusts for my sisters, too. They were supposed to be for our benefit but we recently found out he's been using our money for his business, this house, maybe his shopping sprees. My sisters won't talk to him. He apologized and said he'll pay every cent back. As far as I'm concerned, he stole the money. My Mom says she didn't know about this. But I recently found out anything they've bought me or paid for—my car, my therapy, my clothes—they've paid out of my trust. So, nothing they've ever given me was really a gift from them—it was a gift from me, my own trust! Things kind of came to a head recently when I used their credit card. I guess I wanted them to see how it felt for me. Now they're saying I can't go to college.

On Day 2, Bristol's mother picked me up in her white Mercedes SUV. I did some psycho-educational work with Bristol about shopping and stealing. Later, I met Bristol's Dad, a top businessman, who proudly gave me a tour of the family compound which he'd helped design and custom-built over the last several years. He gleefully showed me his spacious private office, accessible only by spiral staircase up to the third floor, filled with all kinds of vintage and kitsch memorabilia. *"It's like being a kid in a candy store, isn't it?"* A ping of envy coursed through me—I couldn't deny it; but I quickly came back to my senses as I thought: this is a perfect lesson about how all the money and beautiful things in the world mean little to nothing when there's a dysfunctional family and a child in distress.

At the end of Day 2, I reminded Bristol we had one more day together. I wanted to have her parents join us at some point tomorrow to discuss what we've learned and where to go next. I asked Bristol how she felt about that and, also, if there was anything important she'd yet neglected to share with me.

I don't know if it's going to do any good to have them join us. We've had family sessions with my therapists before. They tend to sugar coat and minimize their part of the equation. Their hypocrisy is appalling. They try to buy my love with money and things all the time and then I find out that it's actually my money they're using. But what hurts even more is something I haven't really talked about with my therapists. I've tried to forget about it but I can't. My parents used to hit me and beat me when I was younger, especially my Mom; she also called me horrible names. They'll deny it or say they don't remember. Why can't they just admit it and apologize? I want to be closer to them but I can't. So, I settle for stuff, money and stuff—because inside, I just feel like shit.

I asked Bristol if she felt she could bring up her feelings about this physical abuse during a family session at some point tomorrow. She said she didn't know. I told her we could have a family session and start with less threatening discussion. We agreed on a sign she would give to indicate if she felt ready for me to bring up this tender subject.

On Day 3, Bristol picked me up in her Black Range Rover SUV. She and I spent time going over some ancillary issues such as a plan for finishing her art portfolio and application for college; distinguishing healthy from unhealthy friends and peers; and processing how she'd apologize for misusing her parents' credit card even though her parents' had already deducted the money from her trust to pay the bill.

We had a 2-hour family session at the end of the day where Bristol apologized for abusing her parents' credit card. I explain that, in my opinion, Bristol wasn't a shopaholic but had acted out her anger and frustration and helplessness through shopping and stealing. Bristol did a wonderful job of expressing her feeling that it was unfair for either parent to use money from her trust without her permission or input. Then, I looked over at Bristol to see if she'd give the signal to proceed in confronting her parents about her past physical and verbal abuse; she nodded and went right into it.

Over the next half hour, Bristol poured out her heart about the pain and hurt she felt at both of their hands and recounted specific abuses that most impacted her. I glanced over at her regularly, giving her a look of encouragement and a sign that reminded her to take deep breaths and then exhale. Her parents sat frozen and expressionless as if in disbelief.

When Bristol was finished, her parents took turns speaking. They both denied any physical abuse whatsoever. Bristol's Mom mentioned one incident where she admitted slapping Bristol across her face but said she apologized for that a long time ago. Her tone resonated with anger and defiance. Bristol's Dad spoke in gentler tones, expressing sorrow that Bristol had these memories. He shared that if there was anything he or her mother did to make her feel unloved or unsafe that they apologized for this. He didn't admit abuse.

Bristol expressed how she felt very disappointed that neither of her parents had enough courage or respect for her to just admit the truth. So, there was no "fluffy reconciliation" this time but, when I had a moment alone with Bristol afterwards, I hugged her and told her how proud I was of her. She broke down and cried for the first time and thanked me. If everything she related was true—she grew up that day. It seemed this recent family drama was co-created over the parents' empty nest fear of being left with each other. Bristol likely had mixed feelings about leaving them, too.

Post-script: A few days after I returned home, I spoke to Bristol's therapists by phone. Then, Bristol's mother called me: *"Well, I don't know what good you did. Where do we go from here?"* I told her I'm sorry she feels that way and I didn't choose to talk to her without Bristol present, that they might be best to deal with all of this with their local therapists. Bristol kept in touch periodically by e-mail. I was in their state about a month and a half later on business and the parents had tentatively booked me to stop by for a few hours to follow-up with them and Bristol but they canceled at the last minute. Finally, I heard Bristol got accepted to college and moved out of state to attend but only lasted one year before coming home.

Art's Story

Art, 60, a retired, soft-spoken, well-to-do, gay man, worked for years in a high-powered business empire. He had a long history of living double-lives—initially, by hiding his sexual orientation and, later, by engaging in random credit card thefts where he'd buy useless items and discard the cards. These thefts continued for years until he recently was arrested twice and faced two felony charges in different states when he contacted me. He had no idea why he stole and was very distressed about losing his freedom, job, and reputation.

Art was one of my earliest phone clients as well as one of my longer-term ones. He was from the Tri-State area of the east coast and first contacted me in mid-2004. We worked together intensively for about a year and kept in touch with periodic sessions over the next two years—until mid-2007.

Art was a high-powered business executive who'd just retired from working for an even higher-powered mogul. He'd been stealing in one shape or form, most of his life; it worsened over the last 15 years—partly due to increasing work stress. But it spiraled out of control during the last two years and resulted in two felony charges for credit card theft and fraud. Art was a multi-millionaire. He was on the eve of enjoying his retirement with his partner in a new home they'd just built in an exclusive town by the sea; all this was threatened by his reckless theft of credit cards—out of the coats or wallets of veritable strangers—with which he charged meaningless things. His story began to emerge...

I'm on an electronic tether for felony credit card theft in one state and I just picked up another charge in a neighboring state, so I violated my probation in the first state. I've hired a well-known attorney who's charging me an arm and a leg.

I have two court dates next month. I may need you to fly in to appear in court as an expert.

I grew up with a family of Holocaust survivors; my parents' families perished in the camps. They came to the U.S. through Canada. My parents expected me to be perfect. We weren't religious but they used to tell me: "We expect you to be Jesus Christ!" Yet, they had absolutely no standards for my older sister. I remember my folks were going to adopt some children from Germany and bring them here. But my Mom got pregnant and my Dad was too busy making money. I always asked them: "Why did you let those kids die?" It still tears my heart apart to know my own people didn't do enough. My folks were hypocrites. They were self-absorbed. I still have a lot of anger about this. I have some survivor's guilt, too. I think this has something to do with my stealing.

I had my first sexual experience at age 10 or 11; I was seduced by an older woman, a friend of the family. I didn't tell anyone. A couple years later, I started becoming sexual with various boys in the neighborhood. At age 15, I told my parents I was gay and they put me in therapy to "cure me." My therapist took advantage of my sexually after a few sessions. This continued for six months. I never told anyone. I saw several therapists over the next few years and they all took advantage of me, too. I started shoplifting things during this period. Then, in my late teens and 20s, I started stealing more from people than from stores. When we had relatives over—or if we'd go to their homes—I always had the urge to take something: money, cash, jewelry, knick-knacks. I felt like nobody was paying attention to me. I was never caught.

I enrolled in business school; my parents wanted me to be successful and make a lot of money. I've never really cared that much about money. I've always had money but I was really looking for love. I ended up becoming a city planner— this was the mid 80's. I enjoyed my work, was making a decent living, but lived with a boyfriend for five years who was a chronic alcoholic. I tried to save him but had to leave. I'm always trying to help people. I think I developed a messiah complex. I also had a Robin Hood complex: I began stealing from the rich to give to the poor. Mostly, I'd steal wallets from rich people's coats or purses. I'd use the cash or credit cards to buy gifts for my boyfriend, co-workers, friends, even strangers. I rationalized my stealing because I was always helping people who were down and out. Then, I'd feel guilty which made me want to help people even more; it was a vicious cycle.

After I left my boyfriend, around 1990, I got an opportunity to work for a high-profile, high-powered business. I took the job and worked there until about a year ago. Talk about being in the belly of the beast! I think I sold my soul working that job. I saw so much corruption, greed, and stealing—my thievery was small potatoes. There was so much stress—I worked seven days a week and my boss kept upping the ante for me. It was the same feeling as in my family: I had to be perfect and make everyone else look good.

During this time, my father passed away and my mother fell ill, so my sister and I put her in a nursing home. We'd visit her every Sunday. It was a tough time. I was grieving and, yet, I was so busy I don't even think I had time to grieve. I started to take cash and credit cards when I traveled out of town for work. It's like I had a split personality; I'd become a different person. I'd get some kind of rush or satisfaction. One time, I even swiped my boss's credit card.

Well, somehow I managed to avoid arrest until I retired; I thought maybe it would stop when I had less stress. But I was more addicted to it than I realized. Also, my mother died less than a year ago and this may be a factor why it continued. I steal when I get angry, anxious or depressed. It's just like being an alcoholic. I started seeing another man a few years ago. He's 20 years younger and a doctor. He's very sweet. But I don't know what to tell him about my stealing or my

66

legal issues. I'm afraid I'm going to wind up in prison, alone. I don't want to be abused again... (Tears)

Over the next few months, Art and I peeled back the layers of his life to make sense of his stealing and worked toward developing a recovery program. He read *Something for Nothing* and *Biting The Hand That Feeds* and related to much of the material about shoplifting and employee theft.

I worked with Art to muster the courage to tell his current partner about his problems—especially since they'd talked about building a house together. Art was surprised and relieved to find his partner was very loving and supportive. He was tearful when recounting this. Here was this 60+ year old man finally receiving the unconditional love he'd always desired. We included his partner on a phone session and this helped, too. I also encouraged Art to see a local psychiatrist for mood disorders and sleep problems. He followed through and was put on medications which seemed to help.

I traveled twice to the Tri-State area to be an expert witness in both of Art's court cases. It was good to meet Art face-to-face: he had such a warm and gentle spirit. I also got to meet Art's partner—a wonderful man. Both of Art's court cases settled favorably—no incarceration period, just fines, probation, community service and therapy. I continued to work with Art for two more years. He made great progress and reported occasional temptations but no relapses.

Post-script: Art and I still keep in touch by e-mail on a regular basis. He finished his probation several years ago and is enjoying retirement, his relationship, volunteer work, and his mischievous mutt. He's contemplated writing a book about his life. I've encouraged him to do so.

Notes & Reflections:

Part Three
Bought Out and $pent!
Compulsive Shopping and Spending

You can never get enough of what you don't really need.—Dr. April Benson

We used to build civilizations. Now we build shopping malls.—Bill Bryson

I always say shopping is cheaper than a psychiatrist.—Tammy Faye Bakker

Most compulsive shoppers and spenders report early memories of either emotional and/or material deprivation, or emotional deprivation and material overindulgence or spoiling or, on occasion, emotional and material overindulgence or smothering. Compulsive spending can be quite insidious.

When shopping or spending becomes a drug, it's important to engage in intensive, specialized, and ongoing treatment. Similar to recovery from overeating, recovery from overspending may be a long, up and down journey; but it doesn't have to be. In recovery from compulsive overspending—again, like overeating—the goal isn't complete abstinence but to gain balance, integration, and harmony through insight into what issues or emotions fuel the shopping/spending (or eating) and what new awareness and coping skills can help one stay alert and relapse-free.

The good news is that more and more people consider themselves recovering shopaholics and, in a sense, the recession has made being thrifty and frugal "cool" again.

A bargain is something you can't use at a price you can't resist.—Franklin P. Jones

The Freedom Lighthouse 5/26/11 (excerpt)

What should one make of the report on Newt Gingrich's reported purchases of $500,000 worth of jewelry from the upscale store "Tiffany's"? Gingrich maintains he does not understand what all the fuss is about, because he owes no debt and he paid for the jewelry promptly. It's not like he ran up the bill and then did not pay it. But Gingrich continues to maintain they are very "frugal," and says he is "mystified" by all the attention to his jewelry purchases. The problem for Gingrich is that this only serves to further distance him from average people. Most Americans won't make $500,000 in 8-10 years; much less buy jewelry for that amount. That kind of spending on does not normally conjure up thoughts of the word, "frugal." To be sure, Gingrich has a right to spend his money how he sees fit. But Americans are also free to form their attitudes based on those decisions.

Nicolas Cage Losing His Treasures (excerpt)

People Magazine, December 7. 2009

Big and expensive easily describe two things in Nicolas Cage's world: his blockbusters and his lifestyle. But after racking up 15 palatial homes, 22 cars and four yachts over the years, the actor owes $6.3 million in back taxes. To pay his debts (including a $2 million loan default), the actor is selling properties and seeking $20 million in damages from his former financial adviser Samuel Levin, whom he accuses of sending him towards "financial ruin." Countersuing for $129,000 in back pay, Levin claims he warned Cage he was "living beyond his means." Cage will probably be able to bail himself out with his up-to-$20-million-a-movie salary. But will he stop shopping? Some of his recent purchases:
*$33,000,000 on 3 new homes in 2007
*$3,000,000 on a Bahamian island
*47 pieces of artwork
*A reported $276,000 on a dinosaur skull
*Priceless shrunken heads
*$1.6 million on comic books
*22 pricey automobiles and 4 yachts

Long Island Wal-Mart Worker Dies in Black Friday Stampede (excerpt)
New York Post, November 28, 2008

A Wal-Mart worker died early Friday after an "out-of-control" mob of frenzied shoppers smashed through the Long Island store's front doors and trampled him, police said. The Black Friday stampede plunged the Valley Stream outlet into chaos, knocking several employees to the ground and sending others scurrying atop vending machines to avoid the horde. When the madness ended, 34-year-old Jdimytai Damour was dead and four shoppers, including a woman eight months pregnant, were injured.

Top 10 Reasons People Compulsively Spend*

1. To feel better about self, soothe or life mood
2. To avoid dealing with something important
3. In response to life stress or trauma
4. To rebel or express anger/vengeance
5. To hold onto love/avoid abandonment
6. To project image of wealth/power/status
7. To fit in to an appearance-obsessed society
8. To escape painful self-awareness
9. To feel more in control
10. To deny death/mortality *Thanks to Dr. April Benson*

All of the key dynamics in couples and groups play themselves out in the financial arena. There are five principle areas that are noteworthy: *

1. *power and control*
2. *trust and mistrust*
3. *commitment*
4. *belonging*
5. *caring*

If we can discuss these aspects as they relate to money and spending, we can use them as a window into fully understanding the dynamics of the relationship and how to heal that relationship. *Thanks to Dr. Natasha Kendal*

SUB-CATEGORIES OF SHOPAHOLICS

Compulsive shoppers – *tend to shop to avoid or suppress painful feelings—usually from loss or trauma. They may shop continuously or when they get particularly triggered.*

Trophy shoppers – *tend to need to have the best of everything; they seek out that perfect object, be it fashion, art, car, etc— the more special, unique or rare, the better.*

Image shoppers – *similar to trophy shoppers but their motivation is less about the inherent value of the objects than for the image those objects project to and impress others.*

Bargain shoppers – *tend to be driven by the deal (regardless of income level); need to feel competent and victorious in finding or negotiating that discount.*

Codependent shoppers – *tend to buy things/gifts primarily for others to secure love, approval, avoid abandonment; often, gifts are given with (secret) strings attached.*

Bulimic shoppers – *tend to buy and return repeatedly (similar to the eating disorder bulimia); initial buying is cathartic but then extreme "buyers remorse" sets in.*

Collector shoppers – *tend to focus on attaining sets of things or multiples/variations of similar objects;*

Experience vs. object spender – *tend to spend money more on events like dining out, theater, vacation, parties than on things; may overdo occasional large events such as weddings or on occasional expenses like on a home or car.*

Note: Under-shoppers or under-spenders (potentially problematic in their own right) often pair up with overshopppers and overspenders.

20 QUESTION

Assessment for Compulsive Shopping/Spending

1. Have you ever lost time from work or school due to shopping/spending?

2. Has shopping/spending caused relationship problems?

3. Has shopping/spending ever affected your reputation or people's opinion of you?

4. Have you ever felt guilt, shame, or remorse after shopping/spending?

5. Did you ever shoplift or steal from work to get money to pay debts or to solve money issues?

6. Did shopping/spending ever cause a decrease in your ambition or efficiency?

7. Did you ever experience a "high" or "rush" of excitement when you shop or spend?

8. Have you ever shopped/spent to escape worries?

9. Has shopping/spending caused eating/sleeping problems?

10. Do arguments, disappointments or frustrations create an urge to shop or spend?

11. Have you noticed you began shopping or spending more frequently over time?

12. Have you ever considered self-destruction or suicide as a result of your shopping/spending?

13. Upon stopping over shopping or overspending did you continue to be tempted/preoccupied by it?

14. Have you kept your shopping/spending a secret from most of those you are close to?

15. Have you told yourself "this is my last time" and still over shopped or overspent again?

16. Have you continued to shop/spend despite having had legal issues such as bankruptcy or divorce?

17. Do you often feel angry or feel a need for control?

18. Do you often have feelings of life being unfair?

19. Do you have persistent feelings of entitlement?

20. Do you have trouble speaking up for yourself, asking for help, or saying "no"?

Most compulsive shoppers/spenders will answer "yes" to *at least 7* of these questions.

Virginia's Story

Virginia is a 60ish divorced woman, with three grown children, who came from modest beginnings, but received tens of millions of dollars in a divorce settlement. She lives in a major east coast city and is an artist. She began overshopping at an early age but it worsened near the end of her marriage and after her divorce. She doesn't have debt but her shopping is taking time and energy away from her work and she feels constant pressure to buy gifts for others.

Virginia contacted me because of her concern over her compulsive spending—especially on gifts for others. She only completed half of my 10-session program but her story vividly illustrates the shopaholic who has plenty of money but whose spending was causing distress nonetheless...

I was married for many years to a very wealthy man but we divorced nine years ago. He had concerns about my spending while we were married. I received a very generous divorce settlement—I'm talking tens of millions of dollars. But my spending has gotten really bad over the last ten years. I've seen some of the best doctors in the city and been on medications for 10 years but they don't seem to be able to help me with my spending. I'm hoping you can. I'm an artist and it's interfering with my work. I have a big show coming up in a few months and I can't concentrate. I'm worried it'll be a flop. I can't let that happen. I have three grown children; one has mental health issues. My family always turns to me for advice and help. I'm supporting a sister financially; she's a starving artist and a shopaholic, too.

I grew up in an upper-middle class family. My father came from wealth but my mother's family was pretty poor. But both of them had money issues. My father was a spendthrift who lost all his money a couple of times. My mother would buy gifts for us on occasions but make us feel guilty about wanting things. I was mocked for not wear the best brands of clothes. While my Mom tried to dress us nicely, it wasn't the same. So, I have this deep fear of not measuring up. My brother has always been very frugal and my sister spends every dime I give her. My kids have a trust fund so they're taken care of. I'm concerned about my son who has mental health problems. He's coming into his trust money; I'm worried he'll blow it. My others sons are penny pinchers. I haven't been the best example to any of them.

I went to college and worked in advertising and then in investments. I had my own money when I met my husband. I've always had expensive tastes—especially when it comes to clothing, jewelry, and decorating my home. My husband always gave mixed messages about spending. On the one hand, he'd say things like "you can have whatever you want," but then he'd be like my mother and make me feel guilty or question my purchases. He made so much money he couldn't possibly spend it all. How could he justify being so frugal and controlling? So, we had constant arguments and power struggles. He also made large donations but wouldn't tell me or wouldn't include my name on the donation, too. I was going through menopause, I also had skin cancer. Then, right before my surgery, my husband left me for a younger woman. That was the final straw; I filed for divorce. My husband fought me tooth and nail and I spent a small fortune on attorneys. He also spread rumors about me around town.

After my divorce was final, there was this endless streak of tragedies. My half-sister died. I was hit by a truck and badly injured. I had a terrible theft of my jewelry four years ago.. I suspected it was the doorman at my building or somebody he knew. I tried to prove it but the residents and the condo board sided against me. I hired a private investigator to find evidence but he dropped the ball. Even my insurance company didn't pay out. I got maybe 15% of what was the *jewelry was worth, forget that they were antiques and irreplaceable. I felt very betrayed and unsupported. This led me on a shopping binge to hunt for and buy similar pieces.*

Then, I started buying a lot of gifts for people. I felt very vulnerable. I like being creative and love the feeling of making others happy but it's gotten out of hand. There's twenty staff in my building and they all seem to expect gifts—especially around the holidays. I'm being bled to death. I think my problem is that I'm always thinking of the perfect gifts. I'm an unusually attractive woman—even for my age. My husband used to put me down and say I was fat or ugly. My father always complimented me. I got a facelift a few months ago by the most extraordinary plastic surgeon around but nobody noticed. But it's women, mostly, who judge other women's looks and fashion. I shop to nurture myself but then feel guilty and conflicted. I shop for others and feel good at first but then feel resentful.

I love getting compliments, so I'm constantly buying clothes and jewelry. I only recently started to date again. I've been afraid to risk rejection. But I'm lonely and depressed. I try to stay busy; I think I fill the emotional void with shopping. Sometimes, I feel guilty because I have all this money but haven't really earned it; it's like I'm trying to get rid of it. But, I was like a prisoner while married. He reminded me of my mother. So, maybe I've rebelled in the other direction. I don't even know how much money I have or spend or what my bills are; my accountants deal with that. Maybe I need to have them make a budget for me. I feel so confused still....

Postscript: After Virginia went AWOL half-way through my treatment program, I sent her an e-mail asking how her exhibition went. A few weeks later, she e-mailed me back, asking if she could resume counseling with me. I said yes but expressed I still had some concerns about her commitment and about stopping the program mid-way through. She never contacted me.

Lisbet's Story

Lisbet is a 39-year old mother of two in a wealthy enclave near a major metropolis. She contacted me on the verge of divorce from her husband, an accountant, who was at his wits' ends with her overshopping, lying, and hiding purchases. Lisbet always had a "passion for fashion" as she called it, but her obsession worsened after quitting her job a few years ago to become a full-time Mom. Her parents urged her to get help; their relationship has its own complications.

About a year ago, I got a call from a doctor in distress: *"It's my daughter Lisbet, she's a shopaholic! She's got two kids. Her husband's an accountant and he's about to divorce her! Can you help her? I'll pay for it!"*

I gathered some background and encouraged him to have his daughter call me. Later that day, I spoke with Lisbet and her husband who were at each other's throats. We all agreed this was an emergency situation and it would be best for Lisbet to get away and come to Detroit for my 3-day intensive program. She was on a plane three days later.

When Lisbet met me at my office, I saw a beautiful but broken soul. She was no stranger to therapy—for years, she'd been seeing a local therapist and psychiatrist; yet, her shopping had only worsened over the last 6 years.

Day 1: *I'm a wreck! My OCD has been out of control. I've been taking Lexapro for a couple of years but either it's not working anymore or I need another approach. I'm not a big fan of medicine. I'm so glad you were able to see me on such short notice; I couldn't stand another day around my husband. I know I have a problem with shopping but he's got a problem, too: he's a total control freak! I feel bad about leaving my two young kids with him but maybe he needs to see how hard it is to take care of them all day! Nobody seems to understand the stress I'm under. My mother and father are part of the problem, too, but we'll get into that later.*

I come from a pretty well-to-do background and live in an affluent area. I got into shopping as a teenager—what girl didn't? It was mostly clothes—I've always had "a passion for fashion." I always had to go through an interrogation with my father whenever I wanted something. He uses money to control people—he did it then and he still does it. It's giving with strings attached. Of course, he doesn't see it that way. My Mom tends to be passive and sides with him—I think she's afraid of him; she rarely took my side. I have a brother who blew threw money, too. He got into financial trouble and they bailed him out. He's in legal trouble and they've gone to the ends of the earth to help him. I guess you have to be in a crisis before they give you anything. I never felt like I could just have what I wanted—no questions asked.

I got through high school without many troubles and I went to college and got a degree in fashion journalism. So, it's probably no surprise I became a shopaholic. I graduated and started writing and doing other kinds of work in the fashion, jewelry and cosmetics industries. I know a lot of shopaholics, many worse than I am, believe me! But I always seemed to pay my bills on time, well, most of the time. I wanted to prove to my parents I didn't need their help.

After working several years and moving up in my career, I met my husband, Larry. He was handsome, smart, funny, and crazy about me. We seemed to have a lot in common. He was an accountant and had just landed a good job with a major accounting firm. We dated for a year and my parents really liked him. He seemed pretty free with his money at the time— but I guess that's normal when you're dating. Anyway, I thought we complimented each other well. I even thought marrying an accountant might help me with my shopaholic tendencies. I just had no idea how far that would go. Well, we got engaged and it's customary for the bride's parents to pay for the wedding, right? Well, my Dad offers to do so but, here we go again, it's got to be on his terms. He dictated the budget, the venue, just about everything. Larry didn't care, he was hardly involved in it. I wasn't happy but what could I say? I think it was a big mistake looking back on it. I was so resentful; it didn't even feel like it was our wedding day. That's no way to start a life together.

Larry and I discussed starting a family together but I never imagined I'd become a full-time Mom and housewife! I figured, we'd have a few kids and I'd go back to work for a few years in between—or at least find a way to work part-time. I loved my work. I had a bad bout of post-partum depression after my first child was born seven years ago. The depression lingered and I had more trouble adjusting to parenting than I anticipated. I'll be honest: it was stressful. Larry started to work more to make up for my loss of income and I assumed my mother would come over to see me and the baby and give me some advice or a break here and there. But, I couldn't believe it: it was like pulling teeth to get her over! I was on my own. I think I started to shop just for relief—plus my body changed a bit so I needed new clothes.

A couple years later, just as I'm getting my bearings, I got pregnant again. I was really worried I'd have post-partum depression again. Fortunately, I didn't. But I was still overwhelmed—now I've got two kids—and no mother to help me and a husband and a father who are workaholics. I really missed my job, making my own money, working with interesting people. I kept shopping, maybe to fill the void and because I was angry and feeling abandoned. I bought a lot of stuff for my kids, too. I wanted to give them anything they wanted; I didn't want to be like my father.

Larry didn't seem to mind my shopping early on; he was making decent money and working all the time. I think he probably felt guilty I was home alone and he was gone a lot. But then we made a big mistake—well, I think he made the mistake. We were looking for a new home, something bigger for our growing family. I told Larry we don't need to go all out, but either it was his ego or my Dad's offer to help us with a down payment... we bought a million dollar home. I told him we have to be careful about accepting gifts from my parents—it's going to be trouble. I think Larry looked to my Dad like the father he never had—his father was poor, uneducated; I think he admired my father and was just swooped up with his offer to help.

Well, we moved into this house and then the recession hits. Our home value plummets right off the bat, Larry's work starts to slow, no bonuses for a couple of years, and all of the sudden my shopping is the problem. I mean, don't get me wrong, I was overdoing it, but it was nickels and dimes compared to our home expenses. For the last year or so, he's come down with an iron fist! I just can't take it anymore...

In listening to Lisbet's story, it was clear to me why arguments over finances are the number one reason couples fight and part ways. And while it takes two to tango, I wanted to create a safe place for Lisbet to vent about her family and husband; eventually, I brought the topic at hand—shopping addiction—to front and center. While Lisbet acknowledged being a shopaholic, it became clear that neither Lisbet, nor her husband, nor her parents really understood this disorder as no different from other addictions; Lisbet's family saw her shopping and lying as proof of her stubborn, immature and materialistic nature. While she may have had some "character defects," nobody could see that her pain was really driving her spending.

Day 2: I engaged in more psycho-education with Lisbet. We worked through my book and watched video/DVD clips of programs on shopping addiction. I had to impress upon her the serious nature of her addiction and what recovery would entail. I told her about Debtors Anonymous groups and we found two groups online that she could attend weekly near her home. Coincidentally, a new women's shopping addiction support group met a half hour from my office later in the day. I drove Lisbet to the group and dropped her off. The 15-woman group was led by a therapist—a recovering shopaholic herself. Lisbet seemed timid and told me she'd probably just sit and listen. When I picked her up two hours later, she was ecstatic. *"I could relate to everyone there. It was so cool! I shared a lot! I hope I didn't dominate!"*

Day 3: The goal of our last day was to talk about transition back home and the changes she'd need to make to support her recovery. We also planned on talking with Larry and, hopefully, with Lisbet's parents as well. Our phone session with Larry went as well as could be expected. The two were still a bit distant and tentative but there were moments of humor and love that poked through. I explained to Larry that shopping addiction is no different from alcohol, drug or gambling addiction and he'd need to be patient with Lisbet; she was new to recovery and there'd be no quick fix. We discussed and agreed that Larry would have sole access to the credit cards for a while. They also committed to sit down, look at their family budget, and agree to some amount Lisbet could spend per week or month—no questions asked. I reminded Larry that he had to watch his controlling ways, for they'd just feed Lisbet's rebellion and shopping.

As for spending money on their kids, that was a tougher issue. Larry and Lisbet couldn't make much progress on want vs. need in this realm. What Lisbet said the kids needed, Larry replied: *"that's a want."* As for their intimate relationship, they agreed to schedule date nights—even if they had to hire a babysitter. We discussed and made some progress on getting Lisbet some more help in the home. Larry didn't want to hire anybody and it was clear he undervalued Lisbet's contributions, but he agreed to help out with some chores and to have more realistic standards about order, cleanliness, and cooking meals in the home. They also agreed not to argue in front of the kids, for it was clear this had taken its toll. Their daughter was playing cop to Lisbet, telling her not to spend money or daddy will be mad. Their son, sensitive to yelling, was overly anxious.

Our session with Lisbet's folks went less well than we had hoped, though she wasn't too surprised. I tried to educate them about shopping addiction and some of the childhood origins of her disorder without blaming them for this. I encouraged Lisbet to tell her folks what she learned. In a calm, sometimes shaky, non-blaming tone, I thought she did well in expressing how she felt money was used for control; how she felt frustrated she rarely got what she wanted; and how the last several years had been full of stressful changes, depression, anxiety and loneliness. She expressed her hurts about not having the wedding she wanted and about not having her mother help her with her kids more.

When Lisbet's parents got their chance to share, it was clear they felt hurt; they were defensive and reactive. They affirmed their love for Lisbet; then her father stated "I wasn't going to pay $250,000 for a wedding! When someone accepts a gift, they don't have any right to complain about the amount." Lisbet's mother told her she just didn't have the energy to be around young children anymore.

Lisbet absorbed her parents' remarks. I could feel her heart close up. When we got off the phone, we talked about how hard it was for her to see the limits of those she loved. She had to admit her own limits as well. When we wrapped up our last day, Lisbet realized she had to want recovery for herself, not her husband or her parents—just for her.

Post-script: Lisbet and I continued to have sessions by phone intermittently over the next four months. She had many relapses, dragged her feet about attending DA meetings, and continued arguing with Larry. She fell out of touch with me.

Gretchen's Story

Gretchen, a mid-western part-time school teacher in her mid-50's, never married, no children, contacted me after many years of struggling both with compulsive eating and compulsive spending. Due to a decrease in her employment and income, and an increase in hormonal and other health issues, she'd become more aware of her financial distress. She feared she'd have no money for retirement and had little support—financially or emotionally—from family or friends. She wanted to know what was really driving her shopping.

Gretchen contacted me a year ago—two months after reading my book *Bought Out and $pent!*—after having just hit the $50,000 credit card debt mark. It was hard for her to believe the mess she'd made. Gretchen had a wonderful sense of humor, a sharp intellect, a good heart; yet, her wounds ran deep and she seemed quite childlike at times. She had some borderline personality tendencies—she was particularly sensitive to rejection and abandonment—and I was concerned she might unconsciously stay stuck in her addictions in order to keep from losing our therapeutic bond. Her story came in bits and pieces over time…

I'm a tough nut. You have your work cut out for you. I was adopted at six weeks old. My older brother was adopted, too. He was mentally ill and physically, emotionally abused me when I was young. There were sexual overtones, too. I also have a younger brother who was a "miracle baby." My parents knew my brother was abusing me but all they did was tell him to quit. That didn't really stop it. My Mom was emotionally abusive herself. My Dad was a workaholic and wasn't around much. My older brother lives nearby. I've got a restraining order against him; I'm closer to my younger brother and have always been kind of his protector.

I never really wanted to know who my biological parents were. I'm pretty sure I was an unplanned pregnancy. I once went to a psychic who told me my birth Mom committed suicide. I don't know anything about my birth father. My adoptive father died suddenly of a massive heart attack 30 years ago and my adoptive mother died about 10 years ago. I've felt alone most of my life.

I think my binge eating started when I was about 12—right around puberty. I've heard a lot of kids gain weight when they've been abused. I think that's probably part of it—a kind of protection. I'm sure I used food early on to soothe myself emotionally, too. Right now, I'm the heaviest I've been: probably a good 70 lbs overweight. I was diagnosed with body dysmorphic syndrome back in my 20s. This is around the time I found OA—Overeaters Anonymous. I think this group has helped me more than therapy. I started to date a little and actually was engaged once. When that didn't work out, I think I switched addictions and started to shop more. I bought clothes, books, music. I'm a voracious reader—I've bought more self-help books than I'll ever read. I attended church for a while, too, but I've always had a conflicted relationship with God and organized religion.

I taught elementary and junior high school for many years but chose to retire six years ago when I got ill. I still regret that decision because it put me in a hole financially. I receive a small pension and started working again part-time in the last year. Teaching got so stressful but the loss of structure led to more eating and shopping. Now I feel like I'm barely getting by. My anxiety leads to more eating and shopping. I'm caught in a vicious cycle. Also, I've been going through the menopause from hell! It's never-ending— my hormones are going up and down constantly—and I've been to doctor after doctor and trying diet after diet and can't seem to find prolonged balance.

By the time I turned 35—about twenty years ago—I made

peace with the idea I'd never get married. I used food and shopping to fill the void and to reward myself after stressful days at work. I was in a small apartment (I'd later have my own home) and I didn't have too many expenses, so I didn't have any debt problems early on. When I stopped dating, I got lonely; so, I started finding female friends to hang out with. I gravitated toward friends who had problems and who I tried to rescue. I started to take them out to eat and buy them things. It was draining my time, energy, bank account, and self-esteem. I finally put a stop to this just recently.

For a long time, I worked a pretty good recovery program through OA. I was the poster child—the one who recovered where others kept struggling. But my spending and codependency were running wild. I was so in denial. Right now I'm more concerned about my debt than my weight.

When my mother died ten years ago, this triggered some pretty deep feelings of grief and abandonment. I fell off my OA program and started eating again. I started to have health issues myself and this prevented me from feeling more physically active. I discovered Internet shopping—which was like putting crack in front of a cocaine addict! I bought books, DVDs, CDs and even various vitamins and supplements. Amazon should send me a big "thank you" card! I knew I was getting out of control so I even bought every book I could find on shopping addiction. I read parts of a few of them but that didn't help much. Then I took Dave Ramsey's course and also found a local Debtors Anonymous meeting which were helpful.

Six years ago, I got really sick and had to deal with that. I made the really tough decision to retire. I just didn't have the energy to work. I'd accumulated about ten thousand dollars of debt. I figured, without much income, I'd have to curtail my spending—both on food and things—so maybe it would be a blessing in disguise. But—thank God or the Devil for credit cards—it didn't work out that way. On average,

I've rung up about ten grand a year in debt over the last five years; so, I've been spending about a thousand a month more than I'm earning and putting nothing away for retirement. My apartment is full of clutter. I still have some money in a couple of CDs and in my 401(k). I don't want to touch those but I might have to. Even working part-time and doing some tutoring on the side, I don't know how I'm going to get out of this debt—the interest alone is killing me. Why do I do this to myself?

As I learned about Gretchen over the first few sessions, I heard clearly the vicious cycle of addiction. She understood what her eating and her spending were doing to her but she hadn't quite found the deep desire or the support and accountability to change. She admitted there was a big part of her that just didn't care anymore. She felt tired, past her prime, her faith in God, life, and in herself had been slipping. Thus, I told Gretchen: I know you want help or you wouldn't have contacted me. But I can only do so much. I will do my best to help you understand why you keep undermining your life and what you can do to stop this, but you have to do the work. I asked her: Are you willing to commit three months to my program? Then we'll see where you are at that time and whether it's worth continuing. Gretchen agreed.

Over the next three months, Gretchen and I spoke once a week and I had her check-in with my by e-mail almost daily about her progress. She got back involved with Debtors Anonymous and Overeaters Anonymous and I added her to my private online group for recovering shoppers and spenders. She renewed her commitment to find a food plan that worked and to take regular blood tests with her hormone doctor. I coached her to take as many substitute jobs as she could handle to fill up her time and increase her income to pay her debt down. I supported her in setting boundaries with two of her friends who were draining her in every way.

Gretchen responded fairly well to the treatment goals and,

though she had some ups and downs, she began eating more healthily and spending far less money than she had. She began to go through her apartment and discover all kinds of items she'd forgotten she'd bought. She also threw out, donated, or gave as gifts much of the clutter. Setting boundaries with friends proved to be harder than she thought but she was moving there slowly. Her energy, sense of hope, and self-esteem began to inch up bit by bit.

Once Gretchen was somewhat stronger and more stable, we began to delve into her core issues: what was really at the bottom of the well that was fueling her overeating and overspending. It was hard for her to go there but she did. Through tears of pain and vulnerability, she really understood and believed she was unlovable and undeserving of a good life. She saw the arc of her life: adopted, abused by her brother and her mother; unprotected and neglected by both parents; overweight and unattractive—not marriage material; alone, in poor health, better off dead. It looked and felt pretty bleak to her. But she kept taking it one day at a time, declaring and claiming small and major victories.

As Gretchen and I continue to work together on healing her shame and her grief, she's continued to enhance her eating and spending recoveries. She's made steady progress with a few setbacks. I hope she finds inner peace and acceptance.

Post-script: As Gretchen and I approached one year of counseling together, she continued to progress with her compulsive eating and spending. She was looking forward to summer and had some tutoring, exercise, and fun times planned. *"Life isn't perfect, but it's a helluva lot better when I'm in recovery."*

Lauren's Story

Lauren, 53, works for a major retail chain in a large city. She's had problems with compulsive shopping for over 30 years. She contacted me due to her continued conflicts with her husband about money and her increasing concerns about retirement and her credit card debt. She was smart enough to know she was out of control and needed help.

I've been a shopaholic for about 30 years. I'm $22,000 in debt but I've also been dipping into my savings. I make a lot of money and love my job as buyer for a major retailer. We get such great employee discounts it's kind of like being the proverbial kid in the candy store. I work 60 hours a week and I think I use shopping as a reward. But I know the old saying: "you have to spend money to save money." And I'm not saving money. My boss and my best friend are shopaholics, too. But my husband is the polar opposite of me—he's super frugal even about Kleenex. We've been fighting more and more about money and even though I don't think he'd divorce me, I'm getting tired of it.

I've suspected I've had a shopping problem for a while now—I've tried to stop on my own but it hasn't worked. This is the first time I've sought help. The last time I had any counseling was 15 years ago when I went through a severe depression when I moved to another state for another job. I hated the city and the job. I was on medication for a while. Then I moved to this state and this job which I love.

When I look back on my life, I've tried to see if any events stick out that help me understand my obsession with things— especially clothes. When I was 13, I remember babysitting; every time I got paid, I spent it all on clothes. I even tracked what I wore to school everyday. I certainly didn't save anything. I don't remember my parents having any input on what I should do with my money. It just felt good to do whatever I wanted with it. It's funny: I guess I still feel the same way on some level. I don't like to be told what to do. But I'm not 13 anymore, I'm 53.

You tracked the clothing you wore to school at age 13? That sounds a little like OCD. Was there anything else going on in your life at the time?

You know, there was. My father was in a boating accident and a young boy got killed; I knew him, he was a year older. We had a cottage on the lake. My father was pulling kids on water skis and he accidentally drove his boat over the kid in the water. My parents were really damaged by this, they became more distant. From this time on, my whole life changed. I basically raised myself. My Dad became an alcoholic. My older sister became a functional alcoholic. My younger sister just doesn't remember too much about the accident; she isn't too insightful in general.

I remember telling a good friend about this incident many years later. Her theory is that, after the accident, I became obsessed with perfection. She may be right. But what I really wanted more than anything was my father's love and approval. But he was just never the same after the accident. Also, my family went from upper middle class to just middle class after the accident. I'm not sure how that happened but I think my father just wasn't as ambitious afterwards.

I think my Mom sensed something different in me, too. She offered to buy me things—even a pea coat she knew I wanted—but I only wanted to buy things for myself. I didn't want to burden anyone. It's like I became an adult overnight. I took on the job of cleaning up around the house—I'd even dust around my father's gin bottles. I think cleaning and bringing order to the house soothed me.

As much as I wanted to buy my own things, I also have a memory of borrowing $300 from my Dad when I was young. He was really on me about paying it back and that didn't feel right either. He could be verbally and emotionally abusive. He'd fly off the handle over little things. My Mom never stood up for me. I've never talked to her about this.

My shopping has gone up and down over the years and I think when I get a little depressed I actually shop less. I used to treat myself to a spa day on the weekends. It was $400 but included a massage, a Mani Pedi, a haircut, and few hours in a soothing environment. In some way, I think that was better than just buying more clothes I don't really need. I have trouble distinguishing between want and need. I recently went over some records; I spent about $50,000 on clothes last year and $60,000 the year before. Even if I cut my clothing budget to $2,000/month I could be content and save a lot of money, too. I hope you can help me with that...

I enjoyed working with Lauren. She was forthright, highly motivated, and had already been thinking about her issues and ways to curtail her shopping before we started working together. She read my *Bought Out and $pent!* and identified with much in it. She didn't attend Debtors Anonymous meetings—which I'd suggested. *"I don't think I'm a 12-Step kind of person. I don't even know if I believe in God."* I continued to encourage her to go but you can't force people.

We processed her early trauma: the boating accident and how that changed her life. I told her that I believed she lost something—her father's love and her childhood innocence—she could never replace with shopping or things, no matter how hard she tried. She agreed. We also explored whether she'd become a workaholic as a way of staying busy to keep deep and painful memories at bay; then she'd go shopping to take off that edge. This made sense to her but she reminded me that her job required long hours.

While a $2,000 a month clothing allowance might strike many people as excessive, I'm always careful not to impose my own values on others. If Lauren could save $20-$30k per year, this was a step in the right direction. She came up with the idea of selling some of her clothes on e-Bay or to upscale resale stores and apply any proceeds toward her debt. I had her switch from credit cards to debit cards and keep a spending log so she could track her purchases. She agreed to discard any catalogues that came in the mail and to unsubscribe and remove her credit card numbers from online stores, *"except Rue La La"* she protested.

I asked Lauren if she had any hobbies or if she was interested in learning any new skills. *"I've always wanted to learn how to cook better."* In time, Lauren began to read cook books and filled up some of her time creating new dishes for her and husband. *"He's ecstatic,"* she reported. *"He loves when I cook and it's actually cheaper than going out to eat. I even love baking cookies and bringing them to work."* She also realized since she and her husband argued less, her urges to shop plummeted, too.

We also discussed Lauren's boss, her best friend, and even her step-daughter—all shopaholics. She didn't necessarily have to tell them she was a shopaholic but practiced politely saying *"no, thanks"* when they wanted to go shopping with her and, instead, suggested other fun activities to do together such as going to movies, museums, the park, or out to eat.

Lauren set a timeline by when she wanted to pay off her debt and a schedule for amounts to put toward her retirement. She told her husband so he could help hold her accountable. She had progressed nicely when our treatment concluded. I've kept in touch with Lauren by e-mail every few months.

Post-script: Lauren recently e-mailed me that she'd had one relapse and she'd taken a group phone therapy program and was still moving forward in recovery.

Audrey's Story

Audrey is a 40ish divorced mother of two boys—one with severe autism. She owns a successful business but when she came to me for counseling locally, she was spending like a wild-woman, arguing with her boyfriend and her parents, and had felt like she'd lost the respect of her employees. She seemed to be juggling a thousand balls in the air at once. She needed to restore order and balance to her life quickly.

Audrey was a recent client who counseled with me for over a year. She'd been working with a local counselor on a variety of issues, mostly related to her family of origin and a troubled romantic relationship she'd been in for several years. But she was also over-shopping and spending, causing more problems with her family and her boyfriend, and impeding her ability to focus and manage her business. Her therapist referred her to me for specialized treatment.

In listening to Audrey's story, her excessive shopping was a distress signal: she was buckling under the various pressures of her life, including trying to please her parents; running a business with 20 employees; taking care of two kids, one with severe autism, with little emotional or financial support from her ex; and dealing with a boyfriend who was more needy than giving. She had little time for herself except when she went shopping. As with any addiction, the solution just adds to the problems. She shared her story with me...

I feel so lost and so ridiculous. I buy things I don't even need. Last year, I spent $30,000 on office supplies. I buy food we don't eat, clothes I don't wear. My parents and my boyfriend are livid with me. And my employees must think I'm a space cadet. I think they've lost all respect for me. I haven't been able to manage my books or the business. I feel *embarrassed just being there. I feel like people are talking behind my back. I don't even know how it came to this.*

I grew up in a wealthy family. My Dad is a successful businessman. He and my Mom came to the U.S. when they were very young. I think my Mom is a shopaholic. She has closets-full of clothes I don't think she's ever worn. My brother is successful, too. He has a big house and several fancy cars and motorcycles. He's married to a woman who grew up poor but has expensive tastes. I was a total hippie chick in high school. I wore ripped jeans, smoked a little pot, and was into music and just hanging out with my friends. After I graduated from high school, I went to college and started to make friends with some girls who were a little more style-conscious. I guess that's when I started to get into clothes more. My parents gave me an allowance but I don't think I abused it. I got my own credit card and got into a little bit of debt. My Dad paid it off and I got a lecture. I graduated and thought about going to graduate school, ironically, to become a therapist.

Then I met a guy and fell in love. We were engaged to be married, so I put school on hold. My parents loved the guy. I still don't know what happened, but things were moving too fast and I got cold feet. I was in my early 20s; I just needed a little more time. But he took it the wrong way and he broke up with me. Instead of comforting me, my parents really beat me up about it. On rare occasions my Mom still brings it up: "Your biggest mistake was not marrying Gary!" I went through a really confusing period for a few years afterwards. I dated a bit again. I think I was in a hurry to meet another guy and marry him this time around. I think I wanted to redeem myself. I wanted my parents' approval. So, I met this guy and we dated for a short time. I wasn't sure if I really loved him but he proposed and I accepted. My parents seemed lukewarm about him—it was like I couldn't win. I married him and—other than giving me two wonderful kids—that was a bigger mistake than not marrying Gary.

My youngest son was born with severe autism. I think my ex-husband just couldn't handle it. We divorced and he's been virtually useless since. He hardly sees his kids and pays minimal child support. I have to take him to court at least a twice a year. So, I had to grow up pretty quickly. I love being a Mom but I wanted to do something more with my life; so, my father helped buy a business for me to run. I found out quickly that running a business is a lot harder than I thought. Then I started dating a musician. I was trying to live in two worlds—recapturing my youth while running a business and raising two kids. My boyfriend was fun but he was needy and self-centered. I felt alone and unsupported. Pretty soon, I felt like I was taking care of everybody; but who was taking care of me? My folks mostly showed their love through helping me financially. They're pretty hard at times. So, I think when I felt scared or overwhelmed, I went shopping. Part of it was just an escape, a mindless escape but part of it was kind of like I was both parent and child: I'd buy myself something, just like my parents used to do for me. Eventually, it got so out of hand it was clearly a cry for help.

Unfortunately, it took several years of spiraling with my spending before I even realized I'd become addicted to shopping. I mean, I've heard the term shopaholic before but I guess I thought it was a joke. My Mom is a shopaholic but it never seemed to cause much trouble for her and my Dad. I just looked at it like it was silly. But I'm in debt, I've lost a lot of respect, and I have some pretty big decisions I need to make soon: whether to break-up with my boyfriend and whether to go back to college or continue running my business. My father wants to buy a building for me to move my business to but I don't think he'll do it if I don't have my act together. I need to figure out what I really want.

Over the course of therapy, Audrey began to peel back the layers of her life and connect the dots. She had to learn how to take life one day at a time and how to ask for help in her personal life and in her business. She set some limits with her boyfriend and asked him to come join us for a therapy session but he made excuses. We included Audrey's parents for a session. I tried to educate them about her addiction and underlying stress. I saw first-hand, however, how they paid lip-service to the idea their daughter needed therapy but focused more on how frustrated and let down they felt over her spending binges and what it cost them to bail her out. As they spoke, I saw Audrey shrivel up like she was 5-years old. We processed this session later. It was hard for Audrey to hear but she also understood her parents' feelings. She worked hard to take responsibility for her behavior. We also worked on having her speak up or walk away if her parents became abusive. She went to a couple of Debtors Anonymous meetings but found more value in Alanon meetings. She returned to doing yoga, she had other people shop for her, and she sat down with her accountant and got her head into the books of her business to really understand what goes on. In time, she regained her parents' confidence; they invested almost a million dollars to buy a new building for her business. Audrey broke up with her boyfriend and took charge at work, regaining the respect of her staff.

Post-script: Audrey had a few more sessions with me after breaking up with her boyfriend. She was set up on a date and within a short period of time, began seeing this doctor who was newly divorced. I always feel concerned when people get out of long-term relationships and jump right into a new ones. The way Audrey described her new beau seemed too good to be true. They ended up moving in together a few months later—another warning sign. Sure enough, things got chaotic in Audrey's life very quickly. Her new boyfriend seemed to be everything her old boyfriend wasn't—helpful, giving, and attentive—but he was also codependent and a control freak. Audrey stopped counseling with me, bounced her last check, and last emailed me a few months ago to tell me she'd be in touch when things settled down. She made no mention of the particulars but I hope she regains her equilibrium and makes her recovery a priority again.

Notes & Reflections:

Part Four
You Can't Take it with You
Hoarding Disorder

You can't take it with you.—Kaufman and Hart

Compulsive hoarding (a.k.a. pathological hoarding or disposophobia) is a hard condition to pin down. While no clear clinical definition or set of diagnostic criteria exist in the current DSM-IV, certain defining features have been identified by researchers in dealing with chronic hoarders. *These criteria include:*

1. The acquisition of and failure to discard a large number of possessions that appear to be useless or of limited value;
2. Living spaces sufficiently cluttered so as to preclude activities for which those spaces were designed;
3. Significant distress or impairment in function by hoarding;
4. Reluctance or inability to return borrowed items; as boundaries blur, impulsive acquisitiveness could sometimes lead to stealing or kleptomania.

Although not commonly used by clinical psychologists, criteria for five levels of hoarding have been set forth by the National Study Group on Chronic Disorganization (NSGCD) entitled the NGSCD Clutter Hoarding Scale. Using the perspective of a professional organizer, this scale distinguishes five levels of hoarding with Level I being the least severe and Level V being the worst. Within each level there are four specific categories which define the severity of clutter and hoarding potential:

-Structure and zoning
-Pets and rodents;
-Household functions; and
-Sanitation and cleanliness.

Level I Hoarder
Household is considered standard. No special knowledge in working with the Chronically Disorganized is necessary.

Level II Hoarder
Household requires professional organizers or related professionals to have additional knowledge and understanding of Chronic Disorganization.

Level III Hoarder
Household may require services in addition to those a professional organizer and related professional can provide. Professional organizers and related professionals working with Level III households should have significant training in Chronic Disorganization and have a helpful community network of resources, especially mental health providers.

Level IV Hoarder
Household needs the help of a professional organizer and a coordinated team of service providers. Psychological, medical issues or financial hardships are generally involved. Resources will be necessary to bring a household to a functional level. These services may include pest control services, "crime scene cleaners," financial counseling and licensed contractors and handy persons.

Level V Hoarder
Household will require intervention from a wide range of agencies. Professional organizers should not venture directly into working solo with this type of household. The Level V household may be under the care of a conservator or be an inherited estate of a mentally ill individual. A team needs to be assembled and members should be identified before beginning work. These members may include social services and psychological/mental health representative, conservator or trustee, building and zoning, fire and safety, landlord, and legal representatives. A written strategy needs to be outlined and contractual agreements made before proceeding.

Beauty is Nature's coin, must not be hoarded, must be current.—John Milton

Top Ten Reasons People Hoard
1. Get high from accumulating/pain from discarding
2. Reaction to trauma, loss, PTSD—control over little things
3. Social anxiety/phobia, isolation/protection
4. Perfectionism/Procrastination/Avoidance
5. Shaky sense of self and over-identification with objects
6. Problems with attention/organization
7. Problems processing info/categorizing
8. Problems making decisions
9. Problems with memory (too much/too little)
10. Safety, security, control

Reality TV's New Wave: Trash Picking, With a Smile (excerpt)
New York Times, January 8, 2011 by Jon Caramanica
Our stuff is suffocating us: at least that's what reality television has told us in recent years. Shows like "Hoarders" and "Clean House" serve as virtual purges for over-consumers. Here, having too much is more than just a problem of limited space—it's a failure of psychology. The things themselves don't matter so much—could be cans, cars, or cats. Anything that fills a room can ruin a life. The past year, though, has seen a shift in perspective. No longer is clutter the enemy, but a potential gold mine. The new reality television hero is the picker, someone willing to face the accumulation the owner just can't and squeeze value out of it. There's potential liberation in them thar piles. The question is no longer how to get rid of it, but instead, what can be gotten for it? Even though this shift swaps one reality television archetype for another, it still counts as a turn for the optimistic. Hoarding shows—and also the many recent shows about hyper-consumption—mirrored a society that had hit rock bottom, and had no tools with which to dig out.

We are hoarding potentials so great they are just about unimaginable.—Jack Schwartz

99

20 QUESTION
Assessment for Hoarding/Cluttering Disorders

1. Are some living areas in your home cluttered?
2. Do you have trouble controlling urges to acquire things?
3. Does the clutter in your home prevent you from using some of your living space?
4. Do you have trouble controlling your urges to save things?
5. Do you have trouble walking through areas of your house because of clutter?
6. Do you have trouble throwing away or discarding things?
7. Do you experience distress throwing away or discarding possessions?
8. Do you feel distressed or uncomfortable when I can not acquire something you want?
9. Does the clutter in your home interfere with your social, work or everyday functioning?
10. Do you have strong urges to buy or acquire free things for which you have no immediate use?
11. Does the clutter in my home causes you distress?
12. Do you have strong urges to save things you know you may never use?
13. Do you feel upset/distressed about your acquiring habits?
14. Do you feel unable to control the clutter in your home?
15. Has compulsive buying resulted in financial difficulties?
16. Do you often avoid trying to discard possessions because it is too stressful or time consuming?
17. Do you often decide to keep things you do not need and have little space for?
18. Does the clutter in your home prevent you from inviting people to visit?
19. Do you often buy or acquire for free things for which you have no immediate use or need?
20. Do you often feel unable to discard a possession or possessions you would like to get rid of?

Most compulsive hoarders will answer "yes" to *at least 7* of these questions.

Cathy's Story

Cathy is a 50ish married mother of three children. She works part-time and had been overshopping and hoarding for 20 years—starting around the time her first daughter became very ill at age 3. Her husband, Don, was an overspender, too, but eventually became a penny-pinching workaholic. He's been increasingly angry and controlling and has thrown out some of Cathy's things without asking her, yelling: "It's me or the stuff!" Prior to contacting me, Cathy had been on medication and saw two local therapists— including a marriage counselor—but her problems persisted.

Cathy called me on the verge of tears. She had been suffering from compulsive shopping and hoarding for nearly twenty years, she'd been in an out of counseling with little progress, and her husband, Don, recently gave her, what she feared was, a final ultimatum: "It's me or the stuff!" I asked her if she acknowledged her own shopping and hoarding problems. She assured me she had but she was quick to describe Don as a periodic shopaholic, too. *"Not to mention, a workaholic and a control freak!"* she added.

Indeed, within the first couple weeks of counseling with Cathy by phone, Don called and e-mailed me several times to both make sure Cathy was keeping her appointments as well as to complain she wasn't getting rid of her stuff quickly enough. I tried to reassure him but he exclaimed in frustration: *"She's been to two therapists in the last six years with no progress. She's got $100,000 worth of stuff she never uses. Even her last therapist sided with me. She's gotta get rid of it!"* I knew I had my work cut out for me.

Cathy felt assaulted and helpless, trapped and apathetic. She didn't want a divorce; yet, the way Don was treating her, she found it hard to get motivated to clean up her clutter for him or for her. She felt paralyzed. I worked to create a safe place for her to tell her story to see if I could find a way to help her break this cycle. I also asked whether her children had exhibited any signs of overshopping or hoarding. She acknowledged they had, which seemed to concern her more deeply than her husband's ire. Her story began to unfold…

I started to have problems with overshopping and hoarding about twenty years ago—around the time my 22-year old daughter was three. She was diagnosed with leukemia; we thought it was a death sentence. I was pregnant with my second child at the time and was worried about my newborn, too. The shock of and the uncertainty of the outcome left me so helpless and anxious—like I lost all control. I suffered depression, too, and was diagnosed later with post-traumatic stress disorder. Fortunately, my daughter was cured, my pregnancy and birth went smoothly, and my next daughter was healthy. My husband and I had a healthy son shortly afterwards, too. But I guess the aftershocks lingered.

My shopping and hoarding was actually my husband's fault, in a way. I think he even blames himself—though he'd never admit it—that's why he's so mad. He also projects onto me because he has some of the same problems but won't acknowledge this. During the time our daughter was ill, Don encouraged me to get out of the house and go shopping; I think he meant "window shopping." Anyways, I started off window shopping but I had money and credit cards and we were doing pretty well financially at that time. It was innocent shopping at first, nothing passive-aggressive—that came later; it was just stuff for the kids, especially our sick daughter. I wanted to make her feel better. I guess I wanted to feel better, too. And it seemed to help.

The other thing that complicated matters was that we moved several times during this period because of my husband's work. We moved further away from our families who really could have helped more had they been closer. And we kept moving to nicer areas where status and appearances were more important. I felt a certain pressure to keep up; I think Don did, too. I think, especially given the stress with our daughter's illness, we just wanted to fit in, be normal. In some way, focusing on material stuff kept our minds off the emotional stuff. Plus, neither of us was ever good at organizing or getting rid of things before moving; we just brought it all to the new home. Don started to work more and more—I don't know if he was avoiding things at home or if his workaholic tendencies just increased. That was hard on me. We got into this cycle: I felt rejected and unsupported— he was gone so much—and he felt unappreciated which, I guess, made him work harder and avoid me more.

Don started to spend more and buy more, too, though mostly for himself: expensive cars and motorcycles. I mean, he worked hard so I didn't begrudge him at first; but I guess I felt: if he can spend money, so can I. Eventually, he started keeping tabs on my spending and making little comments, so I started to become more secretive about my shopping, lying about where I'd been, and hiding purchases. At some level, I knew I was shopping to fill the void in our relationship as we drifted apart. It was my way of loving my kids and myself. When I felt unloved, I went shopping. I tried to talk to Don about this but it didn't sink in. My Dad was a workaholic, too. They say you marry your parents. Don's Dad was an alcoholic; I think he feels like he married his father.

I asked Cathy to tell me about her early life and her life before she met Don some twenty plus years ago.

We grew up middle-class, not poor but not rich. I feel like, even though my Dad worked a lot, we were emotionally attended to. I think my Dad was a bit of a hoarder and Mom was a bit of a spender; but she always orchestrated garage sales, so I don't remember there being constant clutter. I collected a few things like books, pictures in frames, and beanie babies. Now, I collect clothes, kitchenware, figurines, and a few other things. Most of it's stored in our basement— I don't have a room to call my own. I think Don really wants my stuff out of there so he can store his stuff down there, like his motorcycles and parts. I buy a lot of relatively small and inexpensive items and he buys fewer things, but they're bigger and more expensive. Anyway, I can't recall anything that significant about my upbringing. My other counselors asked me the same thing. I've never been abused. I'm not sure my upbringing had any influence on how I reacted to my daughter's illness but I just lost it. But, you know, when you're told your child won't live past first grade, well...

I continued to ask questions about Cathy's childhood...

I guess if there was anything that upset me was that I did feel my brother and sister were a bit more spoiled than I was. I felt there was unfair treatment at times. I suppose there were times when I envied the other girls at school who dressed, as they used to say "fresh." We didn't get many extras in our family. Neither my sister nor brother has any addictions that I'm aware of. They know I'm a bit of a shopper/hoarder though; they just want me to get help. I think I innocently stumbled into this mess but it's been made worse by this power struggle with my husband. I worked for several years before we had kids and I gave up a lot to be a full-time Mom. I even help at home with Don's business but he acts like everything we own is all because of him. That's not right. I feel he's projecting his rage toward his alcoholic father onto me. He's still got issues. He was angry at his father's drinking and angry at his mother for putting his father down. He's acting like his mother, belittling me. It wasn't like this earlier. He was very sensitive when our daughter was ill. I don't know what changed. We both changed.

I know I need to stop shopping and get rid of a ton of stuff. I just need some support and for Don to back off. He'll say he's leaving me alone but then, at the slightest whim, he goes into my stuff down the basement or in the kitchen and makes impromptu executive decisions to get rid of things! That just pisses me off and stalls the whole process. He yells at me in front of the kids: it's like he's trying to turn them against me. I wish I started working with you ten years ago, Terry.

I told Cathy: "You wouldn't have been ready. Now, you're ready." But I asked her: "What do you think needs to happen in therapy this time for there to be a different outcome than the last two times?" She hit the nail on the head: *"This time, it's got to be about me, not Don."* Bingo. Part of what makes my therapy effective—besides having some specialization in certain lesser treated addictions—is that the initial phase of my program is time-limited: 90 days. This motivates clients to focus and not drag their feet. Cathy read my book *Bought Out and $pent!* which helped her understand the origins of her shopping and hoarding. I also added her to my online support group for recovering shopaholics and hoarders which helped her feel less alone.

I asked Cathy what she really wanted from her life. She paused, initially unclear, then asserted: *"I really want to feel confident about myself again; somewhere along the line, I lost that. I want to be able to stand my ground again with Don and be equals."* Their relationship had regressed to a parent-child dynamic. Don acted as parent but his style of parenting—yelling, belittling, controlling—was hardly mature, loving or effective. I asked her if she wanted to stay married to Don. *"I don't know,"* she confessed. *"My kids are almost old enough to be on their own. I'll probably go through empty nest syndrome. I can't expect Don to be sensitive; he'll just expect me to go back to work full-time."*

Then it really hit Cathy: she needed to reclaim her own power–whether she stayed with Don or not. For the first time, she really saw how her shopping and hoarding had drained her power. This scared her. We made our primary goal to stop accumulating things. Next, she'd spend short

105

blocks of time each day locating items she could return to stores for a refund or credit. She had many unworn articles of clothing from her favorite clothing store that—because she'd been such a good customer over the years—let her return many items for a full refund beyond the usual policy. *I told my favorite saleswoman that I regret all the returns but that I'm a recovering compulsive shopper and in therapy for this. She understood. She told me I wasn't the only one.*

A remarkable process began to take root: Cathy began to feel new hope and—with each item returned, donated, recycled, or tossed—new lightness. She enrolled her kids to help her and was happy they were so supportive. As expected, Don did his best not to praise Cathy and even tried to undermine her progress with snide remarks and by continuing to throw things out on a whim. Cathy practiced not reacting. I told her it's a common dynamic for a spouse to say he wants his partner to change but part of him doesn't. He wants the status quo; he wants to feel superior; he wants to complain; he wants to control. I told her: "When you change, he feels threatened, he feels lost; he doesn't know his lines in this new script." Cathy felt good about not getting too triggered but she still felt sad. She wanted his praise and wanted to believe he could change, too. She held out hope that they might recapture some early passion and partnership.

Eventually, Don joined us on a couples' phone session. I had Cathy tell him what she was learning about herself and she asked him how he thought things were going. He praised her mildly, admitted he had issues, too, and said he'd seek out therapy. When I followed-up with Cathy a week later, not much had changed with Don. Time would tell if they'd stay together or drift apart. But Cathy continued to move forward and, as our treatment ended, she had made great progress in her insights, her self-esteem, and her change of behavior.

Post-script: Cathy resumed working with her local therapist. Last I talked to her, she was still doing well.

Billie's Story

Billie is a 65-year old homemaker, wife, mother and grandmother. She lives in a rural suburb and is married to Hank, a retired auto engineer. She is strong though childlike and emotional at times. She's been in recovery from shoplifting addiction since 1995 but has had co-occurring shopping and hoarding problems. Her basement is bursting at the seams with boxes of knick-knacks she's accumulated over the years. Hank is loyal and committed but continues to be frustrated with Billie's difficulty letting go of things. Note: Billie is an acquaintance of mine, not a client.

I'm 66 and I'm not exactly sure when I became a shopaholic and a hoarder but it happened gradually over time. As a child, I didn't know where I belonged. My brother and I went back and forth between foster homes and our biological mother; I was finally adopted at age 5. I used to shoplift and steal when I was little. The first time I ever stole anything, I was 7 or 8-years old. I stole a candy bar. I stole it for a girl who I wanted to be my friend. I got caught. It was from a little Mom and Pop store on my way to school. My parents were called but I don't remember if I was punished.

When I was 12-years old I was molested. I was abducted from my parents' house and before I was returned, I took twenty dollars from the guy; it was probably the twenty dollars he was going to pay the taxi to drive me home. I never even got to keep the twenty dollars; I hid it in my underwear and my Mom found it in the bathroom. I denied it was mine. I never said anything to her about the incident. I just blocked it out of my mind. The memories only came back much later when I was married in my early 20s; then I started shoplifting things like spices, small things, expensive. I was on a budget, twenty-five dollars a week to spend on food. I found I just couldn't stretch it. It was just a few spices. Then it was a little bit more, like a package of ham. It started to be like a rush, something that was a secret, my secret. My husband never suspected anything. Looking back, I see I was depressed and anxious. We had three children within a short period of time. Hank worked full-time and I felt lost. He'd come home for dinner and I was just finishing watching soap operas all day. That's how it all began.

I didn't have any real idea why I was stealing. I stole things for my two daughters, things from the grocery store, cards— cards were expensive. It ballooned later on. It was hard to make ends meet. Then I was arrested and I remember feeling cheated and angry with the court for having to pay high fines. Then I discovered a loophole where I could return merchandise without a receipt and get money back. Later, I'd take things from the store and bring them to the counter and get money back for them without even buying them.

During this time, I also got into the flea market and resale business. I worked at a resale shop when the kids started school. I was buying things from catalogues and from garage sales, buying cheap and selling reasonable. At one point, it was fun and profitable but, after a few years, it really didn't end up being worth it because of the expenses. I bought certain things—knick-knacks and household items— over and over that I knew would sell in the stores. A lot of times they'd stay in the bags. It's surprising Hank and the kids didn't say much about this. I must have had some need to collect or hoard things because my basement has been filled with boxes of knickknacks for decades. Eventually, my husband came to hate the clutter. I've been working gradually on getting rid of the stuff but it's hard to let go. I kept shoplifting along the way as well.

My kids were growing up and were in school or with friends more and Hank was still working full-time so I think I felt lonely. Then we moved to another house in 1987 that we built over a few years. It was even bigger and out in the boonies. I had all this stuff, so I opened another resale business to get rid of it. Looking back, I was definitely manic. I put so much time into buying and selling things, it can't believe it. I was also a coupon hoarder. I think it was all some kind of need for control. But I was out of control. I regret not having spent more time with children.

In addition to my hoarding, I was arrested a few more times and each time I felt more and more ashamed and lost. Everybody in my family knew but nobody really understood why I was stealing. It was almost always unplanned and I stole small things I could've paid for. In 1995, I began seeing a psychiatrist and was diagnosed as bipolar, manic-depressive. Eventually, I was put on anti-depressant and anti-anxiety medications. The doctor found out about C.A.S.A. (Cleptomaniacs And Shoplifters Anonymous) support groups. I've attended faithfully for over 15 years. While my recovery from shoplifting has been pretty solid, I still get triggered and tempted—especially when conflicts or relationship problems arise. I still use shopping and hoarding as an outlet. I go to the Dollar Store more than flea markets or garage sales now. But it's still easy to spend $50 - $100 an outing—most of which I don't really need.

It's strange because I seem to have this obsession with accumulating stuff but then I also have an obsession with getting rid of the stuff. I know I have to have different categories for things: trash, gifts, recycling, donations, keepers. But I become paralyzed. I'm also easily distracted. We've had a lot of family issues over the years—health issues and other things—which have taken my attention. The other issue is that all my stuff is primarily in the basement and my knees have gotten really bad, so I can't really get down there easily to sort through things.

I've been watching the hoarding shows on TV and I can relate to those stories and I know my thinking is irrational but I just have to go slow. I get rid of one thing and it seems I have to replace it with another. The shows also got me thinking about my family. My brother is a hoarder, too. He had a stroke a few years ago. He took better care of his stuff than his health. My adoptive parents were hoarders in some ways. They grew up during the Great Depression so they didn't waste anything. I'm sure this rubbed off on me. I've also heard that children who are adopted tend to hoard more than kids who aren't. Maybe it has to do with insecurity or abandonment. I grew up feeling emotionally deprived. It's like I never have enough to feel full. It's like needing more and more but not really needing. And I can't talk to Hank about this because his feeling is "the past is the past."

I tell myself I'm ready to de-clutter but I still get anxious. Ninety-nine percent of my stuff is in our basement so it's kind of like out-of-sight-out-of mind but Hank has been on me for years now to clean it out so he can set up his Lionel train set there. I feel bad because he deserves to have some more fun in his retirement and he still does so much work on the house and the property. I'd be very happy to see him happy.

I've thought about hiring a professional organizer and have a few friends who are hoarders who have offered to help me. It's funny: I've offered to help them, too. One of them is too embarrassed to have me over. Hank and the kids have offered to just send me away for a week or two and just go through all my stuff and get rid of what they think is junk. I'm just not ready for that. I feel like I need to have some involvement in this process. Even if we just donate it all to charity I'd feel such a relief, such a weight lifted. Most of it is junk, I know, but there are a few things in there that would make nice gifts.

Post-script: I last spoke with Billie just after her interview with me in April 2011. She and Hank were making plans for a leisurely summer, and one big garage sale!

Mark's Story

Mark is a 40-year old single father with a 10-year old son he sees on weekends. He's smart, charming, and creative but has drifted since graduating college over 15 years ago. He's had issues with depression, anxiety, OCD, and low self-esteem. He'd been very orderly and neat until his son's birth ten years ago. Since that time, he's struggled with overshopping and, more recently, hoarding. Note: Mark is an acquaintance of mine, not a counseling client.

My hoarding could have started when I was 8 or 9 years old. I had a toy pile in my bedroom and I when I got a new toy, I'd throw it on top of the pile. But it began increasing when my son was taken from me by his mother about 8 years ago. I thought I dealt with it—we ended up separating—but maybe not. My hoarding is made worse by the fact I've been in the same small apartment—a 3-level townhome—for nine years. I don't have much storage space; I keep things piled up in my basement and have quite a few things in my attic crawl space—which isn't allowed, it's a fire hazard. I get anxious about moving all these things. I stopped buying my son gifts all the time a couple of years ago. I used to buy him 2-3 toys every weekend he'd visit. I started to buy myself toys, too.

I have bipolar disorder and obsessive-compulsive disorder. Hoarding and OCD seem very similar and tied in together. I also have a lot of anxiety. When I acquire things, this alleviates my anxiety but the thought of getting rid of things causes me anxiety. I actually got a "high" from shopping for my son—like someone who goes to garage sales and finds treasures. I'd go to 3-4 stores a day to find him certain toys or action figures. I make calls or looked things up on the Internet. I drove all over town! Sometimes I called ahead and sometimes I just drove somewhere and took a chance. If

I found what I was looking for, I got a high; then I'd collect it and hoard it. I'd need that high again and I'd seek out that next treasure. I wasted a lot of time and money.

Interestingly, before my son was born—when I lived with my fiancée—I was very good about throwing things away and being neat. I was content and proud of myself. I had people over regularly. My fiancée was very neat, too. I remember when we had our baby shower; her family bought a lot of gifts, including a baby swing and a playpen. She set them up in the living room before I came home from work. I felt a lot of anxiety when I saw all that clutter. Now, I've been accumulating clutter for eight years. I feel paralyzed. When I think about moving to a bigger place, most people would want to get rid of a lot of things when they move; I want to keep everything and then have a big garage sale! I probably wouldn't get much money for any of my junk, even the collectibles I've gathered over the years, including some of my prized possessions. But now they're just taking up space!

I think my hoarding filled a void and brought me comfort. When my fiancée took my son, I was lonely and sad. I wanted to fill up the house with things that made me feel loved to compensate for my son not being here. I definitely overdid it, though. I used to save up and buy all these gifts for my son during the year and then give him 17-20 gifts for his birthday all at once. I got a big high seeing him open them up and seeing his excitement. He got a high, too. But that high would wear off for both of us; he'd get tired of his gifts in a week or two and expect me to get him more stuff. My spending and hoarding got really bad as my son got older and I started buying wrestling action figures. They came out with these series of figures which were very intricate and detailed; I bought a few of the wrestlers I grew up with. I never got to the point where I'd collect the whole set of 8-10 action figures per series so, maybe I'm different from a real collector; I just wanted some of my favorite wrestlers. There were times I'd go to Toys 'R Us and buy 6 or 7 action figures which could cost $100. Sometimes, I was even thought about shoplifting when money was tight. I bought over 100 action figures for my son. Most of them have been opened. I can't seem to get rid of them, give them away, or sell them on e-Bay—which seems like an ordeal. I've thrown away a few things but it doesn't feel as good as you'd think. If I got a high from throwing things away I'd be doing it more. Maybe I haven't gotten rid of enough; if I got down and dirty and cleaned up my basement maybe I'd feel good. Something keeps it from being that pressing.

I was frequently depressed growing up but my anxiety came on later in life. I think my spending and the rush of going out to find these toys was a bit manic. My bipolar disorder was only diagnosed about 4 years ago. My father was an alcoholic, had bipolar, and was hoarder, too. I think there's a genetic or hereditary cause. I remember he had a lot of things in his closet that he already had, much of it unused or unopened. His house always had a bit more clutter than the other houses I visited. My parents divorced when I was about 5 and I have an older brother. My father died when I was 22. I don't think it fully hit me when it happened; I'm still grieving. He kind of died, in my eyes, when he had a stroke when I was 18 and wound up helpless in a wheelchair.

For a while, I tried to buy my son's love with gifts but I've also tried to give him a lot of my time and attention. This probably relates to why I haven't been able to be successful in my life—move out of this place, have a good job, and buy a house like most of my friends. I wanted to spend a lot of time with my son, especially since I just see him on weekends. I didn't want to work too hard and have no energy left when I saw him. I haven't been able to find a balance. A lot of kids grow up never seeing their Dad; this was true for me. Now I see many fathers enjoyed their careers and were earning money to send their kids to college and provide for them. I definitely wanted to give my son what my father didn't give me, which is a lot of love, love with no judgment, *no hostility—love and acceptance. It's been almost 20 years since his death. He occasionally gave me things but I rarely heard him tell me he loved me or heard him say "I love you" or "I'm proud of you." He seemed disappointed in me. I don't know if losing him relates to my hoarding but it made me want to show my son the love my Dad didn't show me.*

My hoarding also takes other forms. I have trouble throwing out food. I have bottles of hot sauce in my refrigerator that I know are old and expired; yet, I can't throw them away. I feel a sense of relief—probably more than a normal person would—when I force myself to throw something out of the fridge. If things get a little moldy, my girlfriend likes to throw them out; I cut around it. When we go grocery shopping and there's no room in our fridge, I'll throw some old things out. I know there are things in my cupboards that are pretty old, but I feel anxious throwing them out, too. I also don't like people throwing things out without my permission. My girlfriend won't even throw out a crumbled piece of paper because I've yelled at her in the past.

I've also had trouble throwing out papers and receipts since I started buying toys and action figures in case I needed to return them. I have a box for all my receipts—even for things I bought years ago that I know I can't take back. I can't seem to throw them out; I'd have to go through everything. I also have a big problem hoarding the empty boxes or packaging from the toys or action figures in case I want to sell them—they're worth more in their packages. Sometimes, I'd put a figure back in its package if my son was tired of it and return it to the store I got it from or a store in the same chain where no one would recognize me. It took a lot of time. I have this circular file under my desk with papers that are over 10 years old. It's actually a garbage can full of papers I might need but it's mostly trash. I'd like to go through every little piece of paper. I think I'm going to have to just throw away the whole circular file. A perfect analogy would be the "trash can" on your computer desktop—you can delete things but then they go into your "trash." You have to "empty your trash" to permanently delete it and free up space on your hard drive. I also "collect" newspapers and have to read the whole paper before I can throw it away. Sometimes, I've put some of them away to read again later because I couldn't remember if I'd read them or not.

I'm very meticulous, however, about my bills and can throw them away more easily since I do most of my bill-paying online. I've been using a computer program since 2000. It has information and graphs that show how you spend your money. I'm OCD about this, too. When I get a few months' behind, it takes me a lot of time to enter the data. If I just entered the amounts in each category, that'd be easy, but there's a space for a memo with a 50-character limit. I have to fill up that whole space; I can't just put in five words. The problem with OCD—I explained to my girlfriend—is that it's so time-consuming, it causes me to procrastinate. Then it's paralyzing because, four months down the road, you know you have a big task ahead of you. I wish I could take a shorter amount of time and not put so much detail into things. But what happens is there are a few times a year where I'm really thankful I put in all that detail because I needed the name of a mechanic I wrote down somewhere in the memo; it reinforces that my efforts were valuable.

My handwriting has gotten worse over the years, so I tend to go over it. It doesn't have to be perfect but it has to be readable; if it isn't, I have to redo it. A few times I couldn't read one word and it was frustrating; so, that reinforces the fact I need to go over the words. It takes longer for me to take notes because I write slowly to begin with, and then I recheck it along the way and afterwards so it's readable; likely, it's readable but I still feel obsessive about it. I've also been keeping a log on the computer every time my son comes over. I started this many years ago because the Friend of the Court wanted me to document how many nights I had him. Then I thought it might be fun to do, so when my son grows up he could see the things we did together and how much I loved him. But it's gotten so bad that I have to write down every minute detail of what we did; most of it's useless. I don't know if it's more for him or for me; he probably won't care much. But I've been doing it for eight years and now it's hard to just stop. I also hoard emails. I have to go through every single email and see if there's an online coupon worth using. When I find one, it, reinforces the behavior. But I have useless emails I can't delete.

OCD and DVRs make a deadly combination. I find it very difficult to delete TV programs, even ones I've watched! I'm afraid they'll never air again. Since you can rewind what you're watching on a DVR, I play things over and over again in case I was distracted and missed an important line or a sports play or if I didn't understand something during a show. It's not uncommon for a half-hour show to take me over an hour to watch. My videotapes are a whole different issue. I started recording things when I was in high school and my collection grew and grew. My rationale was that I was paying all this money for cable TV, so I'd tape movies to watch later. I could get four movies on a tape and labeled them, too. But I rarely got around to watching them. Then I started recording music videos on tapes. I had one music video project that lasted 4-5 years. I was very perfectionist about it, it got frustrating at times, but I finally completed it in 1999. I still have the master tapes and the other tapes I made from the master tapes! They just sit on my shelves, taking up space. It's nice to know I have hard copies of some of the classics, even though I'll probably never watch them again; I can't even tape over them with more recent stuff.

Sometimes, I think about how I'd feel if my apartment burned down or if it were broken into and my stuff was stolen. I'd be pretty devastated—I think anyone would be. But I'd live; I don't think I'd go on a rampage to re-accumulate. It might even be a blessing in disguise. I've got a fire hazard going on right now—especially in my basement—that concerns me.

I don't really know many hoarders. I have an aunt who's a hoarder; I saw her house many years ago. Her daughter has a lot of things, too, but she has a bigger house and two boys. I lived with a college roommate who had massive amounts of papers on his desk; nobody could touch them. It's hard to believe I took pride in being one of the most organized people in my college fraternity. My son's aware of my hoarding and my OCD. He knows it's hard for me to throw things away. I've yelled at him a lot when he loses or breaks things because I don't want to have to look for them again or buy them again. I feel bad when I yell at him. When something gets lost or broken, I feel like a part of me is lost or broken. I should think of it like "good, one less thing in the house," but I don't. I can't let it go. My son doesn't seem to be a hoarder but he's a perfectionist and has some OCD symptoms; for instance, he's a really picky eater.

I think my OCD prevents me from throwing things out. I don't feel in control. I hear there's some medication for OCD but I know it affects people differently. I've been taking anti-depressants for a while but they don't seem to help my hoarding. I'm talking to my doctor about this. I saw a counselor for a while; that helped some. But right now, my funds are limited. I hear there are support groups but my time is limited, too. I'd like to try to work on it a little more myself. It's not totally out of control but it's not in control.

Post-script: Mark recently graduated from an 8-month technical school. He said: *"I'm hoping I can channel my perfectionist ways into this. I need to get more organized. I recently wasted the week off. I wanted to get all my finances in order; I wanted to get my son's journal in order: this is all part of the problem. I want to get things done but I get too overwhelmed and anxious—I don't know where to start. My perfection leads to my procrastination which leads to paralysis which is why my hoarding isn't going away."*

Bonnie's Story

Bonnie is a 50ish divorced woman who's been a certified financial planner and advisor for ten years. Her mother passed away around this time, too, and Bonnie's shopping and hoarding escalated. She's also a workaholic and recently wound up in the hospital from exhaustion and poor diet. She started dating a man, Claude, two years ago; they moved in together a year ago. He's concerned about her shopping, hoarding, and her health. Note: Bonnie is an acquaintance of mine, not a counseling client.

I've spent at least $24,000 in rent over ten years on one meaningless storage unit. I have four other units in three states—two of them for ten years. I added up the rest of my storage bills and it's over $37,000. This doesn't include the money I spent flying out to try to go through things or the people I've hired to help me. So, it's at least $50,000 total. As a financial planner and advisor, if I had clients engaged in this behavior I'd tell them they're insane! But money doesn't seem to move me. I have mixed feelings about money and things—they seem both important and unimportant. I know relationships are more important to me than money and things, yet money and things are impacting my relationships and my future.

I know it's stupid to have stuff you say you care about packed away in storage units or the bottoms of drawers. But, I think I do that because I think I'll use them later. I don't love or need any of the stuff that's in storage except for I some photographs. I may have trouble categorizing the better photos from the lesser photos but even if I could, that doesn't mean I could throw away the rejects. I could never imagine getting rid of pictures of other people; that's the same thing as saying you don't care about them. I take other

118

people's photos out of the garbage; I can't believe they'd throw away pictures of their dead friends or relatives. That's just so wrong it screams at me! I've tried walking away but I have to go back. It's like throwing away a person's life!

One of my storage units contains a bunch of stuff from my family home I grew up in. I went through it several years ago and planned on getting rid of most of it, but there were things I felt were valuable, such as my grandparents' visas and papers. Nobody else in my family offered to help me go through this stuff, so I felt it was my responsibility. I couldn't decide what to keep and what to throw out. I just recently coerced my sister to help pay some of the storage fees; she's not working and has time to help but doesn't. The easiest storage unit to get rid of is the one here that I rented three years ago. I haven't done the California storage unit. I don't have enough time and money to do the job. I went there a couple of years ago and spent $5,000 trying to go through it. There were just a few things in there I wanted, but it took so much time I couldn't finish. I considered paying $4,000 to have the contents shipped here but I thought that was too much money; maybe I should have done it.

It's a miracle I've been able to get rid of anything and condense it as much as I've done. Several years ago, I cleared out my family home and moved my Dad into a new home. I have this ritual where I donate a lot of stuff to Goodwill on December 31st every year. My Mom kept everything, including everyone's pictures. But I think she'd be happy if I got rid of all this stuff. She doesn't want me carrying the weight she carried. She died ten years ago... (Tears) Maybe I don't want to let go of her. I've known this for many years but this doesn't seem to help. What's the difference between someone who can let go and someone who can't? I've done grief counseling and spent time processing things. I'm scared of what's going to happen when my father dies; I'm already thinking about it. What am I going to do with his house and the things in it? This is the

119

reason I'm trying to spend a lot of time with him now—so I won't have regrets later. He's not as thing-oriented as my mother was, so getting rid of his things shouldn't be as hard.

My Mom couldn't let go of her own parents' things. She valued history and where she came from. I feel this way, too, but I'd feel it more strongly if I had kids and there was a sense of continuity. I feel like all of my family is behind me; so, there's a piece of me that I'm keeping. Maybe, if I had kids, I wouldn't be as intent on keeping so many things because there'd be new things happening all the time. I definitely didn't have enough time with my Mom. I was at the point of my life where I was going out and doing things. I wasn't ready for her to disappear... (Tears) Nobody was. It's the loss of something very special. I had to choose between money and time with her; that's why I hate money. I resent money—the time it takes to make it and what it keeps you from. I regret that the best things in my life took me away from time I could have been with her. Maybe I was selfish, pursuing my own goals. I didn't realize her time was so short. I guess I was in denial. She was always so strong and miraculously came back so many times. We all thought she'd keep coming back because she fought so hard for so long.

I lived in California ten years ago and had to leave prematurely because of my Mom's illness and subsequent death. Even though I've processed her death a lot more than my siblings have, maybe I still shove things under the rug. My hoarding seems to come from a combination of holding onto memories, pieces of life; not wanting to admit mistakes; and not wanting to go back and confront painful emotions. I felt compelled to pursue a career and make money and I resent that. I don't feel like I should have had to. But I was the smart child, so it was expected. I feel I have to keep working so hard because I've already invested so much time and energy, I have to justify why I went to school and went into this field. It's like investing in the storage units; I have to justify keeping them. It would be too hard to admit that any of this isn't that important. It's all tied together. I can accept the fact my Mom's gone but I can't accept the fact I didn't get to spend as much time with her as I wanted to.

Letting go of things is like a muscle you need to exercise; you have to practice and I haven't done that much. I think my hoarding also has to do with having big ideas. I've been going through things in my current home—it's the smallest space I've lived in—and I always get these ideas of what I want to do with things. I have trouble admitting I'm not going to do what I said I'd do. I don't give up. Part of my problem is that I want to do too many things. My Dad has as saying: "I never take on more than I can do. That's how I stay content." He says it so matter-of-factly. I always take on more than I can do—I take on ten times more than I can do. My Dad is very well-balanced and doesn't have much stress. He and my Mom were opposites. She always did more than she could do. But I envy my Dad because he's content. I have to learn how to let go of things, people, even dreams.

Sometimes I've thought about what I'd do if I knew I had just a short time to live. I imagine I'd let go of things much easier because I wouldn't have time to do things with them. I'd just stop working and spend time with my Dad, family, friends, people I want to spend time with. I don't like the fact that I'm all of nothing. This is my personality and I resent that I can't change this. In order to have less stress and more time, I'd have to quit working completely. But, right now, I can't.

Having a partner the last two years has made me see how my relationship with shopping, spending and hoarding has taken a toll on him. If we really have a future together, it may be a deal breaker. We have different values. I know it comes between us and it keeps me from being more present. Maybe it's a convenient excuse to avoid commitment. We live in a really small place which helps minimize my accumulation but it also makes it appear more cluttered. I often feel resentful I don't have a larger home where I could spread my stuff out and hang my pictures on the wall. I feel like I don't have my own place; if I wasn't spending all this money on shopping and storage, I probably could. There's a correlation between time and money. I want to spend because I don't get time to experienced things I want to experience. Claude says he doesn't feel the need to spend because he's already done most of what he wants to do; I've postponed a lot of adventures because of school, work, and time with family. I have trouble getting rid of things because I'm not done with them—I might use them later. But you have to take care of the stuff you own. That takes time and energy, too. Do I own my stuff or does my stuff own me?

There's probably a correlation between high achievement and shopaholics and hoarders. I bet people like me who put all their time in energy into achieving goals tend to lack balance and satisfaction. I bet there's a correlation between people who can say "I've done an okay job and that's good enough" vs. someone who always has to feel he's done his best. Claude and I had a discussion the other day: he said when he took tests, he'd figure out how to study just enough to pass; he spent more time figuring that out than it would have taken to get a really good grade. His teachers wondered how he managed to get the same scores. I know more people like me—who always want to get 100%! I bet people who strive for perfection are more likely to desire and hold onto things. Maybe being okay with "good enough" means you don't need to have more and more.

For example, I buy lots of clothes not because I want or need them but because I'm never satisfied with the ones I have. If I find a perfect outfit, I don't mind wearing it twenty times; but I have to buy a hundred to get that one. I usually don't have enough time to find that perfect outfit, so I settle for other outfits. But settling never really satisfies me. I'm always searching for perfection. The few times I've experienced "perfection"—like the perfect vacation or the perfect outfit, it doesn't even have to be expensive—it feels so good that I feel content and don't want anything else! The trick is: how do you figure out how to spend less time and money to get that feeling? And, I know, it doesn't last. By the next week, I want something else. But when I find something perfect, it seems to last a little longer. The clothes or things I don't use, I eventually donate or give to friends.

I recently altered my diet dramatically after many years of bad eating. I'm not sure what happened that's made me change this behavior but not my shopping or hoarding. I guess I'm an all-or-nothing kind of person. I'd like to say my recent hospitalization finally got my attention, but I'm not really convinced. I just came out of denial and was shocked at how far I'd gotten out of control, how much weight I'd gained. I just got that feeling if I didn't break the cycle, I'd never get out of it. The same thing happened to me years ago when I got addicted to pain killers after a surgery. I had no idea I was addicted but then, when I realized it, I just had this inner feeling that if I don't do it now, I'm going to die. It was more of an internal knowing. I've always believed you have to go "cold turkey." When you're ready, you're ready.

I understand the negative consequences of my spending and hoarding. I waste a lot of money and time. I worry. I can't enjoy what's in front of me because there's so much around me—it scrambles your brain waves. I can't go on trips as much—I wish my bags would get lost so I wouldn't have to carry them. I know it's as detrimental to my health to be carrying around all the weight of my debt and my things as it is to be carrying around the weight on my body. It's something I carry on my shoulders everywhere I go. I also know I'm not in integrity with my higher values or in alignment with my higher self. It affects me every day in some way but this doesn't seem to be enough to cure it. I think it's more an emotional thing I have to go through. I haven't figured out what's going to click inside me to call it quits, enough is enough. I want it to happen but ... (Tears)

I don't think I'll ever feel like I've lived long enough. My partner can say "I'm done; I've already lived long enough." And he's only 31! I think it's an attitude about life, the importance of life. I think about whether I'll have an impact on the world. A lot of people don't think about this.

I also understand that shopping/spending and hoarding are learned behaviors. It was taught to me by my mother and other relatives. I saw the negative side of hoarding growing up in my family. I thought I was better because I could throw some things out but they couldn't. They couldn't even throw away used Kleenex—it just got thrown in the corner, in the drawer, in a suitcase. Some of them came from nothing or had to leave their whole life behind to flee a country. They had to use everything ten million times because they didn't have anything because of The Great Depression. All of our relatives dumped things on my folks because they knew they wouldn't throw things away. They got rid of their junk by dumping it on us—at our house; it wouldn't go anywhere. Hoarding didn't seem to bother my family. I tried to help throw things away—it's often easier to get rid of other people's things—except for pictures. We had more things than anyone I knew. When I had friends over our house, I'd clean up but, sometimes, I'd just show it to people as a warning. I had to clean it up—that was my job in the family; maybe I think that the next person is going to do that for me.

I think what will resolve this is when I really want something I can't afford and I stop paying on the storage units to have that money for this new thing. But even then, I think I'd have to have someone else handle this. I wouldn't want to go back and look at things because it would bring up feelings, memories, sad things, happy things. I don't know. Maybe you can only go forward by dealing with the past, letting go of things. I believe this but it doesn't seem to motivate me. But, at this point, I still can't imagine just stopping paying the rental fees on my storage units—maybe if I died. If they were broken into or demolished by a tornado, that would be

124

better, that would be great; then I wouldn't have to do it, I wouldn't have to make the decision. It's making the decision that's hard. I don't have trouble making decisions generally, but I prefer to leave my options open; having things in storage leaves my options open. About six months ago, I made a hard decision to let go of a condo in Florida I co-owned with a former friend. It still bothers me because I feel something that was taken away from me. But I needed to let go for my own sanity—he was literally driving me crazy!

If someone can use something I have, I can give it to them easily. But I have this fear of not being able to acquire things in the future, so I have to be prepared to reuse the old things. It's like this Depression mentality. Let's say I couldn't make money the rest of my life: then I could go back and use my storage stuff. It gives me a sense of security. Also, if I regret having bought things in the first place, then I have to keep them to make it worth while if I can use them later. It's circular thinking; it's a control thing. It's like I'm trying to make sure things come out right, that I'll be redeemed.

I realize all this preoccupation with keeping options open in the future by holding onto things from the past keeps me from living in the present. It doesn't feel good. There are things I wish I could do but I can't. Take my photographs: I'd love to be able to go through them and pick some out to display or make a collage from, but I can't seem to find the time or motivation to do it. It's insane, I know. If I knew back then what I know now—that ten years would pass and I'd have no use for those things in storage—I would've done it differently. But, having come this far, it's like an investment. It's like holding onto a stock that's going down in value; instead of selling it and cutting my losses, I keep holding on. It's like admitting I've failed. Yet, with my clients, I tell them all the time: "you just have to let go."

Post-script: Last I spoke with Bonnie, her goal was to either clean out or let go of her storage units by year's end.

125

Claude – Bonnie's Partner

Bonnie and I met several years ago when we were housemates. We've been together two years and lived together over a year. I'm from Hong Kong but moved to Toronto in my 20s, then to Windsor (Ontario) for college. When I left Windsor, I left my stuff behind. I told myself: "I have enough." I didn't want to have to find a place to store them. I didn't even have the money. I could use credit cards, but that's not what I do. I rather spend my money on myself. I packed two suitcases and left furniture, clothes, food. I even left pictures behind. If I had to spend an hour looking through them, I consider that a waste of time. The memory is there, the event is gone. Close your eyes and picture it in your mind. If I forget things, they're meant to be forgotten. If I remember it, there must be a reason. Do you need to remember everything and everyone? No!

So, not spending so money, I save time and money. Time equals money. I can enjoy myself. Storage units waste time and money. You can act different if you want to. I don't say I don't like things—I'm not Buddha—but I watch what I want. Also, I only buy few things—that makes what I have more special. If I want something, I buy things that are unique or special; otherwise, why would I want it?

After college, I spent two years doing nothing. It was like early retirement. I had a little money and worked when I needed to. I went to the movies a lot—I go in the morning and stay all day—especially when my friend worked. He let me in. I admit: I love breaking rules. I hate rules. I never liked rules I don't create myself. Why should I have to follow them? I don't like the law; I am the law.

I never regret things I done and I never regret things I buy or get rid of. In China—even in Hong Kong—it's different from here. When you go shopping there, they don't have refunds or return. You must think before you buy something; you can't take it back—they think you crazy! Even if I'm 31-year old, I already bought what I wanted to buy. I already had fun and experience most of what I want to experience. After I graduated from college, I travel two years around the world, playing. I race cars, I went scuba diving, I fly planes. I can't live this way now. I'm older. I got a girlfriend, a home, and a job here. I don't understand people who cheat on their husband or wife. They should make sure they have fun and explore before they marry. It's like buy something and then to return it. It's like a child.

I learn certain values and behavior from my parents, of course. When I was a kid, I wanted everything. That's normal. You want, want, want! It's greed. I learned not to want so much—especially when I have no money or am low on money. My parents didn't buy much for me or for them. But I grew up in China. If you can achieve a state of not wanting things, it's like the state of Buddha. You have to let go. My parents didn't teach me this, nobody can teach you this; you have to experience yourself. Nobody can tell you what's good or bad, you have to decide yourself. My Mom used to tell me all the time and money she spent on me. I tell her: "It's not my fault I was born. You should have used a condom!" This is why I don't want children. It consumes time and money. If I won million dollars, maybe that be different. I don't want kids because I sacrifice too much for them—like my parents do for me. I do things to the extreme. I rather not have something if I can't have it my way.

I love my partner and we have lot in common: we both work hard and both strong-willed. But shopping and hoarding, I'm the opposite. I hate mess and junk. She spends four hours shopping, grab a lot of clothes, not try them on until she gets home. I don't do that. I narrow down to one or two outfits to try and, if I like them I buy them, if I don't I don't. If it's a little not perfect, I don't buy it. If I'm not satisfied, I don't buy it. I tell her, you have to tell yourself: "I have enough."

127

Corinne's Story

Corrine is a 60ish writer, never married, no kids, with a long history of overshopping and overspending—especially bargain hunting—which created debt and led to losing her long-time home a year ago. In the process of moving, she confronted her hoarding disorder and her attachment to stuff. It's been a difficult but illuminating process. Note: Corinne is an acquaintance of mine, not a counseling client.

My happiest times growing up were rummaging for bargains with my mother which netted great goods but led to a lifelong desire to overshop and overspend. I'd come home with my booty of bargains and try them on and model them for my family; then I'd have to thank Mom 15 or 20 times for being the best mother on the planet because she'd purchased these things for me. She'd ask me: "Are you grateful?" And I'd say "Yes, mummy," again and again. It was such a charge to get stuff that sometimes I'd provoke a fight to make her feel guilty, so she'd buy me stuff. Then she'd realize I didn't really need it and she'd make me feel guilty by telling me I should be even more grateful she'd bought me stuff I didn't really need! She created a monster!

Later on, at low points in my life, throbbing with unhappiness or uncertainty, I'd shop. Bright lights, happy clerks, pretty stuff! If I'm afraid to do my work, I take a courage break and go to a garage-sale. So, it becomes a way "I use" and I probably "use" more when I'm lost. This is what contributed to the great amount of debt I've been in.

My old house was twice as big as my new apartment; I knew it was too big for me. It was over my head budget-wise and everything that could go wrong mechanically did go wrong. A big house led me to buy more to fill it up; and the expenses and repairs led to more stress which led to more shopping. It's the same vicious cycle as with an alcoholic: whatever you use is whatever you use until you figure out you don't need it—it's a crutch. It's not the solution, it's the problem. The next thing I know, I'm making less and less money as there's more and more turbulence in the economy. Then I had more time on my hands, so I shopped more when I really should have been looking for more work. I started shopping for cheaper things—I went from Nordstrom's to TJ Maxx, then Salvation Army to Value Village. But it's still shopping, acquiring. I dream of adventures with my new acquisitions which look strangely akin to the old acquisitions.

I still enjoy looking at various things and imagining having them. But I just leave and say, "thank you." It's kind of fun even though it's also kind of dangerous. I used to say: "Yes! I have to have it all!" But here I had all this crap that I had no use for, really. I filled up my space with pretty things because it was devoid of people. One Christmas, I went to a friend's sister's house where a giant Christmas tree filled the living room. Her husband folded laundry, her kids played with their hand-held games, and the wife was cooking dinner. There were few things but much happiness. It was like a Dickens holiday tale; but I was Scrooge with multiples of everything. What or who was I buying for?

Stuff became the all-encompassing substitute for anything or anyone I couldn't have. I'm not married—I don't take up easily with people—and, in a sense, clutter is a way to say: "Don't get too close to me." I have my shield of clutter and hoarding was my hobby: arranging my clutter, washing my clutter, holding my clutter. My clutter became my lover. There were times I opened up my old home to parties and gatherings. I hired an organizer to balance my home. He was very good at redistributing my clutter but I didn't get rid of much. Telling some people to get rid of their clutter is like telling them to get rid of their kids.

Losing my home in a short sale was shattering emotionally but liberating environmentally. With half as much space and one quarter the closets, I have nowhere to put the stuff I have, let alone more. It was really hard trying to figure out how to fit all my clutter in my new space. Now, I shop far less; I mean, I still have a problem—going cold turkey is so damn hard. I give myself one hour to garage-sale rather than a day or two, and the maximum I'll spend is ten dollars. If you cut every piece of chocolate out of your diet—you'd go crazy! Having a much smaller place helps reinforce my minimalist decisions. I was surprised to find out how much stuff I didn't really want because the new place was so beautiful—it overlooked nature. It's been much more gratifying to look at nature than it was to look at all my stuff. I gave away a bunch of art to a charity I support which helped raise a few hundred dollars.

I got a little storage locker and my new game was how to purge. Each month I let go of a little more stuff. My dining room table and chairs fit well in a friend's house, a few bags of clothes helped prosper a resale store. I keep asking myself if I can purge more. Then I moved again—from my new home to an even smaller one. My work and income had dwindled further and I needed to downsize again. I was surprised that letting go of more stuff the second time I moved was even more painful. I suffered a mild depression. I've always had a gregarious and humorous nature but underneath was this core loneliness; I used stuff to cover it up. I have to clean my office here—that's my next task. I still have some de-cluttering to do in the living room and the dining room—the public places—so guests don't trip over things when they visit. If I could find the time and energy I devoted to accumulating the clutter and apply it to getting rid of the clutter, I'd be successful.

Having less clutter and more space has actually been nice. I didn't need six purses. Some of the people who were helped me pack and move said, "Oh, my God, you have five graters!" You just never know when you're going to need one! Some of the things I had multiples of were so silly. When you collect, hoard or bargain hunt, you tend to buy the same things. That's why Dollar Stores are everywhere! I don't like them because there's no thrill of the bargain if everything is the same price! It's not the same feeling as getting something really nice that's cheap.

You know, with all the changes I've been making in my life, it would be absolutely dandy to be in a healthy, loving relationship one day. I'm much more open to this now. But I need to hold it lightly; if I get disappointed, it might trigger a relapse into shopping and hoarding. But living in a smaller place has simplified my life and allowed me to focus on new goals and new friendships, including a few who're helping me get physically fit and financially and emotionally healthy.

I don't see many of the people I used to "use with/go shopping with." Some have modified their spending in this economy. When we hang together, we cook a meal instead of going to a restaurant at a shopping mall. When I do visit shops, they no longer have that "candy store" feel. I look around, admire the pretty colors and styles, but it just feels like a warehouse full of stuff. I'd sooner invite people to my home since it's comfortable and inviting now. Also, I'm not as caught up in comparing my stuff to other people's stuff.

When I was overshopping and hoarding, I felt ashamed and uncertain in my life. Nothing really good happened except that my credit card got lots of exercise. Now, each day, I get out and walk daily in the park I breathe in nature and exhale all my silly fears. Hardly a week goes by without invitations to do fun things at minimal cost. The darkness threatens from time to time but it doesn't take over. Neither does the stuff.

Post-script: Corinne moved again after our interview. She still feels guilt and sadness around letting go but was maintaining her progress and dating a new man.

131

Ralph's Story

Ralph is a retired husband, father and grandfather in his 60s living a middle-class life in a Midwest town. His life exploded recently when his wife and children discovered a myriad of secret lives he'd been keeping over the last several years. He'd been accused of embezzling thousands of dollars from his church, where he'd been a volunteer bookkeeper for many years, to buy all sorts of things which he stored in public storage units close to his home. By the time Ralph's family contacted me, the church had confronted him and his wife was on the verge of leaving him.

A couple of years ago, I got an e-mail from a woman looking for help for her father as well as her family:

Dear Mr. Shulman,
I'm hoping you can help us. I saw your websites and you seem to specialize in several of the addictions my father suffers from, including shopping, hoarding, and embezzlement. We found out about his secret life (or lives) last month. He finally saw a psychiatrist. He's on medication now and we think he may be ready for therapy. We need help immediately! Please respond ASAP. Thank you! Tanya

I promptly emailed Tanya back and then we spoke by phone. If ever there was a complex, sad, and severe case—this was it. Ralph's world came crashing down when his church's pastor and treasurer recently contacted his family and disclosed they'd just discovered proof that Ralph had embezzled about one hundred thousand dollars while he was a volunteer bookkeeper. When his family confronted him with this, Ralph broke down and began confessing to a myriad of out-of-control behaviors.

Over the last few years, Ralph had misappropriated church funds and purchased hundreds of gift cards with the money. Many of these cards were just bundled up and thrown into the trunk of his car; however, he used many to purchase an odd assortment of items including ceramic collectibles, clothing, office supplies, diapers, and kitchenware, all stored in hard plastic tubs in several large public storage units not far from his family's home. Ralph's family was in total shock. Who was this person they thought they knew? Word spread like wildfire throughout the church community. This decent family endured gossip, was ostracized and—worse— faced possible legal prosecution.

By the time I met with Ralph, his wife, and Tanya, Ralph had essentially confessed to the embezzlement. In working with him and his family over two months, I witnessed their collective shame and stress as their world turned upside down. Ralph had no idea how much he stole and no reasonable explanation (as if there could ever be one) for why he'd done what he'd done. To make matters worse, some church officials were baffled Ralph didn't even seem remorseful for his actions. It's understandable they expected tears and pleadings for forgiveness. I saw Ralph's flatness as proof of his overwhelming shame and numbness, which often accompanies a person's misdeeds, especially if that person wasn't really himself when he committed those actions. Besides, Ralph was pretty heavily medicated.

The church officials also felt Ralph was relatively uncooperative. But by the time I arrived in the picture, Ralph and his family had allowed the officials to search their home and all the storage units; they reclaimed wads of cash and gift cards, huge jars full of coins, and their pick of valuables from the public storage units, which they'd left in utter disarray. I made a special trip to visit the units with Ralph, his wife and Tanya, and was stunned by the scope the mess. The money, gift cards, coins, and stored objects reclaimed came to roughly half of what Ralph may have embezzled.

133

As I saw it, the family had three immediate concerns: keeping church officials from filing a police report; helping them understand how and why Ralph engaged in these bizarre behaviors in the first place; and enacting a plan to dispose of the "junk" in the storage units, which was about to cost the family another $2,000 in monthly rental fees.

I told the family I couldn't guarantee the church wouldn't go to the police. I instructed them to notify the church that Ralph had begun specialized counseling with me. I told them if the church had any kind of theft or indemnity insurance, their losses might be covered; however, it was likely a police report might need to be filed for the insurance to pay out. As for helping Ralph and the family understand how and why this all happened, I felt fairly confident we could at least arrive at some sensible working theories to explain the nonsensical—but this would take some time. Finally, I couldn't tell them what to do or what not to do with about the storage units; but I shared that, generally speaking, it can be very traumatic and counter-productive when a hoarder's things are removed or disposed of too quickly and without his involvement. I understood this was a fairly unique situation but I encouraged them to pay one month's storage to allow me time to get to know Ralph and their family and to ask Ralph if would help us commit to dispose of the contents within 30 days. The family agreed, as did Ralph.

Over the course of therapy, I learned that Ralph had always had a penchant for shopping and collecting. He grew up both materially and emotionally impoverished. His mother died of cancer when he was a young boy and his father, an alcoholic, was absent physically and emotionally. In essence, Ralph had been abandoned by both his parents, raised himself, and was a bit of a loner. He found work, moved to another state and married his current wife of 40 years, Roberta. They attended church together and had three children in relatively quick succession. In counseling, he assured me he loved his children and felt he'd been a good father.

It's likely Ralph had been suffering from depression and obsessive-compulsive disorder for many years and should have been diagnosed much earlier. He'd recently had a battery of brain scans and neurological tests which revealed evidence of early organic disease, which also may have contributed to his impaired thinking, mood, and behavior.

Ralph's family all agreed that Ralph had always been rather passive and that it was hard to get him to talk and express himself. I observed his passivity. Ralph stated that when he'd tried to speak up or ask for what he wants, he frequently felt invalidated and rejected by wife and others, so he preferred to avoid arguments and confrontations. I believed Ralph's overspending, collecting and hoarding developed, in part, to compensate for his financial and emotional impoverishment, and were a means of soothing and rewarding himself. From Ralph's and his wife's account, this led to recurring arguments which led to increasingly secretive behavior.

Ralph's life began to further unravel about ten years ago when, after several decades working two full-time jobs, he retired. He felt a huge void. He'd been volunteering as his local church's bookkeeper for many years and, since he had more time, he devoted more of his energy there. He then developed several health issues which left him feeling even more vulnerable; he got treatment but it didn't help much. He also shared he felt he and his wife were continuing to drift apart. Ralph felt he always came last but, consistent with his passivity, he'd rarely spoken up.

A couple years later, Roberta's mother came to live with them, in a hospice situation, until her death. While Ralph attended to her, Roberta spent most of the time visiting their daughter Tanya who was going through some issues. As expected, Ralph took on this burden without complaint. But he shared it was very stressful: he was close to his mother-in-law and her death was traumatic and triggered feelings about his own mother's death. Around this time, Ralph began

135

shopping more and secretly rented his first storage unit not far from home.

Over the next few years, Ralph spiraled out of control, ringing up credit card debt and renting more storage units for his purchases. He was forced to dip into his 401(k) savings to pay these debts as well as the normal bills. His spending and hoarding were cries for help, attempts to fill a deep emptiness, and somehow bring order to the chaos in his life. Ralph recounted the first time he stole from the church was about 4 years ago; he maintained it was a desperate and impulsive attempt to "borrow" some money to ease his financial stress. Once he stepped over the line, however, his stealing—like his spending and hoarding—snowballed beyond his control; before he realized it, he was in too deep. The objects he purchased hoarded and stored—hundreds of gift cards, all sorts of home goods and various tzotchkes— illustrated Ralph's internal madness.

Things finally came crashing down several months ago; Ralph finally admitted he needed help. Ralph shared he even felt angry that people from the church didn't seem to understand he was sick. I've found it quite common that my clients—and Ralph was no exception—possess limited empathy for the victims of their shocking offenses. They remain stuck, at least initially, in their own sense of victimization; a key part of my therapy involves exploring and resolving this.

During my work with Ralph and his family, they were able to give up the storage units within a month. They retrieved some belongings they wished to salvage but, after having several plans that didn't pan-out, they hired a local auction company which sold the contents of the units. They received a couple hundred dollars total. Ralph was involved in this process and, while he felt some sense of loss, his anxiety was low and he realized he had other more important things on which to focus.

Without assigning blame, I helped the family understand how this crisis likely developed. It made sense to them on some level. Ralph and Roberta decided to get marriage counseling and, so, our therapy took a pause. I remained concerned about Ralph's fragile state. I encouraged him to speak up and I encouraged the family to listen to his feelings and involve him as much as possible in the unfolding process. I felt fairly confident the family would evolve and survive whatever came next.

Post-script: I kept in periodic contact with Tanya, Ralph's daughter who initially contacted me. She told me the church had filed a police report but Ralph was never formally charged with embezzlement. This unfortunate situation was tragic for all involved. It never ceases to amaze me how such secret lives can go unnoticed for so long. I hope Ralph and his family found a way to work through their crisis and find some new wisdom and love with which to rebuild their lives.

Sabrina's Story

Sabrina is a 50-ish attractive married woman—no children—with two older sisters. She's been self-employed for 25 years and still works part-time. She's a very spiritual and loving soul and has many friends. Her father died ten years ago; her mother died just over a year ago. Her parents were hoarders and she still feels the effects of this in her life. Note: Sabrina is an acquaintance, not a client of mine.

I'm the youngest of three sisters and both of my parents were hoarders. I have some anxiety about revealing this family secret. There was also a cycle of abuse in my family. I still feel a lot of shame about all of this. It's so deeply ingrained that my nervous system automatically reacts. (Tears) The effect it had on me was anger, frustration, resentment, powerlessness. Even today, I don't know how to reconcile those feelings. All I wanted was a clean home; and they couldn't even provide that for me. I never felt like it was my home. I couldn't bring friends home because the house had an odor to it; I was afraid my clothes had an odor, too. I was always conscious of that. I was always clean—if you looked at us, we were clean and tidy. What went on in our house wasn't necessarily reflected in how we looked. My folks were of modest means. We were on welfare and my parents grew up during The Depression. I always said: "The Depression is alive and well in the house I lived in."

I have hoarding in my DNA. I have to set up systems in my own home. When my husband and I bought our home, I didn't want a basement because I knew I'd probably hoard things down there. I wanted very little storage space so I couldn't store things. So, I had these mechanisms which I purposely planted. In our laundry room, I have a particular space I call "the Salvation Army space" which I regularly

138

fill up with things from around the house to donate later. Sometimes, I'll look at an object—and I'll just keep looking at it—and I don't even know what I'm feeling but it's like I feel: "how can I get rid of you?" Then, I try to say to myself: "well, I'll let Salvation Army store it; I'll let them store it." Sometimes, that's how I need to think about it. I still have piles of papers in a few different places in my home—though I'm much better than I used to be and an improvement from how I grew up. My home isn't clutter-filled—I can walk through the hallways—but sometimes I look at the piles and think to myself: "Who is that person? Why are these things so important to me?" I feel this immediate frustration inside me and I don't know what to do, I don't know what to say, or how to resolve it, so I kind of walk away from it.

I recall throughout my life that my sisters and I, individually and collectively, cleaned up our family home and cleaned out the basement. It seemed like we were always cleaning up after our parents. We found used furniture in the basement. My Dad was a trailblazer in dumpster diving—they call it free-cycling now—but it was all junk as far as I was concerned. He just brought it home because it was free and I guess he thought he'd use it some day. There was this gas pipe that ran the length of our basement that was filled with my Dad's clothes on hangers. You couldn't touch them. But he only wore certain clothes, like uniforms. In the furnace room, he had a lot of tools, nuts and bolts, parts of machinery—really, useless stuff he just collected. With my Mom, my sister and I found a lot of unopened mail, canning jars, plastic bags, a lot of clothes, and dead plants.

My father also used to shoplift regularly. He stole batteries, hearing aid batteries, vitamins, toiletries, ointments. He used to try to push me into stealing, too. He'd tell me: "Go ahead; it's there for the taking." Even though I was young, I knew there was something wrong about this. When my father passed away, about ten years ago, my sister and I had to clean out the house in order to sell it. We filled two and a half long dumpsters-full of toxic, moldy, hoarded and stolen junk. I felt sad and angry. How selfish is that to leave us with all this junk to clean up? It was selfish of them.

We moved my Mom from a three-bedroom, full basement home to a one-bedroom apartment. I was relieved because I thought she couldn't junk up her new place; but, somehow, she did. She was only allowed one animal but she ended up with two; people would give her food and the food went to waste; they'd give her clothes and my sister and I constantly had to clear things out. One time, my sister collected 100 garbage bags full of things to throw out: clothing, cards, food, blankets. My Mom rarely slept on her bed because of the clutter. She accumulated decorations she never used.

My Mom, in my opinion, was also addicted to religion. Her relationship to God, to her religion, and to her people at church was most important; everything else came second, including family. So, she really took care of herself and her community at church. Everything else paled in comparison. I believe she was abused; something happened in her life. I think her hoarding and her religious addiction evolved from this. I believe my father was abused when he was young, too. I'm sure growing up during The Depression didn't help. My Mom's family lived in another country; they came to America to be free, but lost everything in the stock crash.

I've had to work through many issues over the years and I'm particularly aware of my hoarding tendencies. I'm hyper vigilant about my home. I have these checks and balances in my own head because I don't want to get into that pattern; it's just too painful. I have a couple of friends who are hoarders and I can feel the frustration in their own lives but I'm glad I feel totally free of the responsibility to clean it up. I don't feel any urges to clean up their stuff; I just feel the sadness of their situations because I know hoarding is a manifestation of some inner pain, loss or trauma. I've had to deal with the pain, loss and trauma of being brought up by hoarders. At times, it repulsed me. My folks were very narcissistic. They had no concept how it affected me.

I've had difficulty making decisions. I still do. Sometimes, I look at an object and have trouble letting it go—I can't even tell you why. As for making life decisions, sometimes I have trouble and sometimes, not. I had to grow up pretty fast. I've had to learn how to shop, organize bills, other things. As part of my healing journey, I've had to learn how to appreciate nature, to get outdoors and enjoy the expansiveness of nature. I was always so focused on cleaning up things; I had to get out and expand my world. I got into gardening, exercise, and therapy.

I was married once before and my ex-husband wasn't a hoarder. But we'd bought his great aunt's home and she'd just left everything in it; so, we inherited 50 years worth of junk and had to clean all that out. I remember keeping this cabinet, though—I had this thing for glass jars, mason jars—and I filled the cabinet with them. I'd go down, open the cabinet, and look at my collection of jars. Later, I got into canning food. So, I went through a brief period of hoarding.

My oldest sister is definitely a hoarder. I've seen it. She lives out of state. I feel bad for her kids because I know how it feels. My other sister does pretty well. She has lots of things but she's well-organized and keeps her home clean. I know I have to keep an eye on my hoarding just like an overeater or overshopper has to keep an eye on those behaviors. It's like being in recovery one day at a time.

I still feel this deep shame and sadness. My home was filled with stuff, but not much love. And even the stuff I did get was old and second-hand. I'm not a shopaholic—I still like getting a bargain—but I do like to buy some new or high-quality things sometimes. And I do want and need and deserve lots of love in my life. I don't want to settle for less.

Notes & Reflections:

Part Five
It Doesn't Apply to Me:
Rule Breaking and Risk Taking

Laws are like cobwebs, which may catch small flies, but let wasps and hornets break through.—Jonathan Swift

The healthy being craves an occasional wildness, a jolt from normality, a sharpening of the edge of appetite... a brief excursion from his way of life.—Robert MacIver

All of us take risks at some point in our life. Some risks are calculated, some impulsive. Some risks relate to basic life choices: getting into a relationship, going to college, applying for a job, buying a home. We take other risks for the feeling of thrill, excitement, or danger: driving fast, sky-diving, having an affair. Rule-breaking can be part of normal development—individuating and rebelling, testing the bounds of authority. But it can get out of control.

We also learn about taking risks and breaking rules from those around us. We appear to live in a world of risks and rule-breaking. The recent financial meltdown was due to high-risks and loose—if any—rules. When the "innocent" pay for the "sins" of the guilty, is it any wonder there's cynicism—not to mention, a whole lot of people walking away from their mortgages whether they had to or chose to.

A couple of recent true stories: I was talking to a good friend of mine whose ex-husband finally went to rehab. He had long-time gambling and spending addictions and had also become hooked on pain pills after a back injury. The way my friend described it, she worried he wasn't going to really get much out of treatment because *"he broke just about every rule they had! I'm surprised they didn't kick him out! He hid his cell phone and called me and our son—not allowed; he paid fellow patients to do his cleaning and chores; and, somehow, he had access to a credit card because he ordered something and had it delivered so he'd have it when he got home."* I worked for seven years as a chemical dependency counselor and our clients always pushed the envelope around rules. I'd often tell them they should go to law school!

Another story involves a client of mine, a doctor, who's had a long history of stealing in various forms. He "picked up" an electronic gadget at one of the hospitals he works at; it belonged to another doctor he didn't even know. This doctor complained, security reviewed in-house security videotape, and found proof my client had taken the item. When confronted by the hospital administrator, he made a confession of sorts, stating he'd been under stress and had begun to seek counseling (he enrolled in my program the next day). It looked like my client was going to be given a warning—since he returned the doctor's gadget within hours.

Then, two weeks later, my client gets a call from the doctor's friend and a lawyer saying, in essence, the doctor wants $10,000 (Ten Thousand Dollars) from my client for his time and suffering and to buy his silence; otherwise, he will go to the police and file both a criminal and civil complaint—thus jeopardizing my client's reputation, medical license, and job. It's pretty close to—if not—extortion. Two wrongs don't make a right. Now who's breaking the rules? On the one hand, my client felt he deserved to be in a pickle and thought $10,000 was a small price to pay given all he had to lose; however, I worried that giving into the extortion would just confirm his belief that most people are dishonest and lead him to steal again later. Dishonesty may be as old as dust but recent studies have noted a decreasing appreciation of honesty as a core value.

The thief, once committed beyond a certain point, he should not worry himself too much about not being a thief anymore. Thieving is God's message to him. Let him try and be a good thief.—Samuel Butler

Top Ten Reasons People Break Rules/Take Risks
1. Weren't taught value of following rules/being careful
2. Had too many rules/too many cautions against taking risks
3. Witnessed rule breaking/risk taking
4. Had own boundaries violated/was abused or betrayed
5. Was let down by authority/saw hypocrisy of authority
6. Narcissistic tendencies: rules don't apply/won't get caught
7. Attention deficit/hyperactivity—easily distracted/restless
8. Feel rules are unjust; therefore, it's just to break them
9. Had to raise self; therefore, little respect for authority
10. Excitement, power, adrenaline from risks/rule-breaking

When The Teachers Cheat (excerpt)
USA Today, March 10, 2011 by Jodi Upton

Educators as well as administrators, cheat for different reasons—to boost scores, earn bonuses or keep enrollment up. But some cheat because the humiliation of not keeping up with peers is stronger than the risk of getting caught. Some districts post class scores publicly, rewarding top teachers and shaming the rest. Parents may use scores to request certain teachers, creating competition among teachers. In 10 states, teachers' pay is tied to improved test scores; six other states are considering doing the same. Whatever the motivation, when seasoned teachers make cheating seem acceptable, others may go along with it.

An Arizona teacher said that, as a student teacher, she was asked by her supervising teacher to erase and correct answers on a test. "I questioned it in my head, but I did not question her," the anonymous teacher said. "I put this teacher on a pedestal. ... Yet I was cheating." Many teachers justified their cheating—especially the more pedestrian forms—as a way of getting back at a low-paying system rigged by impossible standards and unrealistic goals. Other teachers resented that their entire reputation could hinge on a child's performance on a single day.

The cover-up is always worse than the misdeed.—Anonymous

So What If You Don't Pay Your Debts?

The Atlantic by Megan McArdle, re-edited in June 2011 The Week
If you think mortgage payments are voluntary, "go look at your mortgage documents." People figure they can choose not to pay the bank what it is owed, at which point the bank gets to take the house. In fact, mortgage documents don't offer a buyer that option; instead, they obligate you to "avoid a breach at all costs." Yet the pernicious idea that paying back debts is optional is spreading from mortgages to student loans and other personal debts. The line is, "I don't want to pay, and as long as I'm willing to take the hit on my credit score, no one should judge me." But there's a real problem with thinking that you have "no moral obligation to keep your promises." Think of it in other contexts: Is it okay to cheat on your spouse because you can always get a divorce? Is it okay for your boss to shortchange you on your raise because you can always quit? Americans underestimate the "role that norms play in sustaining a modern economy." So, for everybody's sake, make that mortgage payment.

Pentagon Employees Purchased Child Pornography (excerpt)
Caffeinated Thoughts, January 2011
The Pentagon's investigation of defense and intelligence employees who downloaded child pornography is being criticized in Congress after the Department of Defense acknowledged that its investigators failed to check thoroughly whether its employees were on a list of suspected porn viewers. In 2006, the Immigration and Customs Enforcement agency, which conducts Internet pornography investigations, produced a list of 5,200 Pentagon employees suspected of viewing child pornography and asked the Pentagon to review it. But the Pentagon checked only about two-thirds of the names, unearthing roughly 300 defense and intelligence employees who allegedly had viewed child pornography on their work or home computers.

<u>Breaking Rules Makes You Seem Powerful</u> (excerpt)
Science Daily, May 20, 2011

When people have power, they act the part. Powerful people smile less, interrupt others, and speak in a louder voice. When people don't respect the basic rules of social behavior, they lead others to believe that they have power, according to a study in Social Psychological and Personality Science. People with power have a very different experience of the world than people without it. The powerful have fewer rules to follow, and they live in environments of money, knowledge and support. People without power live with threats of punishment and firm limits according to research led by Gerben Van Kleef. Because the powerful are freer to break the rules—does breaking the rules seem more powerful?

People read about a visitor to an office who took a cup of employee coffee without asking or about a bookkeeper that bent accounting rules. The rule breakers were seen as more in control, and powerful compared to people who didn't steal the coffee, or didn't break bookkeeping rules. Acting rudely also leads people to see power. People who saw a video of a man at a sidewalk café put his feet on another chair, drop cigarette ashes on the ground and order a meal brusquely thought the man was more likely to "get to make decisions" and able to "get people to listen to what he says" than the people who saw a video of the same man behaving politely.

What happens when people interact with a rule breaker? Van Kleef and colleagues had people come to the lab, and interact with a rule follower and a rule breaker. The rule follower was polite and acted normally, while the rule breaker arrived late, threw down his bag on a table and put up his feet. After the interaction, people thought the rule breaker had more power and was more likely to "get others to do what he wants. Norm violators are perceived as having the capacity to act as they please" write the researchers. Power may be corrupting, but showing the outward signs of corruption makes people think you're powerful.

147

20 QUESTION
Assessment for Rule Breaking/Risk Taking

1. Do you typically drive above the speed limit?
2. Do you smoke cigarettes?
3. Are you generally an impatient person?
4. Do you tend to live life on the edge?
5. Have you ever cheated on your taxes?
6. Have you ever cheated on an exam?
7. Do you tend to withhold the truth or lie about things?
8. Do you often feel rules are stupid or don't apply to you?
9. Do you tend to run late for appointments or meetings?
10. Do you tend to alternate between perfectionism and not giving a damn?
11. Have you ever snuck into parties, events or movies?
12. Do you tend to find ways to move up your place in lines?
13. Do you pride yourself on being able to get what you want or solve problems even if it requires questionable tactics?
14. Do you feel disdain for people who play by the rules?
15. Are you sensitive to criticism?
16. When offered free samples of food or other items, do you tend to take more than just one?
17. When staying at hotels, do you make a point to keep any items such as shampoos, soaps, lotions, or the like?
18. Is it hard for you to hear "no" when you want something?
19. Have you bought things from stores and used them knowing you were going to return them later?
20. Do you have issues with authority or being told what to do and prefer to be your own boss?

Most compulsive rule breakers/risk takers will answer "yes" to *at least 7* of these questions.

Dustin's Story

Dustin is a 25-year old young man with a long history of anger problems, lying, rule breaking, substance abuse, and stealing (shoplifting, employee theft, and credit card theft/fraud, including from his own mother). He's had most of his trouble with the law since he turned 18; he's spent three years incarcerated since that time. Dustin's behaviors belie his sensitivity and intelligence. He found out about my counseling program a year ago but didn't have the courage or commitment to contact me. He got arrested for shoplifting shortly afterwards and was incarcerated. His mother contacted me and said if Dustin enrolled in my program and lived with her, he'd be released under strict supervision.

In sharing his history, Dustin reported—and his mother confirmed—that he'd been lying and stealing since age five. When such problems occur at such an early age, I'm always concerned the individual might have a personality disorder such as oppositional defiance or anti-social or conduct disorder. I asked Dustin why he thought he had such a problem with stealing. He surmised it was mostly for thrills and due to poor impulse control. When I pressed, he added it might have something to do with anger and feelings of entitlement. I asked him where he thought this came from...

I had trouble with rules and taking things since I was 5-years old. I was diagnosed with ADHD and put on Ritalin and, later, other drugs. I related to your story, Terry, in your book Something for Nothing. I also related to some of the stories in Biting The Hand That Feeds. I think a lot of it has to do with not having a father figure. My Dad was in and out of my life, especially after my parents separated when I was about 11, which was also around the time I moved with my mother from the neighborhood where I grew up to a more affluent

149

area. I missed my friends and had a hard time fitting in with the new kids at school. I felt different, like I didn't quite measure up. I was bullied and made fun of because my clothes were less cool and my Mom's car was older.

I'd already had some troubles with stealing prior to moving; maybe I was reacting to my parents' fighting. I remember the first thing I took—a stuffed animal Tasmanian Devil, you know, from Bugs Bunny. I took it out of a kid's backpack at Catholic School. My Mom found out and made me take it back to school. When my father heard about this, he went out and bought me my own Tasmanian Devil. I think this impacted me—like, if I got in trouble, my Dad would be there for me. That's been true some of the time, but not always.

After we moved, I remember I was at the Mall with my Mom. She was shopping for some new luggage and, while I was in the store with her, I took off the little locks and keys on a couple suitcases. When we were leaving, my Mom noticed me playing with them; again, she made me take them back. I have this memory of a big snowstorm the first winter we arrived at our new home. I was out there, 11 years old, shoveling and using the snow blower; I was really struggling. I remember thinking: my Dad should be here doing this, not me. My parents finally divorced when I was 13; I'd still hoped they'd get back together. I just went wild.

My Mom and Dad always had money problems. I think my Mom was stressing out about money after the divorce and the big move. She'd also borrowed a lot of money to start up her own business. So, I never really wanted to ask them for help; I didn't want to be a burden. But Mom had a business where customers often paid in cash. She'd leave the cash around a lot and I'd take a twenty here and there and that's how my stealing started to escalate. Sometimes, she'd ask whether I was stealing; my first response always was to lie— unless I'd be caught red-handed. Mom would yell at me but not really punish me. She'd always ask me why I didn't just ask her if I needed money, and I'd shrug my shoulders—I didn't know what to say. I also had a real hard time hearing "no." I still do. I don't deal well with rejection. I live by the saying: "It's better to ask for forgiveness than permission."

In my teens, I got into fights and had a juvenile record for disorderly conduct. I also had friends who worked at Best Buy, Radio Shack, and a drug store. They'd let me come in and steal things. Between the ages 13-23, I probably shoplifted over 1,000 times. I didn't really need the stuff; I took it more for the high of getting away with it. In high school, I failed my freshman year—I went to class but just didn't do any homework. I ended up in a special program to redo my first year. I came back my sophomore year and had an aide/tutor who was like my shadow. The other kids made fun of me—yeah, it was embarrassing—but I learned to joke about it, too, so they'd get off my case. I actually got great grades that year. Maybe I got cocky or lazy but I fell off again in my junior and senior years. I was interested in girls. I didn't have a drop of alcohol until I was 21—and then I made up for lost time—but I got into pot pretty heavily.

When I turned 18, I started having really bad arguments with my Mom. We had this power struggle. I think I was afraid of graduating and what I was going to do with my life. When you turn 18, you're considered an adult; you're supposed to be "a man." But I had no idea what that really meant. My Dad still didn't seem to take much interest in me. I think he was using cocaine then, too. He didn't know how to talk to me. I think I was taking a lot of my anger out on my Mom. Well, Mom called the police one day and they arrested me— on my birthday! I guess she was really afraid and got a restraining order against me. I was shocked and angry. I went by her house to talk and she called the police again. I ended up serving 6 months in the county jail. It was awful. All I learned in jail was how to break more rules and become a better criminal.

151

I got out at age 19 and lived with a foster family for a year while I finished my GED. I tried to turn my life around and ended up getting in with the carpenter's union. I had my first real job and was doing well but it was short-lived: I got caught stealing some copper and some tools from a work-site and was fired. I heard the police were looking for me, so I turned myself in and told them the truth. I ended up with fines, restitution and 5-years probation. You'd think I'd have learned my lesson but, as soon as I turned 21, I started drinking heavily and hanging out with friends who drank and drugged. Then, one night, I stole an inflatable boat from the yacht club my Mom belonged to. I was trying to impress some friends and I ended up getting caught; I violated my probation and served some time again.

After a few months, I got out again and my probation was extended. I knew I was on a tight leash and did my best to stay out of trouble. But I kept breaking rules and laws here and there. I also got involved in this very intense but unhealthy relationship with a woman who tried to help me but really was trying to control me. I broke up with her and she started stalking me. I still get occasional calls from her.

Then, about a year ago—in late 2010—I shoplifted and got caught for the first time. It was right after Thanksgiving. I'd just visited my favorite uncle who was in the hospital. I had a feeling this might be the last time I'd see him alive. I was driving home and took another route to avoid paying the toll road; somehow, I ended up in a Wal-Mart parking lot. I went in and took a DVD. I had a knife on me and cut it out of the package but, somehow, they saw me and caught me. This arrest triggered another probation violation and I was incarcerated for three months. My uncle ended up dying and I wasn't able to attend his funeral. That sucked. Eventually, I was told I could get early release and be put on an intensive, probation under certain conditions: I had to live with my mother; have a curfew; keep a job; report regularly; do drug and alcohol testing regularly; and enroll in a specialized

*counseling program that addressed my stealing. That's how I
found you, Terry. I read your books while in jail and I had
hope for the first time that somebody could really help me.*

Dustin was released under a strict probation earlier this year
and our counseling began. Over the next three months, we
spoke weekly by phone. We included his mother on a few
sessions and she kept me updated by e-mail as I knew Dustin
had a tendency to lie. During the first month of treatment, I
tried to gain Dustin's trust. We discussed his life history and
it seemed clear much of his stealing was anger-related,
especially over his father's absence; he knew he had to find a
way to heal this wound to move forward. We discussed my
books, I added him to my private online support group, he
attended a local support group meeting for recovering
shoplifters, and he kept busy with a new job local law
enforcement helped him secure. *"It's funny,"* Dustin said, *"I
have so many people rooting for me, even the police and my
PO."* But he still longed to have father root for him, too.

Using my own story as an example, Dustin and I discussed
how I'd gone through many similar challenges. I was around
his same age—25—when I finally recognized I was making
choices each day about my own life; and if I kept doing what
I was doing, I'd keep getting what I was getting. He got what
I was saying. We also worked hard on practicing asking for
help and permission—especially from his mother. They had
a complicated relationship. It was vital she allow Dustin to
be as independent as possible—his Mom had real
codependency and boundary issues—while making sure to
enforce enough rules, so he respected her and the law.

After the first month of our treatment, Dustin's rule-breaking
tendencies began to re-emerge. First, he got involved with a
new girlfriend. I told him I didn't want to run his life, but
that getting into new relationships early in recovery often
leads to defocusing. This happened. Next, Dustin's mother
started reporting to me that cash was missing and small

credit card charges began to appear on her statements. When confronted, Dustin initially denied this but later confessed that he'd felt anxious about not having enough money for gas for his car. We went over the how to ask for help. Dustin didn't follow-through with sharing on my online support group as I'd suggested. He had various excuses. He had a lot on his plate and couldn't seem to balance everything. I often felt—as did he—that our therapy was just one more thing he "had to do." There were more arguments with his mother about rules—curfew, having his girlfriend overnight, and drinking alcohol. Dustin still had problems following rules and hearing "no." He tested positive for marijuana but was given another chance and was ordered into substance abuse counseling—another thing added to his already full plate.

Dustin's mother emailed me that he was still stealing from her and drinking. She didn't know if she should report this to his probation officer or not. I told her she might have to. I had a session with Dustin to process his situation. I asked *"What is your thinking process about not following rules. Why would you drink alcohol while your probation says: 'No alcohol.'?* Dustin gave the usual answers: *"the rule is stupid," "I didn't think I'd get caught,"* and *"a drink here in there isn't going to hurt anyone,"* I asked him if he thought there was any connection between not following rules and his recurrent legal issues. He concurred. I asked if he could predict where he'd be if this continues: *"Most likely in jail again."* I asked what value there is in following rules even if we don't agree with them. He said *"following rules makes life easier rather than harder; keeps me out of trouble."*

Post-script: Dustin moved out of his mother's home and into his new girlfriend's apartment. Within a week, however, Dustin had violated his probation for lying to his probation office and breaking other rules. It was sad to see both of these women try to save Dustin but, in reality, they probably got in the way. Even my efforts came up short. Dustin will have to learn to take responsibility for saving himself.

Philippe's Story

Philippe is a 35-year old native of France who moved to Spain a few years ago to avoid legal issues and possible physical harm by various people he'd stolen from or double-crossed. He contacted me after a recent investigation commenced into financial misappropriations at his workplace threatened his civil service job, his work status, and his freedom. He reported a long history of stealing and finally felt tired of the drama. We had several long-distance phone counseling sessions over the last year.

I've been stealing since I was 7-years old. My first theft was stealing some money while in another country with my adoptive parents. Then I was caught shoplifting from a store around age 9 but I managed to convince my parents it was a mistake. I kept shoplifting and was caught again at age 11. This time, my adoptive mother beat me and made me bring all the stolen stuff back to the stores and apologize. But I continued to steal from neighbors, from a charity I was collecting money for, and from just about every job I've ever worked for. I've also had a problem with hoarding things.

In my mid-teens, I was caught shoplifting, assaulted the security guard, and managed to escape. Later, I came back and set fire to that store's stock room. I was never caught or charged. I once worked for a company and stole a customer's BMW because he wouldn't say hello to me. Another time, I stole a bus with 70 passengers on it—just for thrills—and later parked it right in front of a police station. I got away with that, too. Recently, I stole a case of CDs and a bag of clothes from a prostitute, and a handbag that had credit cards in it from an ex-employer I resented.

Currently, I'm under investigation for taking property and misappropriating funds at a civil service job I've had the last two years here in Spain. I'm afraid this time I'm screwed. So far, I've been interviewed and denied everything. Even though I've always had a deep hatred of authority and governmental organizations, I've really enjoyed this job and have done well at it; it's been decent work and pay and I like most of the people I work with. I don't know why I risked screwing things up, but I guess that's part of my addiction.

I used to have a drinking and gambling problem but I managed to quit over 12 years ago. I don't know why I can't seem to quit stealing. I've had a history of depression; I saw a doctor and took Prozac for many years, but I stopped taking it a year ago because I wanted to see how I did on my own. I was attending Alcoholics Anonymous and Gamblers Anonymous groups but I had some bad experiences with people in those programs and now I'll never go back. They were trying to run my life for me and were engaged in all kinds of hypocrisy and illegal behavior themselves. I'm not very religious and that turned me off, too: a lot of those people are holy rollers. It seemed too much like a cult to me.

I have a hard time trusting; too many people have let me down. My mother gave me up for adoption when I was 4-months old. I never knew my father. I've tried many times to find their identities but the government keeps interfering with that. When I was a bit older, I found some information about my birth mother but my adoptive parents stole it from me. They were also liars and thieves: they stole and engaged in tax fraud. I had an uncle who was engaged in illegal endeavors. I think all this has a lot to do with why I have such rage and why I've been acting out through theft and violence. I know this but I just don't seem to be able to stop it. I'm hoping I can trust you, Terry, and you can help me because I do want help. I've been in counseling a number of times and I never really found a therapist who could help me. I've always felt judged; several therapists violated my confidentiality. I feel like I've lost faith in humanity.

I need to talk with someone who won't judge me. I need to unload my secrets because they're like poison to me, Terry, they're poison. I want to be free. I read your books and really related to them. They gave me some hope that I'm not alone. I fear, however, that I'm just sicker than most and that I'll put people off. I realize no matter how much I steal or how many fights I get into, it's not helping me heal or move forward in life. But I can't deny that, for a few moments, I feel a rush of adrenaline, excitement, and satisfaction when I steal; that's the hook. I'm filled with doubt that I'll ever have healthy relationships. I don't trust people, yet I don't want to be alone. I've been at war with the world since I was a kid and it seems like the world just won't stop being at war with me. My adoptive father was at war with the world, too. He even had an affair with my first girlfriend I had when I was about 14. I don't trust men or women. Sometimes I feel like I have a death wish. I feel like I abandoned my own mother—it's ironic; I know she's the one who abandoned me. That's the first time I've said this out loud. If I could, somehow, transcend these feelings, I'd be free.

I think I started getting into trouble as a young boy as a cry for help. Ironically, the police were the only ones who listened to me. Getting into trouble made me feel wanted; it was the only time people showed they cared about me. I also think I saw so much lying, cheating and stealing that I felt: why should I be honest if everybody else I know was dishonest? I had some learning disabilities which kept me from being able to sit still and internalize information. I know I have to deal with the here and now—one day at a time, as they say in the program—but I just don't know what to do with all this pain and rage I feel. Stealing has been my primary outlet. Stealing is all about anger for me. I feel like I've been victimized and oppressed and I get a charge out of striking back. I want to be the toughest, scariest guy around.

And so began my counseling with Philippe. I didn't know if I could help him and, as with Dustin and a few of my past clients, I wondered if Philippe suffered from personality disorders that were so ingrained that dramatic change might be impossible. Yet, I sensed in him a flickering flame of hope: he had tenderness, humor, vulnerability, and a desire to change—or at least to stop his deep pain. I had an edge over other past therapists: he could relate to aspects of my own life story and he seemed to feel less worried I'd judge him or not understand him. He also appreciated that my approach with him was not particularly religious/spiritual or 12-Step oriented. We had phone sessions every month or so, based on his budget. I added him to my private online support group which served as a daily reminder of recovery to him. I instructed him to e-mail me at least a few times a week with periodic updates of how he was doing in recovery and how the current investigation against him was proceeding. I built trust, a rapport, and structure over time.

There've been a few bumps in the road during our treatment. Philippe reported strong feelings of rage coming up and he was extremely sensitive to the slightest perceived rejection or judgment. Without invalidating his feelings, I reminded him that when we're giving up an old crutch, our stress level rises. We're naturally more on edge. I asked him if he knew any people he did trust or could confide in. He mentioned he had one or two friends, including one woman he had just re-connected with coincidentally. I asked him if he felt competent or talented at anything other than—in his words— being "a good thief." He told me he liked reading, enjoyed playing and watching sports, and loved music. I encouraged him to fill his life up more with those interests and hobbies and find people with similar interests. He took me up on this and attended a screenwriting class in a neighboring country. *"The people were great!"* he reported.

Philippe told me *"when someone says to me: 'that was a good thing you did,' that means more to me than a million dollars."* I recognized this as an opportunity to praise and encourage him whenever I could—while being careful not to overdo it or pull punches when I had to. Too many of us are deeply wounded by not having received enough praise and blessings. Philippe and I discussed his "addictive need" to punish himself. *"Maybe I've suffered and punished myself enough,"* he wondered. Much of our work together involved breaking this cycle and planting seeds for healthier habits.

Philippe felt an extreme amount of guilt over hurting many people during his life and wanted to make amends. His capacity for regret and remorse distinguished him from a typical sociopath who has little or no ability to empathize with his victims. Still, I suggested he pace himself in making amends and continue to focus on his own amends by getting his life on track. Step by step, Philippe put together days, then weeks, then months without stealing. His self-esteem slowly rose and he seemed to be injected with new life. He avoided most negative people and parts of town he described as *"sunny places with shadowy people."* The police investigation dissolved due to lack of proof. While he still felt guilty about lying and stealing and having gotten away with it, he took this as a "second chance" to prove himself. Philippe has a long road of recovery ahead of him he told me: *"if I'm ever really going to heal my core pain, I've got to learn how to stay sober and honest. It's up to me."*

Post-script: I've kept in touch regularly with Philippe and his life continues to be in turmoil: his emotions, his relationships, his job, his finances are all over the map. He's begun to reach out to the online group more and that's helped him feel a bit more validated and connected. Somehow, he's managed to avoid stealing, but living theft-free is still very new for him. As he put it: *"I am grieving the loss of my criminal identity. Who the hell am I if I can't be a criminal? What do I do now? How will anyone like or respect me? Where do I go from here, starting over after a thirty year criminal career?"*

Notes & Reflections:

Part Six
Interviews with Experts in the Fields

I feel grateful and honored that seven colleagues have generously agreed to share their wisdom with me and my readers. In my three previous books, I'd also included interviews of people with unique and relevant perspectives. With disorders as relatively unplumbed and even as controversial as those herein, it's imperative to consider other expert opinions. Besides, I enjoy highlighting the trailblazing work of others as much as I enjoy trailblazing!

I've known of *Elizabeth Corsale's* pioneering work with kleptomania and shoplifting addiction since 2003. Finding her in our lonely niche of treatment was like water to my soul. In 2004, Elizabeth connected me with her friend—a producer for Oprah Winfrey—which led to my appearance on the show later that year. Elizabeth came to Detroit in fall 2005—along with our colleague Dr. Jon Grant—to co-present with me at The First International Conference on Theft Addictions and Disorders. Elizabeth and I keep in touch regularly. She and a colleague recently launched The Pathways Institute/Bay Area Impulse Control Center.

I heard about the legendary *Jack Hayes* in 2005 when I began research for my book on employee theft. I'd come to know Jack's protégé and current CEO of his company, Mark Doyle. I've appreciated Mark's support in publishing several of my articles in the Jack Hayes Report newsletters and his generosity in permitting me to cite Jack Hayes Annual Theft Survey statistics. When I interviewed Jack by phone in May 2011, I could not have found a more personable and giving soul. I have to say the same about *Gary Zeune,* who contacted me earlier this year after stumbling across my work on the Internet. It gives me hope to talk to loss prevention pros such as Jack and Gary who see the multi-facets of theft and find value in my background as a former "thief" and as a therapist who treats theft disorders; usually, I'm met with suspicion or judgment by Loss Prevention folk.

A former shopaholic, *Dr. April Benson is* a pioneer and developed a niche therapy practice treating her particular affliction: compulsive buying and shopping. I first heard about her work in 2004. A year later, I met April in New York while there on business. She'd just heard of my work, too. I've admired her warmth, wit, and wisdom and am grateful for her gracious mentoring. She's been anything but petty, competitive or territorial—something I encounter often in business. I completed April's 14-week therapist tele-training in 2006. She's dedicated to helping therapists treat compulsive shoppers. We keep in contact regularly.

I first heard of *Dr. Gail Steketee,* a pioneer in the research and treatment of hoarding disorder, in 2008. Since then, I've read all the books she's co-written, as well as many articles, on this subject. When Social Worker Today magazine recently interviewed Gail and me for an article on hoarding and families in its May/June issue, I contacted her and was honored she took the time to share her wisdom here.

I first met *John Prin* in fall 2005 when he traveled from Minneapolis to Detroit to attend The First International Conference on Theft Addictions and Disorders. I was intrigued by his work and books on "secret keeping" and was impressed by his passion and commitment. I met John a year later when I was in Minneapolis. We keep in touch regularly.

I've known *Tom Lietaert* since 1996 when we did the ManKind Project's New Warrior weekend in the Detroit-Windsor area. We reconnected a year later when we joined an ongoing men's support group. We had so much in common it was as if we were long-lost brothers. Tom is a tireless seeker of truth and growth. Tom moved from the Toledo area to Boulder three years ago; I'm happy he's pursuing his dream of coaching on money and worthiness.

ELIZABETH CORSALE, MFT—*Shoplifting*

Ms. Corsale is a therapist in the San Francisco Bay Area. She works with many different impulse control disorders and addictions and is a pioneer in the study and treatment of kleptomania and theft addiction. Ms. Corsale co-presented at The First International Conference on Theft Addictions and Disorders in Detroit in 2005. She co-founded *The Shoplifters Recovery Treatment Program* now part of *The Pathways Institute*. See *www.pathwaysinstitute.net*.

What is your educational and professional background?
I'm a licensed marriage and family therapist and I've worked since 1995 with shoplifters and their families. I've treated a variety of impulsive/addictive disorders. I co-founded The Shoplifters Recovery Treatment Program (SRT)–now a part of Pathways Institute–one of the few nationally recognized treatment programs for compulsive stealing. I'm a member of the California Association of Marriage and Family and I've offered comprehensive education, training, outreach and consultation to clinical professionals and to criminal justice institutions. I also have a private practice in San Francisco.

When and how did you become interested in the study and treatment of kleptomania/shoplifting addiction? I was an intern working with a forensic psychologist. He told me he'd frequently get court referrals to evaluate or treat individuals with significant shoplifting or stealing histories but who had no other criminal profile. He asked me to do some research on any programs, books or literature on this subject. I found very little. Soon, we began developing a treatment model based on successful alcohol and drug treatment programs. In time, the program I now direct has grown and evolved.

What's the difference between a plain thief vs. someone

163

who has kleptomania or a theft disorder? Well, this is a challenging question if you're asking about psychological assessment and treatment. I don't tend to think in terms of plain thieves or plain dishonesty. If someone is stealing or shoplifting, the person has some kind of problem. It's my job to comprehensively assess this using the best research measures and clinical interviewing tools available.

I ask questions such as: Is the stealing impulsive or compulsive? Does the stealing fit the criteria for kleptomania? How often is the stealing? How much or what is stolen? Is the stealing egosyntonic (the stealing is congruent with the person's character/values and he/she isn't distressed much by it) or egodystonic (the stealing is incongruent with the person's character/values and he/she is notably distressed by it). Does the person have a co-occurring mood disorder, eating disorder, or substance abuse history? Does this person have a personality disorder and, if so, does it relate to the stealing? These are a few questions that help me formulate a complete picture of each person.

There's a real distinction between someone with a criminal profile vs. someone with kleptomania or a theft disorder. The criminal or "professional thief" usually has a longer history of dishonesty or is a "booster" who sells stolen merchandise for profit or works with a gang of thieves. The kleptomaniac or theft addict has much more unevenness in his/her life; except for the stealing, this person is completely upstanding. When I see this unevenness, I have to ask: what's going on?

Does your research or clinical experience lead you to believe that kleptomania or shoplifting addiction is on the rise? There's no doubt stealing is a significant problem in our country and around the world. But before we can understand if it's on the rise, we'd need a large scale prevalence study; as far as I know, no one has done this yet.

What are the primary reasons people steal? If we're

speaking about impulsive and compulsive stealing, then we need to think about the etiology of impulse disorders; the neurobiology of the patient; dopamine feedback loops; and the psychological, emotional and developmental context of the patient. We know impulse disorders worsen if there's an increase of stress in an individual's life. If you don't suffer from an impulse disorder but you turn the knob up to high stress, you'll likely become more impulsive while the stress is high; but unlike a person with impulse disorders, you won't repeat the impulsive cycle once the stress has lessened.

I've found that people who suffer from impulsive and compulsive stealing have had to deal with overwhelming stressors. These stressors may be internal or external and can occur at any stage of life. These people often have co-occurring mood disorders which also can create enormous stress. Many of my patients had early childhood attachment loss or trauma and stressful dysfunction family systems. These factors resulted in compensatory behaviors, such as stealing and/or other unhealthy behaviors they use to cope.

What treatments have you found work best for these disorders? People usually need long-term, ongoing treatment, including cognitive-behavioral and/or dialectical-behavioral therapy, psychodynamic treatment, medication, individual/group therapy, and 12-step/self-help programs.

What would people in general be most surprised to know about shoplifting addicts and kleptomaniacs? People who steal often don't know why they're doing what they're doing and they can't just stop without support. Treatment takes a long time both to help them understand and correct their behavior; there are no quick fixes. People with kleptomania and theft disorders are typically upstanding and honest: they usually hold good jobs, go to church or are religious, and are well-respected in their communities. People often think just because someone steals in one context that they're going to steal from anyone, anyplace, anytime. That's rarely the case.

Do you see a relationship between shoplifting and stealing behaviors and other addictive-compulsive behaviors? We definitely see patients with co-occurring hoarding, eating disorders, sexual addictions, and a lot of codependency. I've always been interested in and treated a variety of impulse control disorders and addictions. We're seeing more people with a cluster of addictions. It's quite unusual to find somebody who is just an alcoholic, or even just a shoplifter.

For instance, we see a lot of codependency—a lot of people who steal things for other people because they try to manage how others see them. This is manipulative but that's part of codependency—being seen as nice, generous, and financially affluent. People struggling with codependency often fear feeling out of control if they were to be fully honest with others, or assert their needs, thoughts and feelings. In treatment, we identify and work with this all the time.

What do you think about the way the media occasionally covers kleptomania or shoplifting addiction? I haven't seen many recent programs, so I can't comment. But there's a tremendous amount of stealing going on in our culture. Some of the people stealing are kleptomaniacs by criteria; others are not. But that shouldn't be the focus of the issue. If someone is stealing then there's a serious problem to address. We in the mental health field—as well as those in the media—need to bring awareness and a spirit of non-judgmental inquiry in order for us to understand impulsive and compulsive stealing. I've treated hundreds of people who have stolen; each person is unique and has value.

How do you measure success in your treatment? I think we're successful when a person gains insight into their stealing; they can reduce the harm they're causing themselves and others; and get to abstinence and work a solid program so they don't relapse and return to stealing. That's the first part of the equation. Once they're on their way to living a life "sober" from stealing, there's further measures of success: Can they get back on track developmentally, psychologically and emotionally? Can they begin to have healthy relationships and meaningful work? Are they making their unique contributions to those around them and to the greater community at large? Are they able to become more fully authentic and free from the burdens and traumas of their past as well as their disorders?

Where do you see the future of this area of treatment? I believe the future of treatment will combine therapies & medication. Hopefully, we'll learn more about the brain and neurotransmitters—dopamine especially—and understand how to better regulate it through technological innovations and neuroscientific discoveries.

It's likely that therapeutic treatment will continue to be necessary as we humans create psychological meaning to the context of our lives. Our unique differences make us who we are and this has to be included in the treatment. Treatment can't ever be "one size fits all." Psychotherapy is necessary for people to receive the support and help they need to work through the issues and problems that self-destructive impulses create in their lives.

JACK HAYES—Shoplifting/Employee Theft/Fraud

Mr. Hayes has been in loss prevention for nearly 50 years. He was the founder of Jack L. Hayes International, Inc. and prior to his "retirement" published the Annual Jack L. Hayes Theft Survey and the quarterly Hayes Report on Loss Prevention Newsletter. He continues to assist Mark R. Doyle, owner/C.E.O. of Hayes International on an as needed basis. Mr. Hayes authored the new book *Business Fraud: From Trust to Betrayal. See: www.preventbusinessfraud.com*

What is your educational and professional background?
After leaving the law enforcement profession, I started my security career in the mid-60s in Washington, D.C with a company called Woodward and Lothrop. In 1970, I was hired by Jordan Marsh in Boston as their first corporate security director. In 1974, I was appointed corporate security director of Abraham & Straus, New York which later became part of Macy's when Federated bought Macy's. At the time I went into A & S we had terrible problems with shoplifting in our Brooklyn store. We prosecuted only 3% of shoplifters at that time and the recidivism rate was 5.5. We averaged 125 apprehensions *per week* in the Brooklyn store alone. I remember telling the manager in charge of that store *"we're going to start prosecuting."* He said *"Jack, this is New York; it's not Boston or Washington."* I said, *"Charlie, we're going to start prosecuting."* By the time I left, we prosecuted over 97% of shoplifters and our financial losses had dropped dramatically, which had a tremendously positive impact on our bottom-line. In 1978, I started my consulting company, Jack L. Hayes International, Inc. Today, Mark R. Doyle, after working alongside me for 25 years, is the owner and C.E.O. of Hayes International.

When and how did you become interested in the study and

treatment of employee theft/fraud? Prior to going into loss prevention, I was a detective with the police department in Washington, DC. I specialized in homicide and sex crimes; interviewing and investigating runs in my blood. In 1966, the United States Attorney's Office assigned me to a very big case. I was given the authority to investigate that case within the jurisdictions of Washington, D.C., Maryland and Virginia; I got a top-level security/loss prevention job offer from Woodward and Lothrop that I couldn't turn down.

Prior to working in the retail, I'd never given any thought about the severity of internal fraud and theft. The magnitude and cost of these crimes was eye-opening! It didn't take me long to realize I was in a unique position to learn far more about the commission of internal fraud and theft in actual situations than others who were in law enforcement. So, on an informal basis, I made it a point to talk with perpetrators about their crimes and why they committed them. In 1969, I developed a specific set of questions for interviewing fraud perpetrators; as the years passed, those questions and my discussions with them became more in-depth. Eventually, my interests grew: I began to focus not only on why perpetrators committed their crimes but, also, on what businesses could have done to prevent theft and fraud.

What are the primary reasons people commit fraud or employee theft? When we look into the rapidly growing problem of internal fraud and theft, we hear all sorts of reasons why individuals commit these criminal acts. Some attribute such behavior to emotional problems that manifest themselves in a need for punishment; others say that, through theft and fraud, these employees believe they are getting back what they're due; still, others direct blame at external factors such as a slow economy or poor governmental-aid programs. Attorneys often argue in courts that medications their clients' took—or didn't take—triggered their criminal acts. After completing decades of studies on dishonesty, I've learned that three variables always come into play anytime dishonesty is involved; these variables are 1) the individual's *moral character, 2)* the *situational pressures* that the person is experiencing, and 3) the *opportunities* available for the fraud or theft to occur. Always remember: internal fraud or embezzlement cannot take place without a betrayal of trust.

What preventative measures have you found work best to deter/prevent fraud? The goal of any anti-fraud effort shouldn't be to detect fraud but to prevent it. Internal fraud can't be eliminated but it can be easily controlled! 90-95% of fraud is the fault of management. Managers can't prevent internal fraud if they don't know where their operation's greatest risks are or if they don't know how to create and implement a realistic anti-fraud action plan.

Educating employees is equally important. Back in the 1990's I wrote a video script called "The Up Front Series.". Each segment addressed issues about theft. The video went over well with most employees and consisted of five modules: 1) An Honest and Frank Discussion on Employee Theft; 2) Causes and Effects of Employee Dishonesty; 3) Definition of Honesty; 4) Our Commitment to Honesty; and 5) Our Responsibility to Prevent Dishonesty. Each module focused on a specific aspect of employee dishonesty, actions co-workers could take to prevent it, and ended with a specific question designed to stimulate group discussion.

I'd gained so much knowledge from speaking with all types of honest and dishonest employees about internal fraud. I'd learned that one of the most effective strategies for controlling internal dishonesty was to discuss the problem directly and involve the employees in "problem-solving" discussion groups. Think about it: how can you really deal with a problem of which you're unaware? I believe it's critical to talk to employees about fraud and fraud prevention in a positive way that doesn't leave them feeling accused or mistrusted. Most importantly, when analyzing the risks of a particular position or job, the approach must stress *"it has*

nothing to do with the individual working in the position."
The risk safeguards must be built solely around the duties of
the job rather than around level of trust of the person
performing those duties. The confidential hotline is another
strategy that helps deter theft. It keeps most employees
honest if they know another employee could turn them in.

Prosecution is an effective fraud prevention measure;
however, it can be an expensive endeavor. I'd developed a
good understanding of the legal system and once set-up a
court program that dramatically reduced the time spent by
loss prevention personnel prosecuting shoplifters and
dishonest employees. The program was extremely
successful. My experiences have taught me that prosecution
is a strong deterrent to both internal and external theft.

Public awareness programs are also effective in helping to
prevent theft. I've always been an advocate of awareness
programs and used them effectively in Washington and
Boston. One of the first things I did was put theft awareness
programs in a couple of schools around Boston. They were a
hit! We also had students take tests which revealed their lack
of knowledge about the severity of this crime. They never
thought about the impact theft has on customer pricing, store
employees, or even their future employment if they were
caught stealing. They helped validate the effectiveness of
"anti-shoplifting" signs and were fully aware which stores
were tough on shoplifters and which were "easy targets" that
practiced "catch and release." I didn't set up such programs
in New York because we were dealing more with hardcore
thieves, so prosecution was the primary goal. There are
hardcore and casual thieves; I don't know if you're going to
change those hardcore thieves. I doubt it.

Once I was asked to do a TV show for Nickelodeon. I went
to the studio in New York; I knew I was going to be talking
to a group of teenagers about shoplifting. I got on stage with
the narrator and the first thing he asks the audience is: *"how*

many of you have ever shoplifted?" A few hands slowly rose and then they'd look around and pull them back. He asked it again; same response. The third time he asked, I raised my hand. After I raised my hand, a number of hands went up.

I proceeded to tell the story of when I was around 14—two of my buddies and I went downtown to Woodward and Lothrop. My buddy was trying on pants and we're hanging around, waiting. He comes back and says, *"That checker isn't checking how many pairs of pants you bring in."* He said, *"Let's take some pants."* And I said, *"aw no, I don't want to do that, I'm not going to do that."* And he said, *"C'mon"* and the other guy said to me: *"What, are you chicken?"* And I said, *"No, I ain't chicken!"* So, I took two pair of pants and put them together. When I walked into the dressing room, the checker asked me how many pair I had. I said "one pair." Inside, I put a pair on under my pants, came back out and gave her the other pair. We headed down the escalator and I thought to myself, *"If someone was tipped and stopped me, what would I do?"* I told those teens if I'd gotten caught shoplifting at that day, even if I wasn't prosecuted, the store would have made a record in their file and I wouldn't be here today talking to you because the first job I ever had in retail security was at Woodward and Lothrop—the store I stole those pants from!

What would people in general be most surprised to know about people who commit fraud/employee theft? In my recent book *Business Fraud: From Trust to Betrayal,* I share stories—everyone of them true—about all kinds of people who steal from their organizations for all kinds of different reasons. I think most people who steal and who are court-ordered into therapy or programs usually aren't as sincere about changing as those who seek out help themselves. I do know there are deeper reasons why many people steal and they do need help. In many shoplifting cases, I know it's not usually about the money. We've done various surveys found practically every shoplifter apprehended had money or credit cards on them; I think a number of otherwise good people have deficits in their coping skills which lead to theft. Today's economy is creating financial and situational pressures that may cause a normally trustworthy employee to commit an act of theft. I predict that unless a dramatic reversal takes place in our business and economic conditions, situational and financial pressures will continue to mount and theft and fraud will continue to rise at a dramatic pace.

I'm equally certain that the individual with a criminal record will have a hard time finding new employment. Many companies automatically reject them. But if you've got someone who's convicted of a crime, it's wise to evaluate the type of offense relative to the particular position sought. Throughout my career, personnel and human resources people have asked me to talk to prospective employees. I can usually tell if they're sincere, but you still have to be careful what type of position you put them in. An in-depth interview and a comprehensive background investigation is a must for anybody in positions of trust. Don't rely on a "gut-feeling".

Where do you see the future of fraud prevention? Let's look at the problem of internal fraud and embezzlement. These crimes cost businesses nationwide in excess of $500 billion annually. They happen in every type of operation imaginable: kids' sports leagues, multi-billion dollar corporations, government and law enforcement agencies, non-profit and religious organizations, schools and universities, and medical facilities. *No business is immune!* Anytime organizations lose such huge sums of money, something's seriously wrong. The current approach to fighting internal fraud isn't as effective as it should be. Surveys show the great majority of internal fraud is uncovered by accident or by a tipster, not through the efforts of auditors or other sources. It's well-known that successful internal fraud prevention requires management involvement. Until that day arrives, I predict little progress will be made in defeating this costly and devastating scourge.

GARY ZEUNE—Employee Theft/Fraud

Mr. Zeune is a business fraud professor at Ohio State University as well as a well-respected corporate fraud consultant. He authored *The CEO's Complete Guide to Corporate Fraud, Vol. 1*. See *www.theprosandthecons.com*.

What is your educational and professional background? I started out in college in 1966 and wanted to be an engineer and design cars. But I switched my major to math and did my undergraduate degree in mathematics, physics and psychology. Then I found out you couldn't get a job in math without a PhD. So, I stumbled into the business school one day and I ended up getting a masters degree in accounting. In 1973, I worked for the Ernst & Ernst accounting firm on the auditing staff. I left Ernst and went to Wendy's International in 1977 and was in charge in financial domestic reporting, mergers and acquisitions, and corporate finance. Later, I went into investment banking for several years. Then, in 1986, one morning at breakfast my 8-year old daughter Tiffany asked me why I worked so hard. I'd never thought about that. I soon got out of investment banking and began teaching full-time. I've taught part-time since 1970 and I've taught accounting and honors finance at Ohio State as well as Strategy Formulation and Implementation for 6-7 years. I also write and consult on business fraud and corporate crime.

When and how did you become interested in the study and treatment of employee theft/fraud? When I started teaching full-time in 1986, I taught securities offerings and corporate strategies, among other things. But I stumbled into fraud one day in the spring of 1994. I was teaching in DC. My daughter wanted to go shopping in Virginia and I couldn't remember the exit to the mall. I stopped at this gas station across the street to ask for directions. There was this big hardware store that had closed and there was a used book sale in it. I walked in and the first book that caught my eye was on fraud. I paid two dollars for it. So, something unpredictable happened: I got lost and got interested in fraud. That's a very common way how fraud is uncovered.

The book I bought was called "Faking It in America." It was about Barry Minkow, the 16-year-old high school kid who fooled everyone in the ZZZZ Best Carpet Cleaning fraud: attorneys, bankers, Drexel Burnham, three sets of auditors, and lots of private investors. As I read it, what hit me was that I needed to write a book on fraud for CPAs. I started interviewing malpractice attorneys, the FBI, and a lot of people who worked on Minkow's Ponzi scheme. But it occurred to me that everyone I talked to was working on the case from the outside looking in. I tracked down Minkow in prison and sent him my initial book manuscript in mid-1994. A couple of months later, it came back in the mail one day. I ripped open the envelope and looked at my manuscript. It was all marked up with red ink; a Post-It note on the front read: *"Dear Gary, this is one of the best write-ups of my fraud that I've even seen and I hope you don't mind my editing of it. Good luck with your project! Your friend... Barry Minkow. p.s. if you're going to be in California any time in the near future, stop by and see me."*

As luck would have it, I had to be in California teaching in October 1994 and I spent a day visiting Barry in prison. He spent seven and a half years in federal prison—the first four in maximum security—but was paroled his first time up. He had no prior record, never been to college, but earned a Theology degree in prison. The SEC (Security Exchange Commission) ended up changing its rules because of what Barry did. He spent seven and a half years in federal prison—the first four in maximum security. During my visit with Barry, we sat and talked outside in the California sun. Then Barry said, *"Hey Gary, come on over here, I have someone I want to introduce you to."* Well, I got to meet the former CFO of the Lincoln Savings and Loan which, back in the 1980's, committed a $1.8 billion load fraud in Phoenix.

The reason most fraud goes undetected is because the people in charge of the control systems and financial resources behave in a predictable pattern—all the time. So, no matter how the good controls are, if the controls are predictable then they're not worth much because the people who are subject to the controls will figure out a way to get around them. That's why in a retail environment you walk up and look at the cashier's drawer on a random basis; you check what they're doing to see if they're really doing their job.

I heard a funny story about a restaurant owner who couldn't figure out why his margins or profits were going down in one of his restaurants. So, he hired this forensic guy who'd drop by the restaurant, sit down at the bar and have a couple of beers. He'd watch everything happen and reported back to the owner that all the money seemed to go into the four cash registers and he never saw anyone take any money. The restaurant owner said, *"What do you mean four registers? There's only three registers in that restaurant."* The owner had a routine where he went to the same restaurant on the same night of the week. So, the employees bought an identical cash register to use on the nights he wasn't there. He was stolen blind because he was predictable. No matter what the system is—business, religious, or educational—if you're predictable, it is easy to circumvent the system. Would it be a good idea if the health inspectors showed up every Tuesday before the annual inspection? Of course not! Why do health inspectors show up at random? Because they want to see how it really works.

What are the primary reasons people commit fraud or employee theft? There was a really interesting study I just tripped across called "the coffee study" conducted by the head of the psychology department at the University of Newcastle in England. She put a sign over the coffee pot at work and the words on the sign were the same for ten weeks. The only difference was that every week she would change the graphic above the words which was either a picture of flowers or a pair of eyes. She alternated the eyes and the flowers. The words stated how much people were supposed to pay for a cup of coffee. When the graphic was a pair of eyes, the donation or compliance rate was dramatically more than when the graphic was a few flowers. She alternated pictures of women's eyes and men's eyes; every single time when she put up the men's eyes, there was a higher rate of compliance. Then she put different kinds of men's eyes. On the 10th week, she had a pair of men's eyes that were really mean and the compliance rate skyrocketed! Just a little sign with different pictures on it dramatically changed the rate of compliance for paying for a cup of coffee.

There's a host of things that can lead to people stealing, cheating, and embezzling. One of the answers is because there are poor controls and people don't think they're going to get caught. It's the exact same reason most people speed when they drive their car. It's the same exact psychology. However, most people won't steal just because there's poor controls or just because they don't think they're going to get caught. For example, almost all of us will typically drive 5-10 miles over the speed limit but we won't go 50 over. The reason is because driving 5-10 miles over the speed limit is normalized behavior, whereas most people know going 50 miles is really dangerous and there's a much higher probability of crashing or getting caught. If you're only going 5-10 miles over, so is everybody else! You're just keeping up with the flow of traffic which reduces the accident rate and your chance of getting caught. Further, people actually think it's *"fair"* to go 5-10 miles over the limit. They rationalize it's fair because the speed limit of 65 is really too slow and they're a really safe driver and they're not going to hurt anybody. But let's say they're late for a meeting and, all of the sudden, they may go more than 10 miles over the speed limit. So, now you've got poor controls and they're going to be late for a meeting, so they exceed their normal behavior and go 15 miles an hour over the limit. There has to be a trigger to act more unusually.

So, let's say a bookkeeper and her husband are under a lot of stress because he just lost his job and their house is going through foreclosure, so they're under a lot of financial stress. She might rationalize *"borrowing"* the money from her employer, telling herself when her husband gets another job she'll put it back. Let's say she normally would just take an extra pad of paper or take a long lunch hour or leave work early to go to a parent-teacher meeting without permission when she shouldn't have been gone. That's the equivalent of going 5-10 miles over the speed limit. The moral to the story is that she doesn't think of it as cheating because she thinks everybody does it, just like very few people think driving 5-10 miles over the speed limit is breaking the law but it is, it's illegal. The bookkeeper uses a flawed rationalization: even if she pays it back, she didn't borrow it—it wasn't hers to take; she didn't have permission. So, the entire chain of logic—*"I'll just 'borrow' the money"*—is completely flawed.

It's not just employees. Business owners will say: *"It's my company and I can do whatever I want."* But that's just flat wrong. It may be their company, maybe they even own the whole business—but they can't do whatever they want. They can't pollute the air, they have to pay minimum wage, and they have to comply with OHSA regulations and the EEOC. What people don't understand is that we don't live in a "free market society." We live in a "regulated market society"—that's called "the law." As long as you obey the law, you can run your business any way you want. So, the thinking that *"it's my company and I can do whatever I want"* is just flat wrong. The owner is rationalizing criminal conduct just the same as the employee who 'borrows' the money. And that's why a lot of business owners justify running their personal expenses through their business. And when the lower level employees see the owner running business expenses through, especially when we're going through hard times in this economy—laying people off, not giving pay raises—well, here's the truth then: people behave the way they see people above them behaving. So, the lower level people see the higher level people—even executives at non-profit agencies—cheating, and it gives the lower level people permission to do it, too. And that's one of the ways people talk themselves into fraud and theft—it's like, *"well, I'm just keeping up with traffic."* It's the same reason we speed.

Business people also rationalize "cooking the books"—*"I have to get the bank loan renewed and there's a requirement in the bank loan that I have to have $1 million in income to get the bank loan renewed, and I'm only at $980,000, so I'll just change that estimate. And I'm not doing it for me, I'm doing it for the 100 employees who work here and they depend on me to feed their families."* So, business owners cook the books and give the banks a fraudulent financial statement in order to get the bank loan renewed to keep the business going to keep the payroll going for 100 employees.

What affect does society have on people's attitudes and behavior—especially with the bank/investment scandals and those responsible not getting punished but rewarded? It goes in cycles. We tend to run in crisis mode—whatever's the crisis of the day—and don't act until there's a disaster. What's making people really cynical now is what's happened—or not happened—with the prosecution of the executives of this latest financial meltdown. Compare this to what happened with the Enron and WorldCom frauds of 2001 and 2002. Over 600 executives went to prison during the "Enron" period. There've only been a handful of prosecutions from the sub-prime meltdown. Some mortgage brokers went to prison but nobody from any of the investment banks. People see the Federal government bailing out all these gigantic institutions and nobody's held accountable. They see these executives get tens of millions of dollars in bonuses and they're the ones who caused the whole damn thing! They willfully, deliberately, knowingly bundled securities they said were great deals and knew they weren't and turned around and bet against them knowing they'd fail. This gives the average guy on the street a reason to be real cynical. It poisons the nation's psyche.

What else should people know about employee theft/fraud? There's no such thing as 100% prevention because you have humans involved in every business, every transaction, and every environment. The most important deterrence strategy is "unpredictability." The second most important strategy is "tone at the top"—people will behave the way the top level people act. The third most important strategy—few get this—is compensation structure: what are people being paid to do? This is different than what they are being told to do. If employees are being paid to do "A" but rewarded to do "B", they'll do "B". In other words if an employee has to make a decision to take care of herself or the company, she'll take care of her family, even if it harms the company

For example, salespeople are told to make profitable, collectible sales but they're usually paid a commission based on the sale not whether it's profitable or collectible. So, what the salespeople do is make unprofitable, uncollectible sales to a customer whose credit is really shaky and then say, well, profitability and collectability—that's the company's problem. A way to explain this to business people is really simple: just ask them why they have a credit and collection department? The answer is because of the way you're paying the salespeople. If you're paying someone based on revenue, you're paying a commission for anybody who will place an order; you're not paying them to make sales that are profitable and collectible. With this kind of compensation system, you have what's called "goal incongruence." That means that the behavior we reward on a sale is incongruent with the welfare of the organization. That's the mistake Congress and the lawmakers don't get. Why did we go through the sub-prime meltdown? Up until 20 years ago if you wanted to buy a house you had to trot down to your local bank or savings and loan and do all the paper work and put 10-20% down and the bank kept that loan in their portfolio. But 20 years ago, Congress said, "we'd like to have more people own their own homes—The American Dream—so let's let banks do the loans and sell them off to investment banks as securities." In and of itself, there's nothing wrong with this. But Congress, in changing the system, didn't ask or carefully consider how people are going to change their behavior. Any time you change a system, people are going to change their behavior to maximize the benefit to themselves.

What would have worked? You can take this idea and apply it any place; it's called "linking the behavior to the long-term consequences." All you would have had to do was to pay the people on the front-end of the transaction as the loan was being paid off—then they wouldn't have done these wild loans and non-documentation loans because nobody would want to do all that work just to see the loan default. If it was a 30-year loan and they were paid as the loan was amortized, most of these bad loans would have cost these lenders 90% of their commission. If you change the system, you have to think about how people are going to change their behavior and does that new system create a fraud risk?

Where do you see the future of fraud prevention? It's still lagging. Small businesses, especially, actively push back when you recommend fraud controls. They'll tell you it costs too much to have good internal controls. Yes, there may be costs, but the issue isn't the costs, it's the psychology. If a small business owner all of the sudden starts to put internal controls in, then they have to admit to themselves that when they hired someone they trusted them and made a mistake. Let's say they've had a bookkeeper for 17 years and they don't want to make the bookkeeper mad. One of the most powerful fraud prevention tips is to have the company's bank statements go to the company owner's home instead of to the bookkeeper at the office. The owners aren't going to take that risk because the bookkeeper knows where all the money is and the business owner doesn't want to take the risk of losing the bookkeeper; yet, they'll take the risk of the bookkeeper stealing them blind!

What else can employers do proactively to deter/limit theft? Nightline did a segment about Zappos' shoe company and its founder, Tony Shea, who's in his 30's and sold his company for over a billion dollars. He still works for the company and makes $36,000 a year. He has people in the call center answering the phones that make more money than he does. Employees don't see all the checks being written for the expenses and the payroll. Their only sense of how much the owner is making is based on how much money is coming in. There've been surveys where employees were asked how much they thought the company owner gets paid; they almost always answer about ten times more than what the owner actually makes. If the owner is willing to disclose what he makes—even though it's usually more than the other employees—most employees won't begrudge him; he's the one who started the company or is the one taking all the risk. Employers should also write at the top of any job application form: "By filling out this job application, you are giving us permission to do both a criminal background check and a credit check or whether you are involved in any civil lawsuits." I'm told that about 80% of employees who see this on an application won't fill it out. It's called "self-selection." This eliminates most problems from the get-go.

Do you feel it's ever a good idea or acceptable to keep an employee on who has stolen or bring an employee back who has stolen or who has a record? I have only seen this happen a couple of times but if it does happen, don't put any employee in a position of trust where she can steal again unless you're going to change the system of controls. For example, you have a bookkeeper who's got a sick family member and stole to help pay medical bills; well, get her out of the bookkeeping department and put her somewhere else.

APRIL LANE BENSON, PhD—*Overshopping*

Dr. Benson is a New York City psychologist and author. She is one of the pioneers and foremost experts in the study and treatment of overshopping. She is the editor of *I Shop, Therefore I Am: Compulsive Buying and the Search for Self* and author of *To Buy or Not To Buy? Why We Overshop & How to Stop. See www.shopaholicnomore.com*

What is your educational and professional background? I've had a Ph.D. in psychology for nearly 35 years and, before I started working with overshopppers, spent many years treating people with eating disorders and training therapists. I've done a good deal of post-doctoral training in psychodynamic psychotherapy, psychoanalysis, cognitive behavior therapy, dialectical behavior therapy, and motivational interviewing.

When and how did you become interested in the study and treatment of overshopping/overspending? In the mid-1990's, I became interested in shopping as a process of search, an activity that could promote self-definition, self-expression, creativity, even healing—*if* the shopping is mindful. I began to give workshops in the area of shopping, got even more interested, and eventually edited my first book. I began to get calls from people whose shopping behavior was having negative consequences, people who wanted to understand what was driving their self-defeating behavior and learn how to eliminate it.

Thus, I actually backed into the dark side of shopping, even though this wasn't where I'd thought my interest would lead. Given the fact that I, myself, had issues with overshopping and overspending for years, I probably should have realized I'd have to revisit my own issues if I was going to help other people! In my book, I mention that there are still occasional moments when I get tempted, caught up in the heat of a shopping moment. These moments only rarely lead to overshopping now because it's become ingrained in me to pause and ask myself questions: "Why am I thinking of buying this and how do I feel?" "Do I need this?" "What if I wait?" "Am I likely to want to return it?" If I'm in doubt, I leave it out! It also helps that my favorite clothing store, which I went into several times a week because it was right down my street, closed 15 years ago. So it's not nearly as easy or convenient for me to shop as it used to be. I never had problems with online or TV shopping, because there wasn't as much online or TV shopping back then.

What's the difference between someone with poor money management skills and someone whose debt may be due to addictive shopping/spending? I think a lot of it has to do with the *motivation* for the purchases. Somebody who buys to fill a hole in the soul is quite different from somebody with poor money management skills. Another way to distinguish between them might be the response to this idea "you can never get enough of what you don't really need." For the overshopper, this idea rings starkly true, and understanding it is critical to recovery. Someone with poor money management skills won't relate to it as strongly.

Do your research and/or clinical experience lead you to believe that compulsive buying is on the rise? If so, why? That's a difficult question because it's so much more in the public eye than before and the opportunities for purchasing are so much greater than they used to be. The only longitudinal study we have is from East and West Germany: samples there from 1991 and then 2001 showed a significant increase. Beyond that, we certainly know that more people are having financial difficulties and spending above their means, some due to compulsive buying. The fact that there's much more attention to this problem in the press indicates the rising level of interest in compulsive buying.

What's the difference between compulsive shopping, compulsive buying, and compulsive spending? In both popular and professional literature, these terms are often used interchangeably, but the behaviors they represent are, in fact, distinctly different. Shopping can be a process of search, a pleasurable recreation, and a way to "spend" discretionary time. The activity enables the shopper to gather information for immediate or future use, and it can be a way to satisfy many non-purchase motives. One may buy without shopping—or shop without buying. Even *spending*, though closer to *buying* than *shopping*, is not necessarily the same as acquiring. Spending relates to relinquishing funds, energy, and/or time rather than gathering material objects.

What are the primary reasons people overshop/overspend? For some people, it's an attempt to feel better about themselves, more secure or more in control. For others, it's an attempt at self-soothing or mood repair, a way to avoid dealing with something important or an attempt to buy love. Still others overshop to project an image of wealth and power or to fit into an appearance-obsessed society. Overshopping can be an attempt to heal a loss, a way to express anger, or even an attempt to find meaning in life (or maintain the denial of death). Tennessee Williams' play *Cat on A Hot Tin Roof* has Big Daddy say: "The human animal is a beast that buys, and if he's got money, he buys and buys and I think the reason he buys everything is that in the back of his mind he has the crazy hope that one of his purchases will be life ever-lasting." This idea is not a new one.

Do people who stop overshopping start doing something else self-defeating? I've seen transferring of addictions in both directions—people who have stopped drinking and drugging and are now buying and vice-versa. The relationship between food and eating and buying is a close one; dieting and shopping are the two ways that countless women deal with the ups and downs of life. I've seen people who have food issues they're trying to resolve all of the

185

sudden start buying—like the actress Jennifer Hudson. But I've also seen it go the other way, where people stop buying and start eating, because the underlying muscles to withstand negative emotions and to learn how to find healthier alternatives to the maladaptive behaviors aren't strong enough to withstand the onslaught of negative emotions.

What treatments have you found work best for these disorders? I think a form of treatment that deals simultaneously with this problem on cognitive, affective, and behavioral fronts has the best chance of success, which is what the program we've developed is all about. Specifically, it's important for people to understand why they're overshopping and how it all began—but that's hardly the end of the story. It's also important to know what triggers it and what the consequences are, and how to take that awareness and use it to resist overshopping impulses. Overshoppers need to understand their own ambivalence about their behavior by identifying the short and long-term consequences of both stopping and continuing. Understanding what they are *really* shopping for—what underlying authentic needs are fueling the shopping impulse—and discovering positive ways to meet those authentic needs goes a long way. Overshoppers need to learn not only to record expenditures, but also to evaluate them as how necessary each and every expense really is. It's critical for overshoppers to discover their signature strengths and think about how to harness those strengths in the service of shopping. Finally, identifying their potential relapse triggers and preparing for high-risk situations are quite important.

Before they finish the program, we talk about concepts and ideas that can reinforce their progress. One is acquisition of "true wealth" which includes those non-financial assets that invigorate and vitalize us: strong relationships, community involvement, hobbies, enjoying nature, and caring for animals. The Japanese aesthetic that I've written about— *wabi-sabi*—describes a reverence for the old and the used, a tradition that counters our cultural emphases on acquisition and our obsession with youth and newness; and *danshari,* which has to do with getting rid of emotional and physical junk. We need to think about voluntary simplicity. These are all ideas that can bolster somebody's resolve.

As for medications, the results are equivocal. For example, two identically designed studies with similar antidepressants, Citalopram (Celexa) and Escitalopram (Lexapro), showed contradictory results. In the first study, compulsive buying symptoms vastly improved with the medication; in the other one, puzzlingly, relapse rates were the same whether the compulsive buyers had been on medication or on a placebo. In addition to antidepressants, treatment with mood stabilizers, Naltrexone (Revia)—an opioid antagonist—and Topamax (an anticonvulsant) have also been reported, with varying degrees of success. Due to the high incidence of co-occurring disorders in compulsive buyers, it is difficult to tell whether a drug exerts independent effect on compulsive buying symptoms that is distinguishable from its effects on mood, anxiety, and other underlying conditions.

Support groups are really important to the success of recovering people. I've run several telephone groups and several face-to-face groups. The group setting helps members feel less alone and more understood, as everyone in the group has the same problem. This camaraderie helps members bear their often overwhelming feelings of failure, guilt, pain and humiliation. There's a kind of group watchfulness among the members to keep an eye on those who may fall through the cracks. The group often rallies around a member who's having a particularly hard time. In my last group, one of the women functioned as a kind of "shopping plan guru." The rest of the members went to her and she helped them with formulating healthy and realistic spending plans and to stay with them. Doing this kept her own intention to follow her spending plan on center stage.

The feedback that group members get from each other helps them cut through their denial. Because group members know how compulsive buyers think, feel, and behave, they can help to identify the defenses that some are using to rationalize their behaviors, and minimize the tendency to disown personal responsibility. In a group, individuals can see people at many different stages of recovery and know that others will be there to support them through the trials they'll encounter along the way. In combination, these features of group therapy constitute a powerful rationale for using it with compulsive shoppers.

As for Debtors Anonymous groups, they may be of some help but I've also found that many clients I work with aren't under-earners and aren't chronically or deeply in debt, so some of them feel as though they didn't fit in. Some cities have Debtors Anonymous groups specifically for compulsive spenders, and I think these can be enormously helpful.

Fostering the family's and/or spouses' involvement can be very important but it can also backfire, as in cases where the spouse attempts to be "the shopping police." It's a tricky and delicate balance. For an overshopper to have a shopping support buddy—usually not a spouse, but perhaps a friend, family member, or therapist (somebody to act as the shopper's advocate and be available to them in whatever way the two decide)—can be critical to the success of the work.

What might people be most surprised to know about shopaholics? What do you think of the term "shopaholic"?
I think maybe one of the things that would be most surprising is that at least a third of the people I work with have no debt whatsoever; they're nevertheless concerned enough about their overshopping to seek professional help. I think the term "shopaholic" runs the risk of trivializing the problem. In addition to "overshopper" which I prefer to "shopaholic" or "shopping addict," I also use the term "shopping problem" rather than compulsive buying disorder,

which I try to reserve for professional and scientific arenas.

What do you think about the recent TV programs on shopaholics like "Big Spender"? Some are better than others at bringing this subject to the public's attention and presenting a realistic rather than sensationalized picture. "The Bank of Mom and Dad" and "My Strange Addiction" were very positive because specific, usable techniques were included in the segments. But I felt the MTV True Life segment "Confessions of a Shopaholic" wasn't good at all because the overshopper wasn't really ready for help. Seeing this can really reinforce a compulsive buyer's denial and become a license to keep doing what he or she is doing.

How do you measure success in your treatment? This is pretty easy because I've collected objective data before, during, and immediately after the groups, and then again six months later. If, on those measures, a person's compulsive buying scores are lower or if he no longer scores in the compulsive buying range at all, that's a successful outcome. Our outcome research is finishing its first year—I'll have the data on the first group completed soon and the rest of the data will be complete this fall. My perception, from having seen dozens of people go through this program, is that it's extremely successful. But I want to have the data to prove it.

Where do you see the future of shopping/spending treatment? I think that we certainly need more research and more research money, and we need to recognize that this is a serious problem because it's still looked at as "the smiled upon addiction." I don't believe the upcoming DSM-5 will include a specific category for compulsive buying, but it seems likely that it will be included in a category of process addictions. I am optimistic, however, that this problem is gaining attention. More and more media are focusing on it. More therapists are asking for training to learn how to work with overshoppers as well. So, I think the future of shopping/spending treatment is bright.

GAIL STEKETEE, PhD—*Hoarding Disorder*

Dr. Steketee is a certified social worker in both research and clinical practice, specializing in anxiety disorders and hoarding disorder. She was on the faculty of Temple University and is now at Boston University. She is a pioneer and expert in the study, research, and treatment of hoarding disorder, along with Dr. Randy O. Frost. Dr Steketee has co-authored several books on hoarding disorder with Dr. Frost including *Buried in Treasures* and *Stuff: The Meaning of Things. See www.ocfoundation.org/hoarding*

What is your educational and professional background? I am trained as a social worker so I have both my MSW and my PhD from Bryn Mawr in their graduate school for social work. But I've grown up with psychologists, clinical psychologists, and in psychiatry. My first major academic position was at the Temple University Department of Psychiatry where I worked with a group of faculty who were mainly clinical psychologists working on mental health research, typically the anxiety disorders under Dr. Joseph Wolpe who was one of the fathers of behavior therapy.

When and how did you become interested in the study and treatment of hoarding and cluttering disorders? This came through my work with Randy Frost who is at Smith College. Randy and I began to work together collaboratively on some OCD research in the middle 1980's. He had researched OCD from the perspective of normative samples and populations—for instance, student groups he had ready access to—and was studying "checking behaviors' in students as precursors of OCD symptoms and their relationship to a variety of other conditions. I had been working for some years prior to that at Temple on OCD in patient populations. Randy and I teamed up when I came to

Boston University and began some work on OCD.

At the same time, Randy had led a seminar in OCD at Smith College for advanced undergraduate students. In the course of one of his seminars—in the early 1990's—one of his students wanted to work on hoarding. So, that student's work with him on a case—that became "Irene" in our book—helped them figure out what was going on in people with hoarding. His students also did a community project in which they asked for volunteers for a study on "packrats" and received over 100 responses. At some point, not long afterwards, Randy came to me and said, "You know, I think we have a bigger problem than we thought." It seemed that hoarding was more prevalent than we realized.

What is the difference between hoarding and cluttering? I think "cluttering" is the more colloquial term, like "packrat," that we tend to use to refer to homes that have too much stuff in them. "Hoarding" is the more formal term—and will probably soon be referred to as "hoarding disorder" as the OC Spectrum Working Group advances its research efforts to determine whether this will become part of the next DSM-5. The term "hoarding disorder" refers to the broader array of symptoms that go with hoarding which include: difficulty discarding or getting rid of things; excessive acquisition; and the impairment and distress that come from these problems. In a lot of the literature, we're starting to see the term "de-cluttering" pop-up—not as much in the professional literature but more in the newsletters and in the public press. I think a lot of professional organizers use that term as well: de-cluttering. Professional organizers not only work with hoarders but they also work a lot with people who are simply disorganized—that's their main business.

How is hoarding disorder similar and distinct from anxiety disorder and/or obsessive-compulsive disorder? We've helped generate a fair amount of research to study this question—along with the work of a number of our colleagues. The problem of hoarding generates a lot of difficulty in basic information processing and it's driven by two types of emotions—both positive and negative—and that sets it apart from the anxiety disorders and also sets it apart but, perhaps, links it more closely, to impulse control problems and the addictions but without the behavioral or medical aspects of addiction.

So, if you think about hoarding more like gambling, for example, there is a lot of positive emotion—people get excited, even joyful, and experience positive emotions, about finding new things that they're going to acquire or about uncovering stuff in the piles that they already have. There seems to be a positive drive toward something as opposed to the negative emotions which drive a person away from something. For hoarding, this includes not just anxiety but also guilt—which is a prominent feature—and also sadness. So, those three emotions—anxiety, guilt and sadness— together compromise some of what drive people away from being able to throw things out and to resist acquisition. All of this makes hoarding a more complex problem that straddles a line between our existing diagnostic categories. We are now confident that hoarding is not the same as OCD. There are some overlapping features but they're not more overlapping than other conditions. For example, social phobia and alcoholism—there's an overlap there—but not all alcoholics are social phobic and vice-versa.

What are the primary reasons people hoard or clutter? We know that early onset hoarding is the most common—the largest proportion of hoarders is going to get it by the time they hit their 20's. However, they usually won't display the clutter yet for some time; so, the early onset part makes it quite clear that we have a processing problem here and it's mainly about decision making. Sometimes, it's about keeping your attention on a task or tasks—attention deficit problems but not much hyperactivity—but this represents only about a quarter of the sample. We think the decision making difficulty may be close to 100% of the population. We haven't tested this adequately but that is where we would bet money. We think this is more biological and genetically based or it wouldn't onset so early.

Hoarding runs in families, which implies to our geneticist colleagues that there's a genetic basis to it, but we believe there's also a bit of nurture as well: if you grow up in a hoarding home you may develop a certain relationship with stuff. On the other hand, there are a lot of people who grow up in these homes and don't develop hoarding precisely because they are incredibly frustrated and upset about this.

We often see with mid- to later-onset hoarding that decision making problems were evident early on. So, what happens for most people as well is that sometime in a person's 20's or 30's the clutter begins to accumulate because the decision-making problem is still present, they develop more reasons to save, and they've been able to acquire more than they could have acquired when they were young. A number of people with hoarding disorder have had a loss of their partner or loved one—sometimes they die, sometimes they leave—and, often, they've lost someone who was helping control acquisition and helped manage decision making. So, when the partner or loved one is gone, even if there were difficulties in that relationship, the hoarder is then faced with going it alone, their identity is impacted, and their hoarding escalates. Sometimes, people don't lose this vital relationship until their 50's, 60's or 70's and you see the hoarding, which was either gradual up to that point, or there's just this explosion of accumulating too much stuff.

Does your research and/or clinical experience lead you to believe that hoarding/cluttering is on the rise and, if so, why? Unfortunately, we don't have the data. The only data we have is that the purchase of storage units over time has gone up exponentially over the last 30 years. We know that because when you drive around now you can find them fairly frequently compared to many years ago—or at least there weren't very many of them. We don't have prevalence rates of hoarding early on that would help us with this.

We know we're living in a culture—at least in this country and in Europe and now happening elsewhere—where the drive to accumulate goods is considered "a good" for the country. So, they tell us even now in our economic downturn that the best thing we can do is spend money. I think that's partly driving some of this that might not have otherwise existed; in addition, the availability of cheap goods means you can acquire much more than you could before and, in some cases, it's even harder to get rid of the stuff.

How prevalent is hoarding? We work with the figure from the prevalence data. We know that hoarding in adult populations is somewhere between 4-5% of the population; that's about 1 in every 20-25 people. If you take the population of the U.S. and cut all the children out—and I don't know that figure—but let's say our adult population is 300 million and we take 4% of that, we'll get 12 million people and if we take 5% of that, we're going to get 15 million people. So, it's somewhere in there, but it could be a little less—more like 10 million—if we add the kids in the equation. I wish I knew what percentage of our country are children so we could come up with the number.

What exactly are the criteria for hoarding disorder? When we're admitting people to a research study I can tell you what criteria we require. We require clutter in the home at a moderate or higher level. Our determination of moderate is based on the clutter image rating we use—so it's pictorial in nature. Essentially, the moderate level means that you have to move things off of furniture to sit down or you have to move things off the table to find a comfortable space to spread things out. Also, you have to wind your way around paths of stuff—you can't just walk in the door and walk straight to where you're going to—you're going to have to dodge things in your way. It doesn't have a particular height associated with it but typically there are things piled around the edges of the room and sort of butting into the middle of the room that are, maybe, a foot or two high. So, that's what moderate clutter kind of looks like. The picture shows you pretty well what that looks like from our therapy manual and our book *Buried in Treasures*. A "4 or higher" on the clutter image rating is required.

We also require impairment: that there's something about everyday life that is impaired (social life, family life) or has significant impairment. How you define significant is a little bit hard but it just takes practice in knowing people in those contexts; but the individual would agree, if he or she was not being defensive, that there are things he or she cannot do. There's usually distress but sometimes that distress—especially when that hoarder has been very defensive because people have been attacking—is only in the eyes of the family member or the neighbor and not necessarily in the individual who hoards, although people who seek treatment usually admit distress or they wouldn't be seeking help.

So, those are the three things that are most essential but we also track excessive acquiring which is present for about 80-90% of people we talk to: they don't have any place to put their stuff anymore and they all have difficulty getting rid of things. It's not easy for them to just sort through a pile of things and decide what to keep, what to get rid of, and where to put them. People who have substantial clutter or things that aren't being used but which are not interfering with normal use of living space would not typically qualify for our study. But if their decision making in regard to discarding items is so difficult, or if they could only function if someone else was doing the organizing for them, then they'd qualify for our study.

Are there differences or similarities between types of hoarders such as shopaholic-hoarders, document-hoarders, junk hoarders, food hoarders, animal hoarders? I don't think we have enough data at this point to identify traits of certain kinds of accumulation. We do know there are different reasons for hoarding and that certainly can determine what people hoard. Somebody who is concerned about waste and believes "if I throw these things out I will be a wasteful person and that will make me feel guilty so I just can't tolerate that"—is going to save extra containers that come when you order food out to go; they're going to save anything they might feel is useful now or in the future and, therefore, should not be wasted. They're going to save things that prevent them from feeling like they're being wasteful because that's painful to them.

There are other people who are going to save because they're going to need to remember something and their anxiety is about not having critical information when they need it or when somebody else around them needs it. They're going to save magazines, newspapers, flyers, information acquired through some venue, and it's being driven by the belief they hold. Now, you could have both things in the same person— they don't want to be wasteful and they want to remember information—so they're going to save both things. Those are two examples of beliefs that people hold. There are other folks who save things because they are driven toward beauty, which is obviously in the eye of the beholder. They save things because they'd be upset if they got rid of something they considered "good art" or useful for an art project they plan to produce even if they'd have trouble doing it because their house is too cluttered to sit down and do what they may be quite good at. So, different reasons drive saving.

What would people in general be most surprised to know about hoarders/clutterers? If anything, it's the breadth of the kind of person who can have a hoarding problem. It ranges all the way from people who are really quite organized, for example, at work and they could organize someone else's stuff, but when it comes to their home, they usually can't do it and they can't do it because there's some emotion tied up in the material that they're trying to work with that interferes with their abilities. So, there can be great capability in certain areas and tremendous deficits in others. It's surprising whenever you encounter that. I also believe we think of the classic notion of a hoarder as someone who is quite socially isolated. But a lot of the people we talk to are socially skilled and enjoy their social contacts, but might never let anyone into their home. Some people would be surprised how someone who looks reasonable at work could live like that at home. We see these incredible discrepancies and they're hard to process.

What treatments have you found work best for these disorders? The treatment that we know best because we've tested it most so far is a blended cognitive and behavioral form of treatment that includes several components. And certain pieces seem most important to us—though we've not yet tested whether they are critical. A cognitive piece includes motivational interviewing or motivational enhancement strategies because so many people have such limited insight into their hoarding that they tend to deny it which means we have to avoid triggering denial because it's much harder to move forward with the cognitive and behavioral strategies. Other behavioral pieces include skills training—there are people who just aren't good at organizing and they're not good at planning, problem solving, or decision making—which they can develop with proper training. In addition, we do deliberate exposure to getting rid of things, making choices about how to organize things, in the context of cognitive therapy to help them evaluate what they're thinking and whether that thinking makes sense.

What about medications? There are no good prospective studies with the exception of one by Sanjay Saxena with Paroxetine (Paxil). Paroxetine proved as useful with hoarding as it did for OCD with the two populations he was working with but it wasn't all that effective for either

197

condition to be quite truthful—I think 25-30% benefitted, not a great rate. The other studies, which are retrospective, suggest that, when you throw hoarding into the mix of other OCD symptoms, the SSRI anti-depressants don't work very well or work less well if someone has hoarding. Nobody has studied, for example, attention deficit drugs, so we don't really know what impact those drugs would have on the roughly 25% of the population who have that disorder. We don't have a drug we'd automatically use for decision making. When somebody comes in who's already on medication that's worked, we'll definitely leave them on it.

What is the importance of educating the hoarder's family and whether to include them in the treatment process? We have not tested this at this point. What's clear to us is that family members often react strongly about the hoarding and, although some family members can be quite supportive and perhaps even helpful in facilitating the hoarding problem, other family members are very angry and frustrated about it. So, given a strong family response, it's always wise to include family members in the initial assessment process so they can hear about what the treatment would include, about the nature of hoarding, and why hoarding is so difficult to overcome on one's own. I think a lot of family members, naturally, want to know: Why it's so difficult to throw stuff out, I don't get it? They need to be educated about the nature of the problem and then what can be done about it. Sometimes, family members who have a good relationship with the hoarder can be very helpful in the treatment process. However, if they have a negative, hostile interaction, they probably shouldn't be involved in the treatment but need to be educated and asked to observe when change does occur.

What do you think about the recent TV programs on hoarding? I've only seen some episodes of "Hoarders" and "Buried Alive" and just a snippet or two of "Animal Hoarders." That's probably because it isn't the nature of my work to spend a lot of time watching these as I see these problems up close and personal and I prefer to work from my own understanding and knowledge of talking to people directly. However, I feel these programs serve multiple purposes; some of them are good and, perhaps, some of them are misleading to people. They certainly have educated the public; I mean, there's almost nobody I meet who doesn't know these programs are on TV and many watch them regularly. I think that's because we all have stuff—you can't live without some stuff. We're very curious about our own relationship with objects and our family members' and friends' relationships with stuff. Then there's the horror factor: how can somebody live like this!? There must be some enjoyment we all get out of seeing people struggle because there's many shows on TV that show people struggling hard with one thing or another.

I think TV shows try to sell products. They want good ratings so they have to show things that are somehow exciting or interesting or awful—that tends to illustrate the more serious problems people have and the ones that are also atypical. So, does it represent the full-range of hoarding symptoms? No. It doesn't show you what a more mild level is or even what a more moderate level is. It shows you the weird stuff because that's more interesting, and that's a disservice. These shows also tend to give the impression there's a "quick fix" because they can't actually sit down with someone for 26 weeks and work on the problem with them; it's not interesting to see all the pieces of that. But that's what we have to do with folks. We wouldn't want the public to come away with the notion that you can just clean it up and ship it out and the problem is solved. Some of these programs have become better at providing those who are on the show with at least a few weeks of treatment afterwards, but that treatment is rarely the full treatment adequate to the need. Finally, as most of the cases on these programs are so extreme, there's a danger a hoarder or a hoarder's loved one may minimize the problem compared to what is shown and then stay in denial and avoid getting help.

How do you measure success in hoarding treatment? Well, we haven't that much experience yet with the long period of time but, at least, the immediate outcomes show that somewhere between 70-80% of people who go through a 26-week program—over 6 months to a year—report themselves as much or very much improved. Now, that doesn't mean the problem is entirely gone, and that's where the risk lies: that they can revert to a collecting problem and difficulty discarding without the input of someone who is helping them almost on a weekly basis. We've done a little bit of follow-up at this point and the number drops a bit but it doesn't go below 50-60% of our graduates who still believe they are much or very much improved. We haven't done all the data analysis yet. It looks like we have pretty durable gains with some loss of benefit for some people over a year's time. What happens after three years is a good question. My guess is we'd need "boosters" to help maintain progress.

What about the therapeutic value of group therapy and/or support (self-help) groups for hoarders? We've conducted group therapy where we deliver the cognitive-behavioral treatment in a group context using a clinician, a mental health practitioner who's leading the group, and one additional person who's either a mental health practitioner or someone trained as a coach to assist the people. Those groups we run have about 8-10 people in them. We've learned that 12 weeks is nowhere near enough and even 16-18 weeks isn't enough; 20 weeks starts to be quite useful and results in the benefits I've described for the individual treatment we've done—the 70-80% that are feeling much or very much improved. The trick is how to get enough practice in the home for everyone who is participating in those groups. Having someone who can go to the home with each group member on some regular basis is needed and we keep trying to tinker with methods like coaches who could help them in that way. We run an ongoing support group for people who have finished our CBT treatment—individual or group—who've gone through the entire protocol; they're invited to the support group which currently has 15-20 people in it and seems to be thriving. It meets only monthly to help people maintain those gains.

I know of another person who runs a local group without input from a mental health professional but who is trying to implement the strategies she has learned through the CBT protocols. I don't know how successful this is. I know they have meetings and interested participants but what it takes—just as with the online support groups—is a person who is willing to spend a good deal of effort, who has good people skills, and a commitment to help people gather and keep it going on a regular basis. Randy Frost had a good experience training senior students to lead support groups that have had good outcomes. This may be a good cost-effective strategy.

Where do you see the future of hoarding treatment? I think we have begun to find strategies for training people so that they feel competent and comfortable doing the intervention work with hoarding. I think the number of clinicians who are willing to take this on is slowly increasing, though it's nowhere near adequate for the request for referrals we receive and my colleagues in other parts of the country receive as well. Although the new DSM-5 might be helpful to us, I think the future lies in our better understanding the basis of the problem: Where does this decision making difficulty come from? What can we do about it? If we can help people with that on a very basic level, then we stand to benefit not only the hoarding aspects of their symptoms but some of the other problems they experience: the depression that goes with it—about 50% of our patients suffer from major depression and that's a serious problem for people to keep them motivated and moving forward. The decision making is core and so what do we need to know about that? I think we have a ways to go on understanding hoarding on a basic level, the diagnostic groupings, the interventions, as well as training as many people as we can.

JOHN PRIN, LADC—*Rule Breaking/Risk Taking*

Mr. Prin has a B.A. in English Literature & Theatre Arts and graduated from The Addiction Studies Program in Minnesota. He's been a licensed addictions therapist since 2000 and authored 3 books: *Stolen Hours, Secret Keeping & The Roadmap to Lifelong Recovery. See www.trueyourecovery.com*

When and how did you become interested in the study and treatment of addictions, secret keeping and rule breakers?
My interest in addictions developed after I became sober myself. I'd been a heavy drinker—in secret—for about 15 years; before that, I drank openly. As I got older, I became aware how many times in my life I had to cover up; this was after I gave up marijuana and other things. Alcohol was the last bastion of my secret life. Today, I have over 15 years sober and I have never found a better way to live.

I've written books on the topic of secret keeping with this axiom: "Secret keepers love the following set of emotions: the excitement of breaking rules, the pleasure of indulging in what is forbidden, and the delight in not getting caught." This certainly was true for me but I had to face the truth. Did I break rules? Absolutely! It was appearance first, reality second. I walked a tightrope between two worlds: what I wanted people to see and what I didn't want people to see. But my spiritual life was withering and I knew I couldn't keep this up—the life I was living was so untrue. I had to let the truth come out so I decided it had to stop. I started going to A.A. meetings and about two years after being sober, I began to really feel the positive effects of sobriety. In time, I realized I had to fulfill my gift of teaching, and chemical health education and recovery coaching followed naturally.

One night, a friend of mine in A.A. told me what led him to

become a counselor in the addiction field; he said it was just a logical leap to make based on Step 12. As he talked, I decided that it was also a logical leap for me to make as well. I called Hazelden the next day and talked to a kind fellow named Bruce Larson who talked with me an hour on the phone, and we talked through this whole thing. He was instrumental in starting me in addiction treatment and I'm forever grateful he did. I was smitten and I've never regretted my path since I took that leap. It's one of my main reasons for living today—to help people change their lives.

What is the difference between rule breaking, lying, cheating, secret keeping and addictions? I see people who are addicts and most of them engage in some form of cheating, some form of lying—secretive behaviors. Some people are so blatantly addicted that it's obvious to everyone how addicted they are. But the people who are rule breaking, lying, cheating, secret keeping do these things when no one is looking; they sneak time to indulge in a taboo behavior or ritual and make sure nobody is aware. They may cheat on their taxes or, when they go shopping, they might pick up at least a thing or two off the shelf here and there.

A key factor in secret keeping is entitlement. The DSM-5 is going through a whole reworking regarding changes in the diagnoses of personality disorders. I've met and worked with people who have personality disorders. I'm no expert in this area, but the number one personality disorder that I see regarding rule breaking is narcissism or narcissistic personality disorder—the idea that "I'm the center of the world and everyone's supposed to recognize that and appreciate it and, damn it, if I can do it then I'll do it." We've seen this recently with politicians and their sex scandals.

To me, narcissism is linked to a lack of spirituality, a lack of any sense that there's a bigger world with its own needs than the tiny little world that they've created, the little kingdom they've created in their lives where they are the king or the queen. However, if you look at any faith tradition common to man, there's this idea of a greater, bigger, wiser God out there—or at least divine energy out there—and when we're acting counter to that energy, which is love and peace and order and righteousness, we're in big trouble. When I work with people who have these tendencies, one of my first approaches is to ask them to tell me about their spiritual life. Many will look at me blankly—*"what spiritual life?"* That's my point. *"Do you have a spiritual life?"* They shake their heads and try to change the subject.

Some people are inveterate liars. I don't work with them because that gets into the whole criminal thing. I make a distinction between people who keep secrets or break small rules, and people who do harmful acts and commit crimes or break bigger rules or laws. I distinguish between alcoholics/addicts who do criminal acts to get their drug and criminals who use drugs. The motives are different. There may be a little criminal thinking in every one of us; if we're driving over the speed limit, we're breaking the law and, if you make a fine point of it, we're all a bit criminal at times.

What are the primary reasons people lie, break rules, cheat, keep secrets? Another facet of secret keeping is thrill-seeking. People are pleasure-driven. We all experience pain in life. We all experience distress, disappointment, failure. There's all this tension, friction, conflict and none of it feels good. So, people who break the rules and keep secrets do so to get out of this stressful world and experience, at least for a while, a state of pleasure. Physiologically, it has to do with dopamine, serotonin and brain chemistry. In the end, I think people just want an escape—to escape the reality of harsh living. If you can have a little fun at the casino and forget about life for a while—like the song says—and go where everybody knows your name and eat, drink and be merry even though the whole world is falling apart, and the deficit is growing, and the government can't govern, then fine. It's no secret the world often is unfair. Look at Wall Street and their shenanigans. Those tycoons don't play by the rules; we do. They make their own rules. "The world doesn't play by the rules, so why should I?" People need an escape from this hypocrisy and dissonance, and if they don't have a spiritual outlet and program like the 12 Steps to access that incredible loving, strong, omnipresent, endless, timeless energy that's available, they'll go play bingo or find a prostitute or get drunk and drive—but keep it all hush-hush. That's why we do these things: for thrills, distraction, escape and pleasure.

I've traveled several times in the past ten years to the Balkans for humanitarian work. A Communist system existed there prior to the year 2000. A Communist system ignores reality and says the top elite—the 2% who have all the money and power—don't have to play by the rules, but everybody else has to. So, in that system, you can't be real. In America, though we're not perfect, there's the same tendency but by comparison we have certain freedoms and rights. In a Communist system—and we saw this regularly in Kosovo—there's a huge black market, this whole business of going underground and getting things done that way. Wherever there's this imposed rigidity on people, they find ways around it. People in such cultures have to keep secrets and cover things up. That takes a lot of energy, by the way.

I don't think that any particular religion or culture is more or less secretive than another. But I do believe many family systems keep secrets and foster fuzzy ethics. It's this idea that what happens in the home stays in the home—what happens in Vegas stays in Vegas. So, when we step outside the door and become public, we present a face to the world, a mask: we present ourselves as upright, righteous, law-abiding, and so on. But inside the home there could be domestic abuse, drunkenness, incest, all kinds of nasty things. I note the difference between "shiny" and "slimy." We can be shiny in public and slimy in our own private lives.

There's another element to secrecy, too: shame. Whenever a

child is abused or neglected or there's trauma at a critical age, say from 6-16, there's going to be shame. How many kids, for instance, have been molested by a priest and kept it secret even when nobody asked them to? It's because of shame. If they're lucky, maybe after many years, they begin to process it, become angry, and say "damn it, I want this person to pay for this." Think about that: the abuse that creates shame in the victim can also keep that victim silent. Take the example of someone who is drinking or drugging and keeping it quiet. That behavior or addiction holds them hostage and prevents them from getting help. If that person brings it out in the open and exposes his secret, it brings relief and even a feeling of peace. A heavy burden lifts. However, when we're in recovery, if we still keep secrets it sabotages our best efforts to stay sober. The power of secrets works both in the addictive phase and the recovery phase: double jeopardy. When we're addicted, secrets hold us hostage and prevent our getting help; when we're in recovery, secrets sabotage our best efforts to stay sober.

There's also the person who witnesses something and keeps it a secret. For example, a person who grows up in a Mafia family realizes there's this double-standard going on all the time—two coexisting worlds—and it takes a tight-rope walker to walk between them. Soon, the witness to secret keeping and rule breaking may keep secrets and break rules, too. Just as in the wider culture, Wall Street doesn't play by the rules, Congress doesn't play by the rules, and even our sports figures don't play by the rules—they take steroids, people trying to cheat their way to success—it's everywhere!

Does your research and/or clinical experience lead you to believe that these behaviors are on the rise and, if so, why?
I don't have any real data on this but I just think it's completely inherent in the human heart. People either learn self-control and how to have boundaries around it and remain relatively healthy, or it just starts eating them up. What really brings it out is competitiveness. When you get

involved in a competitive sport or running for elective office, that's when you see a lot of rule breaking. When you're really at the top of your game, that's when it can get tempting to cross over the line. I was just talking to a student who's a high school hockey player here in Minnesota and he was given steroids by the "booster" parents to play better. This was in high school! Some people will cheat their way to success and to be number one. We have this obsession here in the U.S. with being number one. I think we have cultural narcissism, this sense that America is the premier country in the world, and that we only do good in this world—if we do any bad, it's very slight. We grow up with this hubris as Americans. We see this kind of competitiveness in every sport, in the political world, and in the entertainment world. I worked in Hollywood for ten years and I saw a lot of this.

I don't know if rule breaking is increasing; I think it's always been there. It's a combination of the human beings trying to succeed in life and find some sort of satisfaction, and the system they grow up in—whether communism or Wall Street or competitive sports. Cheating's everywhere. Cheating in schools is a real problem; with the Internet, it's become even easier and more widespread. Let's put it this way: I'm not sure if rule breaking is on the rise, but there's more ways to cheat these days than there ever used to be.

What treatments have you found work best for these disorders? One approach I've used with good results is what I call the "Meaning Tree"©. The diagram shows a tree in healthy soil and the basic questions are: "Why are you alive? What purpose does your life serve for you and the rest of the world? Are you seeking the highest and best in your life?" In small group work we start by evaluating that. Most of the time, we're dealing with people in crisis who can list the problems they have like the DUIs and the negative consequences of their using. Then I ask them: "Is this the way you want the rest of your life to go?" Invariably, people will say "No, I'm sick and tired of this, I've had enough."

But when I ask them: *"Okay, then, what do you want?"* There's always this blank stare. "What do I want?" Yeah, what is your dream in life? I start with that. If they can't answer why they think they're alive, or what their purpose in life is, I ask them: *"What is your dream in life?"* They'll usually say: "I don't have one." Then I'll ask: *"When you were 9 years old did you ever dream of becoming a big league baseball player, astronaut, rock star, or great author?"* And they'll often say: *"Oh, yeah."* We go through a whole number of scenarios where we go back to that age of magical thinking when people think they could be anything—a movie star, the President, leaders like Martin Luther King, Mother Teresa, Nelson Mandela, Gandhi.

I ask them: *"Who was your hero?"* Then I ask what made that person a hero? And they may say *"Well, I can't be a major league baseball player now because I'm 40 years old."* So, I'll say: *"Okay,"* but then ask them: *"Can you coach baseball? Can you help kids learn the game you love?"* We go through different possibilities. Maybe it's not even about baseball, maybe there was something else about that hero that triggered it: humility, perseverance, recognition, or achievement. I explore *"Who was your hero, what was your dream then, and what is your dream now?"*

The way I phrase it is: *"Our dream is an ideal, our purpose is how we reach it. We set a dream before us. It's our North Star."* Assume you'll never get there but it points you in the right direction. My purpose is: "when I get out of bed each day I can do something that gets me just a little closer to my dream—even if it's just 20 minutes today." The rest of the time I change diapers, go to work, pay the bills, and clean the stove. But inside the human heart there's a wish: a wish everybody wants to come true. I help awaken that.

Some good movies may inspire us toward our dreams, movies like "Field of Dreams," "The Shawshank Redemption," and "Mr. Holland's Opus." These movies show how one triumphs over life's demands and challenges. Clients need to start reconfiguring their lives to point toward a dream, and then take steps toward that dream by acting with purpose, and how pursuing the best version of oneself—what I call you True You©—creates meaning in their lives. As you meet the goal—if you're a novelist and you write that first draft—there will be a sense of meaning. Or, even if you end up as a Little League coach, it's still baseball! Helping others move toward their dreams also builds meaning in your life. Martin Seligman, a therapist who started the Positive Psychology movement, said "Our lives take on meaning when we serve something larger than ourselves." This is what I try to stir in my clients so they can see there's another way they can choose to live their lives.

What do you think about the recent TV programs which highlight addictions and these problems? Well, shows like "Intervention" spend too much time showing the person being addicted and too little time showing the process of change and recovery. They dwell on the negative, even sensationalize it, while short-changing the positive. They show the guy vomiting on the floor rather than living with hope and purpose. They don't seem balanced right. What about spending the first 10-15 minutes on the problem and the last 45 minutes on recovery and how people can change?

What would people be most surprised to know about rule breakers and secret keepers? They're the person next door, the driver along side of you on the freeway, the shopper in line with you at the supermarket. They're all around you. I estimate that one out of 12 people are secret keepers. What that means is that when you're in a busy big box store or at a major league football game, count every 12 customers or spectators; statistically one of those people is a secret keeper. Open any major newspaper on any given day and you'll find a story about a secret keeper. They're the neighbor next door, or maybe a family member, or a friend you'd never suspect. Believe it. It's true.

Tom Lietaert—*Money and Worthiness*

Tom is a Boulder, Colorado certified money and life coach. He is a former army officer, school teacher, remodeler, and veteran of personal development work. He founded the Sacred Odyssey and Intimacy with Money programs. *See websites: www.sacredodyssey.com and www.intimacywithmoney.com.*

How did you become interested in working with money and money issues? I've done personal development work over the last 15 years and during the course of doing my own work, I kept recognizing there was a constant underlying theme of money issues—not having enough, feeling unworthy around money, fear, shame and inadequacy. At one point, I recall a man saying to me "the relationship you have with money is the same relationship you have with women." While I don't think it's necessarily a universal truth, I found there were some aspects that resonated with me when I really got honest with myself. What I discovered was that I had a craving, a lust, a strong desire to have lots of money in my life much like I had the same desire for women in my life. But I also held deep resentment. "Where the hell is mine? I'm a good guy, doing all the right things and yet I never seem to get mine. Where is my fair share?" I had a relationship with money and women that manifested in my behaviors as a push-pull relationship; I'd draw them near only to push them away.

I reflected on that and observed others. I found it particularly interesting that a lot of people who have done years of personal development work rarely seemed to delve into their money issues. Personal issues with money are transparent to most people. It's often easier for people to talk about sex, religion and politics than it is to talk about money or their relationship with money. As I started studying money, our monetary system and our relationships with it, I learned that the monetary system in which we operate is completely unsustainable individually and collectively. In my assessment, the current paradigm is one of the root causes of all the pain, suffering and destruction in our world. If we truly wish to create a just, harmonious, loving and sustainable world, we have to transform our monetary system. But in order to make this transformation possible we'd need to shift our personal relationship with money.

I see so much dysfunction and pain around money. It's so transparent, yet there's not much awareness of how money is even created in our society. We don't teach this in schools. We don't consider the different monetary systems possible. But if we're not changing our personal relationships with money we won't comprehend the bigger context. There's an emotional attachment to the way things are—a certain security and safety in what's known. It doesn't really matter if it's working or healthy. The status quo serves us by keeping us in our comfort zones. I loosely compare this to the "battered wife syndrome." Why does the wife go back to her abuser again and again and again? It's not because it's working well but because there's a level of comfort in knowing what to expect. It's often easier to go back to the abuse than to take the risk to choose new ways of being that are uncomfortable and unfamiliar.

The first time I watched the movie *The Secret* I remember walking away with the sensation of a twisted knot in my gut. I had a really visceral and negative reaction to it and was astounded to see how many people around me were saying "you've gotta see *The Secret!*" They were really excited about it. I wondered: "what am I not getting here?" Emotions have a golden intention. What was really going on for me was that I had a lot of anger about what was being portrayed in the film. I channeled this into creating what I call "The Three Keys for Manifesting a Rich Life" process. *The Secret* primarily put forth a materialistic expression of manifesting as a means of happiness and well-being in life rather than addressing our deeper spiritual questions and our longings for deeper fulfillment. It never addressed, let alone answered the questions "for the sake of what or whom am I manifesting?" or "how am I making the world a better place through my manifesting?" If we start looking at things with these questions as a starting place, then the kinds of things we manifest take on a whole different form.

The Three Keys Process helps people to examine what is really driving their perceived desires—what I call our "Soul's Desire." What's within me that's unfulfilled? Often we imagine we want material things, the right education, the right job, the right vacation—but what we're actually seeking is a way to fulfill something that's lacking in us or something that's unresolved. When we're looking for this externally, we will never find deep fulfillment or happiness. When I started looking at my *Soul's Wants* (Key 1) I became more in tune with my own desires, their impact on others and the world as a whole. I believe our highest good comes from fulfilling relationships, being in community, and being in harmony. When we start looking at our soul's wants, we're necessarily looking at this from a spiritual perspective and thinking about the broader context of how our wants affect us and those around us. This also really got me interested in looking at the bigger issue of money in our world.

You mentioned that you see how men's relationship to money is like their relationship to women (or vice-versa). Is there a parallel for women and money? What I've most often observed is that women tend to seek a sense of security in money. It's typically an emotional security they imagine money will bring them. I find it interesting that while women are objectified physically men are objectified for what they can provide, how much they earn. This is a gross generalization of course.

Can you give a personal example of how your own money

issues have evolved in your life? I went to a workshop many years ago to dismantle my sense of shame and inadequacy around money. I was a schoolteacher earning $35,000 a year. I actually had women reject me because I wasn't making $80,000 a year! I was aware of being embarrassed about being a teacher because I wasn't making lots of money. I actually felt bad because I didn't have the ability to shower people with money. This played out in many ways in my life. I became timid and chose, often times, not to engage with women because I feared I'd be judged unworthy. At a deeper level I was judging myself unworthy.

I did "The Three Keys" process and asked myself: "What is it I really want?" It wasn't money. I started to look at what I wanted in relationship with women and I recognized a belief that I had to have all of my ducks in a row—that I had to be my perfect ideal of a man—in order to attract the kind of woman I wanted. Further, I believed that if I attracted this woman, it would be evidence that I'd arrived and I was finally worthy. I recognized the absurdity of this assessment as we're all in process—we're all sinners, if you will. Ultimately, I realized that I don't have to wait years—I'm worthy right now! Not long afterwards, I manifested an amazing relationship. Further, I realized that this translates across many domains in my life. I have shifted my perspective about money and now allow money to nourish and fulfill me, supporting my joy and happiness—not just in moments but on a sustained basis.

What is your professional training? I've been an army officer, taught woodshop in junior high, and owned a residential remodeling business. I never found any of these professions fulfilling. I started to get into personal development work about 15 years ago and discovered The ManKind Project. The work I did within *MKP* was where I experienced some of my biggest shifts. I was so impressed with *MKP* that I took all their leadership trainings and got mentoring from many men. Through *MKP* I completed the

Shadow Healing programs with Steve Kushner in Montreal.

Eventually, I made the leap to become a certified life coach and moved from Toledo, Ohio to Boulder, Colorado about 3 years ago. I attended the Gestalt & Applied Existential Therapy training program at The Boulder Psychotherapy Institute as well as The Newfield Network's Ontological Coaching program—one of the best coaching programs in the world. One of the things I love about The Newfield program is that the distinctions in the domains of body, mind and language built upon all my previous studies and personal development work. We look at emotions, language, and body and our habits of being in each of these domains.

For instance, when we are afraid, our bodies actually contract to protect our soft underbellies and if we stay stuck in those body postures, it correspondingly affects our thinking and emotions. The process of making a choice occurs in the limbic center of the brain, which is where most emotions occur. So, when we're in fear mode, the ranges of choices that are available to us are limited. Developing a rich emotional landscape and becoming aware of our habits of being in body, language and emotions is imperative if we are to create our authentic selves.

Have you worked with the issues of shoplifting, employee theft, compulsive shopping/spending, and/or hoarding? Do you see any underlying themes with these behaviors? Of these, I most often address issues related to compulsive spending, though that's not the primary focus of my coaching. I do think there are some common elements between all of these behaviors. There's a deep-rooted sense of shame and unworthiness around money in our culture, which manifests as a wide range of emotions and behaviors. People tend to act out in ways that affirm their sense of unworthiness. Stealing, overspending and hoarding can be understood as habits of being. We often keep manifesting the same events or circumstances in our life until we're ready to look at things from our past and resolve them. These shadows, or unconscious behaviors, can also be understood as the "gold" for they provide opportunities for deeper awareness, personal development, and transformation. Recurring issues allow us the potential to shift the way we are seeing things, doing things, and showing up in the world if we choose to recognize the patterns. There's often a sense of a hole in the soul—an emptiness at the core of our fears—that we're not going to be worthy, loved, or secure, and that we're going to be rejected and abandoned.

Often, I find that people who have a lot of money or who have had a lot of money feel this hole. They're living a lifestyle that, in one regard, is pretty easy—most of their basic needs are met—and they may imagine themselves to be worthy on one level because they have this nice life and these material rewards yet, on another level, they feel empty. Why do we see so many mid-life crises? Most of these people seem to have all of the outward markers of success—money, job, home, partner—and, yet, there's this deep sense of emptiness, longing: "is this all there is?" What's really going on here? What is it about our culture that people have to reevaluate their sense of success or purpose or meaning? I think it reflects back again to this recurrent state of unworthiness we keep feeling. So, I think all these issues are intertwined—shopping, hoarding, stealing—they all seem to be an attempt to fill some hole or meet some deeper need, but they don't. If we look at so called "primitive" cultures, they do not have mid-life crises. What is it about our culture that we would have a crisis of identity after we've reached the pinnacle of society's model of success? I believe it's rooted in our cultural sense of shame and unworthiness.

So what can you recommend for individuals that might help them reconnect with their soul desire and fulfillment? How do we keep from being overly influenced by our culture's messaging and brainwashing to keep up with the Joneses, keep buying, keep competing, keep overworking?

One of the first things I'd say—only little bit sarcastically—is destroy your TVs. Throw them out! We get so many messages from the television about who we're supposed to be. As I mentioned earlier, the process of making choices occurs in the limbic brain, the emotional part of the brain, which is why advertising is so effective. They simply have to create a positive emotional experience of their product. At the same time—and this is really insidious—they do that while suggesting "you will be worthy, you're not good enough as you are, or you need this product and then you'll be happy and joyful and living the good life."

One of the reasons we see so much in our culture and media around "extremes"—extreme sports, extreme violence, extreme drama—is to get people worked up so they can feel something. But they don't really know how to experience joy, so they try to substitute excitement for joy. The problem with going for excitement is that it's a peak feeling and when you have a peak feeling you have to have a valley. So people go up and down. We're creating a bipolar society!

If we start asking ourselves "what is the deeper inner desire that is wanting to be expressed with my perceived external want?" or "what reason do I imagine I need to have these things in order to be happy?" things begin to shift. Often our material wants seem to dissipate and that which we are truly seeking begins to manifest. As we move toward our *soul's wants* we attain genuine satisfaction and fulfillment. I am a spiritual being that seeks relationships to nurture, love, honor, and seek harmony and balance with everything and everyone outside myself. I am finding this sense of sustainable happiness and a joyous path in the world as I continue to get clearer and clearer about my soul's wants.

Notes & Reflections:

Part Seven
Other Research and Theory

That is mine which none can steal from me.—HD Thoreau

<u>Saving Money vs. Hoarding Money</u> (excerpt) By Ryan Puusaari
The Law of Attraction teaches us that "like attracts like" but what does this really mean when it comes to money? You might follow a logical pattern of thought and conclude that having a lot of money stored up in the bank (or in jars buried in your yard) will attract a large amount of money into your life, right? If it's true that like attracts like, then squirreling money away seems like a good idea—until you consider the role beliefs and intentions play in the Law of Attraction. There's a big difference between saving money and hoarding money. These two focuses will create very different outcomes depending on the mind-set of the saver/hoarder. Let's take a closer look at what is happening energetically when you hoard money or save money: **Hoarding Money = a belief in "not enough."** *When you hoard money, you are doing so because of a belief that there will be a shortage or lack of money in the future. You are essentially holding an intention to safeguard against "not having enough"—which must ultimately create the experience of not having enough! This fear-based mind-set drives you to save as much as you can while you can—because you may not have the opportunity later. Because of this focus, you'll end up creating a state of lack because you'll not only attempt to store away as much money as you can, you'll also resist spending money (even on things you really need); and this habit will eventually create a pool of stagnation. If the stagnation becomes big enough or goes on for too long, you'll actually create a blockage in the flow of money through your life. Thus, your belief that there isn't enough to go around will be proven true.* **Saving money = an investment in a better future.** *Saving money, on the other hand, adopts a completely different focus. You're not obsessing about a lack or*

shortage, but rather expressing a belief in your ability to attract abundance and opportunities. How? By setting aside some monetary resources, you're thinking optimistically about the future and creating greater potential for freedom and power in your life. You're not grasping desperately at money; you are creating a pool of abundance that will continue to attract more money, freedom and opportunities into your life. This pool of abundance can create more options for you to employ in many different situations, and it can also empower you to make better choices for your long-term growth rather than acting from a sense of immediate desperation. If you want to increase your bottom line, pay very close attention to your feelings and intentions when you set money aside. Save money with a focus on building wealth, increasing your personal freedom and creating lasting financial security for your family. Develop a habit of investing into a bright and prosperous future. Remember your thoughts, feelings, intentions AND actions will all work together to create your reality–financially and otherwise.

<u>Top 1% Own 42% of Wealth (excerpt) My Budget 360, 12/27/09</u>
Many Americans are not buying the recent stock market rally. This is reflected in multiple polls showing negative attitudes towards the economy and Wall Street. Wall Street is so disconnected from the average American that they fail to see the 27 million Americans that are skeptical about the gospel of financial engineering prosperity. Americans have a reason to be dubious regarding the recovery because jobs are the main push for most Americans. A recent study shows that over 70 percent of Americans derive their monthly income from an actual W-2 job. Work is the prime mover and source of their income. Yet the financial elite have little understanding of this. Why? 42 percent of financial wealth is controlled by the top 1 percent. We'd need to go back to the Great Depression to see such lopsided data. Many Americans still struggle at the depths of this recession. We have 37 million Americans on food stamps. Do you think these people are starring at the stock market?

Questions for Self-Exploration

1. Recall your earliest memory of your problem behaviors?

2. Was anything significant going on in your life then?

3. How did you think/feel when engaged in the behaviors?

4. Was there anything symbolic about the thing/object?

5. Were there any negative/positive consequences for you?

6. Did you develop a habit soon after? If yes, when?

7. When you were a child, did you witness someone else engage in the behavior? Who was it and what did he/she do?

8. What did you think/feel about this person's behaviors?

9. Was anything significant going on in your life then?

10. Do you recall any negative/positive consequences for that person or for you because of his/her behaviors?

11. Did you develop a habit soon after? If yes, when?

12. When you were a child, was anything stolen from you literally or symbolically? What was stolen?

13. Did you know who stole this from you? If so, who?

14. How did you think/feel about being stolen from?

15. Was anything significant going on in your life then?

16. What did you think/feel about yourself?

17. What did you think/feel about the person who stole?

Questions for Self-Exploration (cont.)

18. Are there certain things that seek or keep? What? Why?

19. Did you steal from any jobs? What, when, where why?

20. When did you notice an increase in problem behaviors?

21. Do you tend to engage in the behaviors at a particular time of the day, week, month, or year? When and why?

22. Are you more prone to engaging in the problem behaviors when you're in certain moods? If yes, what mood?

23. Are you more prone to engaging in the problem behaviors when certain events or circumstance occurs?

24. Do you actually derive benefit from things you acquire?

25. Can you distinguish between your desire for what you acquire and your need for it? If so, explain.

26. Do you have strong emotions or physical sensations right before, during, or after you've acquire something?

27. Do you tend to be perfectionist and need control or order? If so, do you think it's a factor in your addiction(s)?

28. Do you have other addictive/compulsive behaviors? What are they and how do they relate to each other?

29. Who knows about your problem behaviors?

30. What prevents you from telling certain people or from elaborating to the ones you have told?

31. List and weigh all the costs and benefits of your addictions. Do you want help? Why and/or why not?

32. What did you learn about yourself from these questions?

Timeline Exercise

Write positive times/events at corresponding age on the lines

1   5   10

11   15   20

21   25   30

31   35   40

41   45   50

51   55   60

61   65   70

Timeline Exercise

Note negative times/events at corresponding age on the lines

1   5   10

11   15   20

21   25   30

31   35   40

41   45   50

51   55   60

61   65   70

1. What is your gender?

	answered question	123
	skipped question	0

	Response Percent	Response Count
Male	9.8%	12
Female	**90.2%**	**111**

2. What is your current age?

20 - 30	1.6%	2
30 - 40	15.6%	19
40 - 50	**41.0%**	**50**
50 - 60	32.0%	39
60 - 70	9.0%	11

3. Marital Status?

Married	**52.8%**	**65**
Single	22.0%	27
Separated	1.6%	2
Divorced	22.0%	27
Widowed	1.6%	2

4. What is your sexual orientation?

Heterosexual	**94.3%**	**115**
Homosexual	1.6%	2
Bisexual	4.1%	5

5. What is your highest level of education?

H.S./GED	11.6%	14
some college	**37.2%**	**45**
undergraduate	28.1%	34
graduate	23.1%	28

6. What is your current employment status?

full-time	**41.5%**	**51**
part-time	17.9%	22
unemployed	17.1%	21
disabled	14.6%	18

7. Do you work for yourself or someone else, or both?

self	31.9%	22

| someone | 56.5% | 39 |
| both | 11.6% | 8 |

8. Children: living, deceased, adopted or step- or half-?

| **Yes** | **76.0%** | **92** |
| No | 24.0% | 29 |

9. If you have children, how many?

1	15.1%	14
2	**43.0%**	**40**
3	20.4%	19
4	12.9%	12
5	6.5%	6
Over 5	2.2%	2

10. What's your current personal household gross income

$0 - $10,000	10%	12
$10k - $30k	15.8%	19
$30k - $50k	17.5%	21
$50k - $75k	**21.7%**	**26**
$75k-$100k	16.7%	20
$100-$250k	15.8%	19

11. How old were you when you first stole something?

1-10	**50.8%**	**61**
11-20	40.0%	48
21-30	7.5%	9
31-40	0.8%	1

12. What did you steal?

money	23.3%	28
food	20.8%	25
clothes	18.3%	22
other	**37.5%**	**45**

13. Who or where did you steal from that first time?

person	26.1%	31
store	**63.9%**	**76**
work	4.2%	5
other	5.9%	7

14. When did stealing become a problem?

1-10	6.0%	7
11-20	26.7%	31
21-30	**29.3%**	**34**

31-40	25.0%	29
41-50	12.1%	14

15. What kinds of stealing have you done during your life
Check ALL that apply:

shoplifting	**94.2%**	**113**
switching tags	70.0%	84
fraud returns	60.8%	73
work theft	57.5%	69
embezzlement	17.5%	21
time theft/	28.3%	34
c card fraud	17.5%	21
identity theft	57.5%	8
from people		50

16. Which form of stealing that has caused you the most
trouble? Choose ONE:

shoplifting	**74.1%**	**86**
switching tags	5.2%	6
fraud returns	1.7%	2
work theft	4.3%	5
embezzlement	5.2%	6
time theft	0.9%	1
c card fraud	1.7%	2
from people	6.9%	8

17. Which form of stealing have you had the most trouble
stopping? Choose ONE:

shoplifting	**79.3%**	**92**
switching tags	5.2%	6
fraud returns	0.9%	1
work theft	2.6%	3
embezzlement	3.4%	4
time theft	0.9%	1
c card fraud	1.7%	2
from people	6.0%	7

18. Check ALL consequences you've suffered as a result
of your stealing:

legal	75.6%	90
arrest	81.5%	97
job firing	33.6%	40

trouble finding job	59.7%	71
marital issues	34.5%	41
divorce	7.6%	9
loss of family friends	31.1%	37
financial	47.1%	56
loss of self-esteem	**89.9%**	**107**
mental health problems	64.7%	77
other	17.6%	21

19. How many times have you been arrested for stealing?

none	14.9%	18
1	14.9%	18
2	**18.2%**	**22**
3	13.2%	16
4	13.2%	16
5	8.3%	10
5+	17.4%	21

20. How many times have you been fired from work for stealing or dishonesty?

none	**63.3%**	**76**
1	19.2%	23
2	6.7%	8
3	7.5%	9
4	0.8%	1
5+	2.5%	3

21. How many times have you served time in jail (at least 1 day) due to stealing?

none	**50.0%**	**60**
1	18.3%	22
2	11.7%	14
3	9.2%	11
4	3.3%	4
5	1.7%	2
5+	5.8%	7

22. If you were incarcerated, what was longest time?

1-10 day	**51.7%**	**31**

23. Did you continue to steal after arrest?

yes	**88.1%**	**89**
no	11.9%	12

24. Did you enroll in counseling as a result of stealing; if so, how many times?

none	14.4%	17
once	28.0%	33
twice	17.8%	21
3 times	9.3%	11
3+ times	**30.5%**	**36**

25. Why do you think you stole? Check ALL that apply:

don't know	25.8%	31
econ need	25.0%	30
finan stress	45.0%	54
relationship problems	53.3%	64
health problems	8.3%	10
abuse issues	35.8%	43
anger issues	61.7%	74
Grief/loss	39.2%	47
depression	70.0%	84
anxiety	60.0%	72
entitlement	**71.7%**	**86**
other	15.0%	18

26. How many times in your life do you think you stole?

1-10 times	4.3%	5
11-50 x	13.0%	15
51-100 x	8.7%	10
101-200 x	11.3%	13
201-500 x	17.4%	20
501-1,000 x	20.9%	24
1,000+times	**24.3%**	**28**

27. If you considered counseling or therapy but either didn't go or dropped out or didn't really stick with it, what were your reservations? Check ALL that apply:

money issues	53.1%	52
time issues	15.3%	15

embarrassed to be honest	55.1%	54
was in denial	35.7%	35
couldn't find a therapist who understood theft	36.7%	36
afraid to feel feelings deal w/ painful issues	41.8%	41
too hard to trust	24.5%	24
other	13.3%	13

28. If you found help for stealing, which did you employ? Check ALL that apply:

individual therapy	**87.0%**	**87**
group therapy	29.0%	29
couples therapy	8.0%	8
family therapy	3.0%	3
self-help groups (theft specific)	52.0%	52
other self-help groups	22.0%	22
medication	48.0%	48
spiritual/religious	41.0%	41
read book(s)	68.0%	68

29.If you had to pick one aspect of help or support which was most important to stopping stealing/recovery from stealing, which would it be?

Individual therapy	**38.2%**	**42**
group therapy	2.7%	3
couples therapy	0.0%	0
family therapy	0.9%	1
Self-help groups (theft specific)	24.5%	27
other self-help groups	2.7%	3
medication	1.8%	2
spiritual/religious	10.9%	12
read book(s)	0.9%	1
avoided people/places	3.6%	4
new hobbies	2.7%	3
stress reduction	5.5%	6

30. What's the longest time you have been truly "honest" from stealing behaviors?

1-30 days	10.3%	12
31-60 days	12.0%	14
61-91 days	14.5%	17
6 mos to a year	14.5%	17
1-2 years	**20.5%**	**24**
3-5 years	10.3%	12
5+ years	17.9%	21

31. How long have you been free or honest from stealing?

1-30 days	**46.0%**	**52**
31-60 days	8.0%	9
61-91 days	8.8%	10
6 mos to a year	13.3%	15
1-2 years	9.7%	11
3-5 years	5.3%	6
over 5 years	8.8%	10

32. Have you had other addictions prior to becoming addicted to stealing? Check ALL that apply:

alcohol	20.4%	20
drugs	24.5%	24
gambling	5.1%	5
eating/food	49.0%	48
shopping/spending	**51.0%**	**50**
hoarding	27.6%	27
work	14.3%	14
sexual addiction	17.3%	17
internet/videogame	9.2%	9
exercise	14.3%	14
TV	25.5%	25
codependency	44.9%	44
other	8.2%	8

33. Did you have co-occurring addictions *during* some or all the time you were addicted to stealing? Check ALL:

alcohol	23.2%	23
drugs	18.2%	18
gambling	3.0%	3
eating/food	**43.4%**	**43**

shopping/spending	42.4%	42
hoarding	25.3%	25
work	14.1%	14
sexual addiction	16.2%	16
internet/videogame	10.1%	10
exercise	12.1%	12
TV	16.2%	16
codependency	37.4%	37
other	6.1%	6

34. Upon stopping stealing, did you go back to or pick up any new addictions? If so, check ALL that apply:

alcohol	13.1%	8
drugs	6.6%	4
gambling	1.6%	1
eating/food	**37.7%**	**23**
shopping/spending	29.5%	18
hoarding	18.0%	11
work	9.8%	6
sexual addiction	14.8%	9
internet/videogame	8.2%	5
exercise	13.1%	8
TV	18.0%	11
codependency	26.2%	16
Other	11.5%	7

35. Since stopping stealing/being in recovery, has your life improved? If so, check ALL that apply:

no or not much change for the better	13.9%	14
better health	24.8%	25
better relationships	43.6%	44
better self-esteem	**69.3%**	**70**
finances got straightened out	13.9%	14
more productive with time	38.6%	39
feel more spiritual/ at peace	61.4%	62
better friend, partner, parent	40.6%	41
more time for fun and goals	30.7%	31
more stable mental/emotional	57.4%	58
other	9.9%	10

36. What are some of your most significant relapse triggers and/or warning signs? Check ALL that apply:

stopping therapy	20.0%	23
stopping attending meetings	13.0%	15
going into stores too much	**56.5%**	**65**
returning to/new addictions	13.9%	16
feeling that life is unfair	51.3%	59
relationship issues	47.8%	55
financial issues	51.3%	59
health issues	10.4%	12
overgiving/codependency	41.7%	48
lying/hiding the truth	54.8%	63
not asking for help	52.2%	60
procrastination/perfectionism	44.3%	51
other	9.6%	11

37. Which is your most dangerous relapse trigger or warning sign below? Choose ONE:

stopping therapy	3.4%	4
stopping attending meetings	6.0%	7
going into stores too much	**23.3%**	**27**
returning to/new addictions	1.7%	2
feeling that life is unfair	14.7%	17
relationship issues	12.9%	15
financial issues	10.3%	12
health issues	1.7%	2
returning to overgiving/codependent	6.0%	7
lying/hiding the truth	7.8%	9
not asking for help	5.2%	6
procrastination/perfectionism	1.7%	42
other	5.2%	6

38. How would you describe the support you generally received from your partner, key family members and/or friends in regards to your recovery from stealing?

none	15.5%	18
hostile or belligerent	10.3%	12
interested but ignorant	18.1%	21
passive or disengaged	15.5%	18
very interested in learning and	**33.6%**	**39**

supporting me

other   6.9%   8

39. Who knows about your stealing problem and/or recovery? Check ALL that apply:

nobody   2.5%   3
just God   18.6%   22
one person   17.8%   21
a select few people   **47.5%** **56**
most close friends/family   23.7%   28
all close friends/family   5.1%   6
everybody   4.2%   5

40. How active and grateful are you for your recovery from stealing on a regular basis?

not very grateful/active   4.6%   5
very grateful very active   **37.0%** **40**
very grateful/ not active   31.5%   34

Online Theft Survey Link:

http:/www.theshulmancenter.com/ShulmanCenterSurvey.pdf

Born into Debt: Gene Linked to Credit-Card Balances (excerpt)
Scientific American, August 2010, by Valerie Ross

A recent study was the first to show that a particular gene affects financial behavior outside the lab. When trying to understand why some people have trouble living within their means, we tend to blame factors such as high interest rates and irresponsible spending. Now, researchers have found another possible culprit: a gene linked to credit-card debt.

Earlier work has shown that genetics plays a role in how we handle money. But a recent study was the first to show that a particular gene affects financial behavior outside the lab. Researchers at the University of California, San Diego, and the London School of Economics looked at genetic data and questionnaires already collected from more than 2,000 young adults age 18-26 as part of the National Longitudinal Study of Adolescent Health. In particular, they looked at whether these young adults said they had any credit-card debt and what version of the MAOA gene they had.

Monoamine oxidase A (MAOA) is an enzyme that breaks down neurotransmitters (signaling chemicals) in the brain. Previous studies have linked the low-efficiency versions of the MAOA gene—the variants that cause less MAOA to be produced by brain cells—to impulsiveness.

In the new study, people with one "low" MAOA gene and one "high" MAOA gene reported having credit-card debt 7.8 percent more often than people with two "high" versions even when they controlled for factors like education and socioeconomic status. For people with two "low" versions of the gene, that number jumped to 15.9 percent.

The researchers were surprised by the magnitude of the difference. "The effect is as big as financial literacy,"—the ability to digest complicated financial information, says Jan-Emmanuel de Neve, an author of the study.

Part Eight
Odds and Ends

More quotes...

There is no reason to repeat bad history.—Eleanor Holmes Norton

Power is of two kinds. One is obtained by the fear of punishment and the other by acts of love. Power based on love is a thousand times more effective and permanent than the one derived from fear of punishment.—Mahatma Gandhi

Shopping is better than sex. If you're not satisfied after shopping you can make an exchange for something you really like.—Adrienne Gusoff

Thank God we're living in a country where the sky's the limit, the stores are open late and you can shop in bed thanks to television.—Joan Rivers

The sage does not hoard. The more he helps others, the more he benefits himself. The more he gives to others, the more he gets himself.—Lao Tzu

That is mine which none can steal from me.—Henry David Thoreau

I have learned to be honest. What a relief! No more ducking or dodging. No more tall tales. No more pretending to be what I am not. My cards are on the table for the entire world to see. I have had an unsavory past. I am sorry. But it can't be changed now. But now my life is an open book. Come and look at it if you want to. I'm trying to do the best I can. I will fail often but I won't make excuses. I will face things as they are and not run away.
—Anonymous

The 12 Steps

1. We admitted we were powerless over (stealing, spending, hoarding), that our lives had become unmanageable.

2. Came to believe that a Power greater than ourselves could restore us to sanity.

3. Made a decision to turn our will and our lives over to the care of God as we understood Him.

4. Made a searching & fearless moral inventory of ourselves.

5. Admitted to God, to ourselves, and to another human being the exact nature of our wrongs.

6. Were entirely ready to have God remove all these defects of character.

7. Humbly asked Him to remove our shortcomings.

8. Made a list of all persons we had harmed and became willing to make amends to them all.

9. Made direct amends to such people wherever possible, except when to do so would injure them or others.

10. Continued to take personal inventory and when we were wrong promptly admitted it.

11. Sought through prayer and meditation to improve our conscious contact with God as we understood Him, praying only for knowledge of His will & the power to carry that out.

12. Having had a spiritual awakening as the result of these steps, we tried to carry this message to compulsive debtors, and to practice these principles in all our affairs.

Starting a Self-Help Group

Here are some ideas I've used successfully:

1. Contact National Office or A.A. World Headquarters
2. Establish a meeting place and time
3. Create flyers and mail, post and fax about town especially to courts, churches, counseling offices, newspapers, criminal defense attorneys, bookstores, coffee shops (include a contact phone number or e-mail)
4. Create a website
5. Post flyers at other support group meetings
6. List your group information with your state's self-help clearinghouse--usually located in your state's capital
7. Write an article (even anonymously) for a paper
8. Notify employers/businesses or employee assistance and human resources departments that may pass on the word
9. Ask for ideas or help from friends/family
10. List in your local newspaper's health calendar

Add some of your ideas:

1.

2.

3.

4.

5.

6.

7.

8.

9.

10.

The Stolen Years (a poem by John S. 5/11)

All my stealing was a cry for love, not a cry for help.

All my addictions have been a cry for love.

I ceased to be a victim the second I got clean. As long as I stay clean, nobody has the right to call me victim ever again.

I am not here to be nice; I am here to be myself, and express my uniqueness which is my gift to the world. I am not "terminally unique." I am one of a kind, as precious and as valuable as any person who has or ever will walk this earth.

I have been hurt. If I am sad, grieving, frustrated, upset, in pain, shocked, afraid or lonely, and I acknowledge that fact, I am being honest, sincere and brave.

If I am then told I am feeling sorry for myself or having a pity party the real pity is that the person who says this closes the door on my beautiful vulnerability—a vulnerability that if they had courage enough to express, would strengthen their soul and soften their heart.

There are no words from a book that will heal me, no platitudes, slogans or affirmations—only the kindness of a wounded warrior that has travelled a similar route.

The slightest encouragement, a joke at a difficult moment, being understood, heard and respected can nourish a desire within me to create where before there only existed hellish confusion and destruction.

My only language for so long was hatred.

Now I know I am made of love.

If Only I Had Not Been Caught Stealing (by S.H. 6/11)

If only I had not been caught stealing, I would never have
gotten to this place that I am right now....
I would have never looked for Terry Shulman! I would have
never started my recovery in therapy with him.
I would have never learned how it feels to be forgiven.
I would have never been able to experience truly forgiving
someone else.
I would have never become closer to my little sister or my
mom.
I would have never been able to understand and forgive my
dad or be able to have such an awesome relationship with
him now.
I would have never met my soul sisters from my phone
group!
I would have never been able to have friends that have
actually experienced what I experience, and who understand
without me even explaining what I do!
I would have never found this group where I have read and
learned so much from people who feel like family to me
even thought I have never even met them!
I would have never been able to hold my head high when
telling my children my rules and really believe that I was
making the right decision.
I would have never been able to teach my children right from
wrong and felt OK doing it!
I would have never been able to trust that God, my Higher
power, knows exactly what He is doing, and that I can get
through it all with a little prayer and a lot of Faith!
I would have never been able to listen to advice given to me
from complete strangers and felt as though they were
speaking from experience, not judging me.
I never would have been able to appreciate what I have
because I never knew what it was like to be in jail and have
nothing!
I never would have appreciated "having no control" does not
mean I am out of control.

I never would have been thankful for all the simple things that I see every day like the flowers, the sun, the clouds, the rain, the wind, the birds, the bees, and the grass.

I never would have fully understood the gift of true friendship and honesty with those friends.

I never would have met Patti, my hypnotist, who took away all of the shameful hurt feelings that I had bottled up inside me since I was 6 years old.

I never would have experienced waking up every morning without the urges of stealing and committing illegal acts.

I never would have been able to relax and be able to laugh at some of my old behavior.

I never would have understood that I will always be IN RECOVERY, and NEVER RECOVERED.

I never would have been grateful to be in recovery instead of mad that I would never be recovered.

I never would have seen that my actions were causing so much pain and agony for me and for those who love me.

I would have always been so selfish in how I treated others by my actions.

I never would have understood why I was crying out by stealing and would have never tried to understand how to stop those actions.

There are so many more the list is never ending, but I must share that I am so glad the I got caught, because I never would have been the true me that I am now, and this is how I hope to stay now and forever, with you all, on-line, on the phone, in therapy, and hopefully one day in person.

Thank you all for helping me to become the happy, content individual I am today. I will always choose the high road from now on, never again the easy road of shoplifting, and dishonesty!

Blessings to each and every one of you!

Sincerely,

S.H. Ohio

Epilogue
Where do we go from here?

This book has been a labor of love to research and write. Having written three books already made this book easy to write in one sense but I worked longer and harder on this book—due to its diverse and expansive scope. As I release it, perfectly imperfect and never quite complete, I hope something in it makes a difference to each reader. Maybe you found a new understanding about yourself, your family of origin, or someone you know.

In this fast-hurtling world of many challenges—where things often seem and feel out-of-control—it's understandable how we reach out for things to soothe and steady us, not much different from when we were toddlers. We are searching and grasping and, as the U2 song lilts: "still haven't found what (we're) looking for." But, perhaps, it's a start to wake-up and realize what we thought we found, probably isn't it.

Sometimes, I look at this so-called conflict between East and West as war between hyper-spiritualism and hyper-materialism. East and West live in each of our souls; and a Civil War has been waged for too long. We need to find a path to peace and reconciliation between all that is temporary and all that is timeless. In the meantime, our children are watching, searching, grasping for guidance, attention, love, and protection. There's a parent and child in each of us.

I'm no psychic, but there are many urgent reasons to put the brakes on our ravenous stuff-lust: financial, environmental, relational, spiritual, and temporal. Madness has many forms. Let us come to our individual and collective senses now. "No-thing" can undo the past and "no-thing" can really save us from the future, except a different way. It's time to wake-up and live like there's "no-thing" to gain and "no-thing" to lose.

The Shulman Center for Compulsive Theft, Spending & Hoarding

The Shulman Center for Compulsive Theft & Spending
Founder/Director: Terrence Daryl Shulman, JD,LMSW,ACSW
PO Box 250008 Franklin, MI 48025
Phone/Fax 248-358-8508
E-mail: terrenceshulman@theshulmancenter.com
Web site: www.theshulmancenter.com / www.terrenceshulman.com
Skype ID: terrence.shulman

Something for Nothing: Shoplifting Addiction and Recovery, T. Shulman (2003)
www.kleptomaniacsanonymous.org
www.somethingfornothingbook.com

Biting The Hand That Feeds: The Employee Theft Epidemic: New Perspectives, New Solutions, T. Shulman (2005)
www.employeetheftsolutions.com
www.bitingthehandthatfeeds.com
http://theshulmancenter@360training.com

Bought Out and $pent! Recovery from Compulsive $hopping and $pending, T. Shulman (2008)
www.shopaholicsanonymous.org
www.boughtoutandspent.com

Cluttered Lives, Empty Souls: Compulsive Theft, Spending and Hoarding, T. Shulman (2011)
www.hoardersanonymous.org
www.hoardingtherapy.com
www.clutteredlives.com

*Specialized counseling in person, by phone or *via Skype*
*Books and Research
*Legal Representation/Expert Letters/Testimony
*Seminars, presentations and trainings
*Corporate Consulting

242

SHOPLIFTING/KLEPTOMANIA

Bay Area Impulse Control Center
Co-Director: Elizabeth Corsale, MFT
Phone: 415-267-2916
E-mail: pathwayshelp@gmail.com
Website: *www.pathwaysinstitute.com*

University of Minnesota Medical Center
Jon Grant, JD, MD
Phone: 612-273-9800
E-mail: grant045@umn.edu

*Stop Me Because I Can't Stop Myself: *Taking Control of Impulsive Behavior*, Jon Grant, MD and S.W. Kim, MD (2004)

*Impulse Control Disorders: A Clinician's Guide, *John Grant, MD (2008

*Compulsive Acts: A Psychiatrist's Tales of Ritual and Obsession, *Elias Aboujaude, MD (2008)

*Pyromania, Kleptomania and Other Impulse Control Disorders, *Julie Williams,* (2002)

*Bee Season,

*Kleptomania, *Marcus Goldman, MD (1997)

www.yahoogroups.com under "kleptomania" / "shoplifting"

Films: Bee Season, The Thomas Crown Affair, Catch Me If You Can, House of Games

EMPLOYEE THEFT/FRAUD/OTHER THEFT

* Business Fraud: From Trust to Betrayal... How to Protect Your Business in 7 Easy Steps, *Jack L. Hayes* (2010)

www.preventbusinessfraud.com
www.hayesinternational.com

*The CEO's Complete Guide to Committing Fraud, Vol. 1, *Gary Zeune* (1994)

www.theprosandthecons.com

*The Silent Crime: What You Need to Know about Identity Theft, *Michael McCoy and Steffen Schmidt* (2008)

*Employee Theft: The Profit Killer, *John Case* (2000)

*The Art of The Steal, *Frank Abagnale* (2001)

*Catch Me If You Can, *Frank Abagnale* (1980)

Films: *An Inside Job, Too Big To Fail, Capitalism: A Love Story, Enron: The Smartest Guys in The Room*

COMPULSIVE SHOPPING/SPENDING

Stopping Overshopping & ShopaholicNoMore Programs
Director: April Benson, PhD
300 Central Park West Suite 1K
New York, NY 10024
Phone: 212-885-6887
E-mail: info@shopaholicnomore.com
Website: *www.shoapaholicnomore.com*

* I Shop Therefore I Am, *April Benson,* PhD, Editor (2000)

*To Buy or Not to Buy: Why We Shop and How To Stop, *April Benson,* PhD, (2008)

*Addicted to Shopping and Other Issues Women Have with Money, *Karen O'Connor* (2005)

*Born to Spend: Overcoming Compulsive Overspending, *Gloria Arenson,* (1991)

*A Currency of Hope, *Debtors Anonymous* (1999)

*Overcoming Overspending: A Winning Plan for Spenders and Their Partners, *Olivia Mellon* (1995)

*Facing Financial Dysfunction, Bert Whitehead,CFP (2002)

Judith Gruber, LCSW, *www.moneyandempowerment.com*

Dave Ramsey
Suze Orman
David Bach

Films: Confessions of A Shopaholic, What Would Jesus Buy? *Affluenza, I Am*

245

HOARDING/CLUTTERING DISORDERS

*Stuff: Compulsive Hoarding and The Meaning of Things,
Randy O. Frost and Gail Steketee (2010)
http://www.ocfoundation.org/hoarding/

*Treatments That Work: Compulsive Hoarding & Acquiring
Randy O. Frost and Gail Steketee (2008)

*Buried in Treasures, *David Tolin, Randy O. Frost and Gail
Steketee* (2007)

*The Secret Life of Hoarders, *Matt Paxton* (2011)
www.theclruttercleaner.com

*106 Ways to Uncomplicate Your Life, *Paul Borthwick* (2007)

*Dirty Secret: A Daughter Comes Clean about Her Mother's
Hoarding, *Jessie Sholl* (2010)

Support groups:
www.messiesanonymous.org
http://sites.google.com/site/clutterersanonymous/Home
www.childrenofhoarders.com

Films: My Mother's Garden, Bee Season

RULE-BREAKING/RISK TAKING

TrueYou Recovery, Inc
Founder: John Prin, MA
Phone: 952-941-1879
E-mail: john@johnprin.com
Website: *www.trueyourecovery.com*

*Stolen Hours, *John Prin* (2004)

*Secret Keeping, *John Prin* (2006)

*Thrilled to Death, *Archibald Hart* (2008)

*Drive!, *Daniel Pink* (2010)

*America Anonymous, *Benoit Denizet-Lewis* (2009)

Films: *Catch Me if You Can,*

RELATED

Sacred Odyssey / Intimacy with Money Programs
Founder/Director: Tom Lietaert
Phone: 419-699-6100
E-mail: info@sacredodyssey.com
Website: *www.sacredodyssey.com*

*Intervention, *Vernon Johnson* (1986)

*The Sociopath Next Door, *Martha Stout*, (2006)

*The Five Love Languages, *Gary Chapman* (1992)

*The Haves and Have-Nots, *Branko Milanovic* (2011)

CPSIA information can be obtained at www.ICGtesting.com
Printed in the USA
LVOW080218071211

258186LV00015B/37/P